The Deals of Warren Buffett

Volume 4

The Deals of Warren Buffett

Volume 4
Making the world's most respected company

Glen Arnold

Harriman House

HARRIMAN HOUSE LTD
3 Viceroy Court
Bedford Road
Petersfield
Hampshire
GU32 3LJ
GREAT BRITAIN
Tel: +44 (0)1730 233870

Email: enquiries@harriman-house.com
Website: harriman.house

First published in 2025 by Harriman House, an imprint of Pan Macmillan
EU Representative: Macmillan Publishers Ireland Limited, 1st Floor, The Liffey Centre, 117–126 Sheriff Street Upper, Dublin 1, D01 YC43
Associated companies throughout the world
www.panmacmillan.com

Copyright © Glen Arnold 2025

The right of Glen Arnold to be identified as the author has been asserted in accordance with the Copyright, Design and Patents Act 1988.

Hardback ISBN: 978-0-85719-655-2
eBook ISBN: 978-0-85719-656-9

British Library Cataloguing in Publication Data
A CIP catalogue record for this book can be obtained from the British Library.

All rights reserved. No part of this publication may be reproduced, stored in a retrieval system, or transmitted in any form or by any means (including without limitation electronic, mechanical, photocopying, recording, or otherwise) without the prior written permission of the publisher. This book is sold subject to the condition that it shall not, by way of trade or otherwise, be lent, hired out, or otherwise circulated without the publisher's prior consent. This work is reserved from text and data mining (Article 4(3) Directive (EU) 2019/790).

Harriman House does not have any control over, or any responsibility for, any author or third-party websites (including without limitation URLs, emails and QR codes) referred to in or on this book. This book is for informational purposes only. Readers are advised to consult an appropriate professional in light of their relevant circumstances and requirements before acting on any information in this book.

No responsibility or liability for loss occasioned to any person or corporate body acting or refraining to act as a result of reading material in this book can be accepted by the publisher, by the author, or by the employers of the author.

To my gorgeous, lively, feisty and adorable grandchildren

Contents

About the Author	ix
Acknowledgements	xi
The Origins of This Book Series	xiii
Preface	xv
Investment 1 – MidAmerican (renamed Berkshire Hathaway Energy in 2014)	1
Investment 2 – CORT Business Services	48
Investment 3 – Moody's	62
Investment 4 – H&R Block	97
Investment 5 – Shaw Industries	125
A Note from the Author	155
Investment 6 – Star Furniture Co.	156
Investment 7 – Jordan's Furniture Stores	164
Investment 8 – Ben Bridge Jeweler	180
Investments 9 and 10 – Justin Boot and Acme Brick	200
Investment 11 – Benjamin Moore	235
Investment 12 – CTB International	254
Notes	283

About the Author

What works in investing?

That is the question Glen Arnold sought to answer in his tenure as professor of investing, drawing on academic insights, great investors' ideas and his own experiences to teach value investing techniques to students and fund managers in the City of London. Along the way, Glen authored the UK's bestselling investment book, many other books on value investing and the leading corporate finance textbook.

In 2013, Glen started a new chapter. Swapping his professorship for the real-world rigours of active investment, he tested his ability to outperform the stock market by investing his own money using the lessons he had learned during his academic career. In doing so, Glen offered full public disclosure of his buy and sell decisions online in a newsletter to followers, sharing each success and struggle along his investment journey.

Glen's new adventure saw him become a Berkshire Hathaway shareholder and attend many annual general meetings in Omaha. Elsewhere in the audience – and unbeknown to Glen – was Tom Spain, another UK Buffett enthusiast building his own reputation for fund management by adopting Buffett and Munger's investment philosophies for his firm, Henry Spain. When several of their other investment choices overlapped, Glen and Tom found themselves attending the same annual general meetings, grilling directors with (polite) questions.

After eight years investing only his own money, Glen was satisfied that he had proven his ability to outperform the stock market by applying the tested value investment techniques he had taught for many years. In 2022, he started to manage Henry Spain's UK Value Managed Portfolio Service, focusing on neglected, unloved and underpriced UK shares.

He is also a director of Zytronic PLC.

Also by Glen Arnold

The Deals of Warren Buffett, Volume 1: The First $100m

The Deals of Warren Buffett, Volume 2: The Making of a Billionaire

The Deals of Warren Buffett, Volume 3: The Making of America's Largest Company

The Financial Times Guide to Value Investing: How to Become a Disciplined Investor

The Financial Times Handbook of Corporate Finance

The Financial Times Guide to Investing: The Definitive Companion to Investment and the Financial Markets

The Great Investors: Lessons on Investing from Master Traders

The Financial Times Guide to Banking

Modern Financial Markets & Institutions: A Practical Perspective

Corporate Financial Management

Essentials of Corporate Financial Management

The Financial Times Guide to Financial Markets

The Financial Times Guide to Bond and Money Markets

Get Started in Shares: Trading for the First-Time Investor

Acknowledgements

This series of books would not have come about without a great deal of help from others. First, I would like to thank Warren Buffett for his willingness to take time to help other investors by writing about and discussing publicly his philosophy and experiences in the adventure of investing. I'd also like to thank him for permitting the use of his material in this book, and for stewarding a portion of my savings held in Berkshire Hathaway shares.

Many scholars have written about Berkshire Hathaway, Warren Buffett and Charlie Munger – not least Robert P. Miles, Carol J. Loomis, Adam J. Mead, Alice Schroeder, Roger Lowenstein, Robert G. Hagstrom, Lawrence A. Cunningham and Andrew Kilpatrick. I am grateful for their work, which creates a bedrock of well-researched and reliable sources of information.

Craig Pearce at Harriman House has been a more supportive and patient editor than I deserved. He did a great job of editing the work and enthusing the rest of the team. Tracy Bundey, Charlotte Staley, Lucy Scott and Carolyn Boyle at Harriman House all played assiduous, creative and energetic roles to ensure the success of the book – thank you all.

The Origins of This Book Series

It all began in 2013, when I took the decision to stop other activities to allow full concentration on stock market investing. This meant giving up a tenured professorship, ceasing teaching in the City of London and, ironically, pulling back sharply on writing books.

To create a record of the logical process in reaching a decision to select a share, I wrote blogs laying out the analysis on a simple website and made it free to all. It was galvanising to be forced to express clearly and publicly the reasoning behind allocating capital in a particular way. And besides, I needed a way to review, a few months down the line, the rationale for the investments made.

The blog became popular, and then the investment website ADVFN asked if I would transfer it to their newsletter page. I accepted, and one strand of my writing there became a series of articles about the rationale behind the investment deals of Warren Buffett.

That's how it started, but it has since taken on a life of its own. So even though I'm now a professional investor and director of a UK company, I continue to learn from the process of writing down the detail of Buffett's investments.

The 'Why?' question

You might think that Warren Buffett has been covered in dozens of published volumes and there is nothing new to say. But having read much of this literature myself, I was left unsatisfied. Other writers address what he invested in and how much he made from it. But I wanted to know why.

What were the special characteristics of the companies Buffett chose that made them stand out? Was it in the balance-sheet numbers, the profit history, the strategic positioning and/or the qualities of management? I wanted to know the detail. How did Buffett go from step to step in rational investing, from having virtually no money to being very rich?

Each investment covered in this book required fresh investigation, tapping many sources. The priority was to focus on the analysis of Buffett's selected companies, which meant very little time spent on his personal life, which has been thoroughly covered elsewhere.

I hope you enjoy reading how Warren Buffett turned Berkshire Hathaway into the world's most respected company.[1]

Glen Arnold
2025

Preface

What to do when a bubble bursts

This book examines 12 fascinating deals in the wake of the bursting of the 2000 dot-com bubble. Warren Buffett had kept plenty of dry powder during the "irrationally exuberant" era from 1997 to 1999, so he was ready to pick up bargains as they appeared while others, frightened, ran away. As most were rushing for the exit, Buffett became emboldened, growing increasingly "greedy when others were fearful".

In the late 1990s, he had renewed his vow to stick to sound value investing principles; to examine business fundamentals and resist the mindset of the speculator. Thus, he found little worth buying. The price of the typical American share had soared so high that people were paying 30 times profits.

That is, investors – or more often, speculators – were willing to accept an earnings yield of just 3.3% and a dividend yield of merely 1.3% for an average company. Why? Because they were absolutely convinced that earnings growth had rocket boosters: the rise of the digital economy, with 'dot-com this' and 'telecom that', would see profits quickly doubling, and then quadrupling.

For some of these companies – the ones only a couple of years old – excited punters would pay ten times sales. That's right: annual *sales*, not a multiple of profits – because there weren't any. They believed that these corporations were destined to become the dominant players in their industries. Webvan would dominate groceries – Walmart didn't stand a chance against Webvan! Of course, by the end of 2001, Webvan was bankrupt.

Two-year-old Pets.com would obviously dominate pet supplies, especially after its lavish Super Bowl advertising. Woe betide the old-fashioned brick-and-mortar pet suppliers as everything moved online. But it turned out that not everyone wanted to buy from a website, and Pets.com shut down in 2000.

Buffett was out of step with the zeitgeist. Indeed, we see that while companies with two minutes of trading history saw climbing shares, shareholders were demoting Berkshire Hathaway. Its shares fell from over $80,000 in March 1999 to $40,800 less than a year later. That's before the dot-com crash – the Nasdaq Composite peaked on 10 March 2000.

Buffett and his approach were old hat, they said. After all, he had long freely admitted that he was unable to analyse these new companies with their whizz-bang tech. He was out of touch, intellectually unfit for the new era, they claimed.

Figure A Berkshire Hathaway 'A' share price 1998–2000 ($)

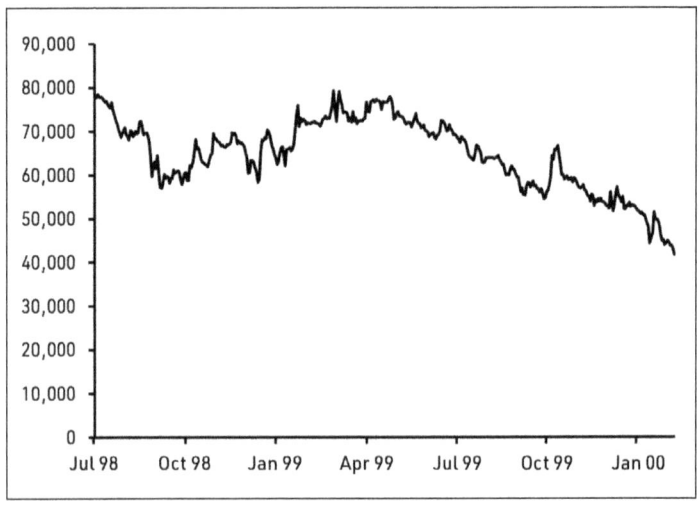

Source: www.ADVFN.com

But was he? There are principles of investment that have stood the test of time through many an up and down, enthusiasms and moments of despair. He and Munger looked at those well-rooted ideas again as they planned the next stage of Berkshire's growth. And it worked. While dot-coms fell by the thousand, in the next two and half decades, one share in Berkshire Hathaway moved from $40,800 to $699,000 (see Figure B). So much for the image of two out-of-touch old men playing an out-of-date game.

Figure B Berkshire Hathaway 'A' share price March 2000–2025 ($)

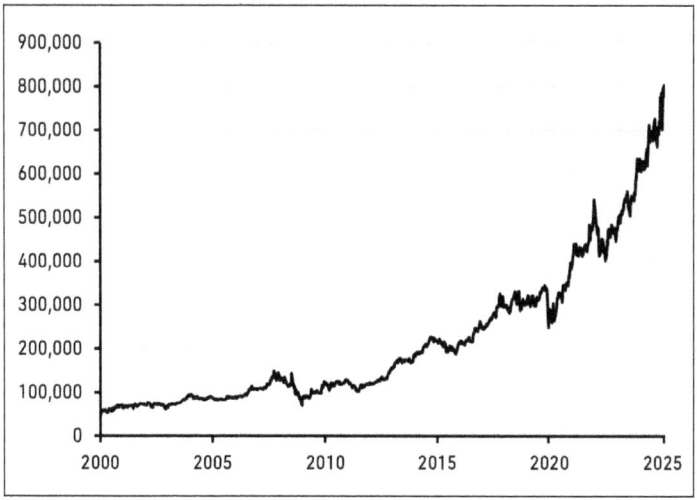

Source: www.ADVFN.com

Recognising an irrationality

Before looking at the key elements of investing, we'll examine Buffett's argument that share buyers were being overoptimistic regarding future returns, reported in a November 1999 *Fortune Magazine* article.[2] The basic point he was making was that people buying equities in 1999 were "expecting far too much".[3] This came from a man who rarely comments publicly on the general level of stock prices; it was just that extreme valuations stirred an instinct within him to warn folk about the dangers.

While Buffett always says that he has no idea where the market will go in the next week, month or year, he does emphasise that markets can behave in ways that "are not linked to value".[4] He referenced a July 1999 survey of investors: those least experienced (less than five years) expected capital returns on equities of more than 22.6% per year on average over a decade. Those who had already been investing for more than two decades were anticipating a much lower figure of 12.9%.

Buffett wrote that even the experienced investors were to be disappointed: "[W]e can't come even remotely close to that 12.9%."[5] The after-tax profit of the average US company as a percentage of gross domestic product (GDP) had been fairly consistently in the 4–6.5% range since 1951. In the late 1990s, the annual figures were just shy of 6%. So 'investors' might expect growth in profits of 12.9% annually, but corporations were only making 6% of GDP:

> When you begin to expect the growth of a component factor to forever outpace that of the aggregate, you get into certain mathematical problems. In my opinion, you have to be wildly optimistic to believe that corporate profit as a percentage of GDP can, for any sustained period, hold much above 6%.[6]

There are two forces working against that:

- Competition among companies: If current competitors or potential entrants to the industry observe incumbents achieving extraordinarily high returns, they will jump in to take market share. Eventually, prices and returns will fall.

- Political objection – and corrective action – to corporate investors eating an ever-growing portion of the American economic pie: If they take more, then workers and/or consumers will get less.

More reasonable working assumptions were 3% real GDP growth and 2% inflation; thus, nominal GDP grows by around 5%:

> If GDP grows at 5% … the aggregate value of equities is not going to grow a whole lot more. Yes, you can add on a bit for dividends [but] … You cannot expect to forever realise a 12% annual increase – much less 22% – in the valuation of American business if its profitability is growing only 5%. The inescapable fact is that the value of an asset, whatever its character cannot over the long term grow faster than its earnings do.[7]

Buffett also pointed out that future returns are always influenced by current valuations. In 1998, the profits of S&P 500 companies totalled $334 billion and the market value of those same firms added up to $10 trillion. Furthermore, US equity investors paid around $100 billion a year to brokers and investment managers, and for advice:

> In other words, investors are dissipating almost a third of everything that the Fortune 500 is earning for them … [to] 'helpers' … investors are reaping less than a $250bn return on their $10trn investment. In my view, that's slim pickings.[8]

So, what could the investors of 1999 expect from equities? The most probable return, Buffett said, was 6% before stripping out an assumed 2% inflation – thus, a 4% annual real-terms return. "And if 4% is wrong, I believe that the percentage is just as likely to be less as more."[9]

And it's not as though you could escape Buffett's logic by picking the winning sectors. This was tried many times before when a revolutionary technology came along, transforming society but often offering poor returns to shareholders. Take automobiles: there were over 2,000 American producers in the early part of the 20th century. By the 1990s, this was down to three – "themselves no lollapaloozas for investors",[10] according to Buffett.

Similarly, airlines have offered a great societal boon, but "the money that had been made since the dawn of aviation by all of this country's airline companies was zero".[11] Then there was the enthusiasm for radios, and then televisions and so on … Sector after sector becomes commoditised unless the players have a moat preventing rivals from entering the industry, putting pressure on prices charged to customers:

> The key to investing is not assessing how much an industry is going to affect society, or how much it will grow, but rather determining the competitive advantage of any given company and, above all, the durability of that advantage. The products or services that have wide, sustainable moats around them are the ones that deliver rewards to investors.[12]

So, what are the fundamentals we should focus on?

In his 2000 letter to shareholders, Buffett set out the absolute basics by relating to them a simple story – a fable written 2,600 years ago by Aesop, which tells us that "a bird in the hand is worth two in the bush". Buffett said you must answer three questions:

1. How certain are you that there are indeed birds in the bush?
2. When will they emerge and how many will there be?
3. What is the risk-free interest rate (which we consider to be the yield on long-term U.S. bonds)?[13]

Could you be at all certain of what was in Webvan's or Pets.com's bush in 1999? By endeavouring to answer these three questions for only those companies where the information is within reasonable bounds of certainty, we can estimate a range of possible values and therefore "the maximum number of the birds you now possess that should be offered for it".[14]

This principle can be applied across a range of assets, from farms and oil royalties to bonds, stocks and manufacturing plants. The arrival of the Internet has not changed this iron rule; just as the advent of the steam engine or electricity or the automobile did not change it. "Just insert the correct numbers, and you can rank the attractiveness of all possible uses of capital throughout the universe."[15]

Metrics commonly used – such as dividend yield, price-earnings ratio (PER) and book value – "have nothing to do with valuation except to the extent they provide clues to the amount and timing of cash flows into and from the business".[16]

Rapid growth in revenue – as we have seen with countless tech companies and other stock market darlings – can actually destroy value in circumstances where cash is being used at such a prodigious rate in the early years of an enterprise that any future cash inflows (after being discounted) are dwarfed by the amount put in.

> Market commentators and investment managers who glibly refer to 'growth' and 'value' styles as contrasting approaches to investment are displaying their ignorance, not their

sophistication. Growth is simply a component – usually a plus, sometimes a minus – in the value equation.[17]

Of course, it's hard work – and it requires good business knowledge – to figure out a reasonable estimate of current birds in the bush and when that flock (cash) might emerge. Buffett advises us not even to attempt at precision here:

> Using precise numbers is, in fact, foolish; working with a range of possibilities is the better approach. Usually, the range must be so wide that no useful conclusion can be reached. Occasionally, though, even very conservative estimates about the future emergence of birds reveal that the price quoted is startlingly low in relation to value. (Let's call this phenomenon the IBT – Inefficient Bush Theory).[18]

Boom and bust

Much of the time, we have to accept that we can't form any conviction about the birds to emerge. This failure to form a conclusion is more likely with young businesses or in rapidly changing industries:

> In cases of this sort, any capital commitment must be labelled speculative. Now, speculation – in which the focus is not on what an asset will produce but rather on what the next fellow will pay for it – is neither illegal, immoral nor un-American. But it is not a game in which Charlie and I wish to play. We bring nothing to the party, so why should we expect to take anything home?[19]

The problem for share buyers in 1999/2000 was that they had experienced a long bull run, and:

> Nothing sedates rationality like large doses of effortless money. After a heady experience of that kind, normally sensible people drift into behavior akin to that of Cinderella at the ball. They know that overstaying the festivities – that is, continuing to speculate in companies that have gigantic valuations relative to the cash they are likely to generate in the future – will eventually bring on pumpkins and mice. But they nevertheless hate to miss a single minute of what is one helluva party. Therefore, the

giddy participants all plan to leave just seconds before midnight. There's a problem, though: They are dancing in a room in which the clocks have no hands.[20]

There was a horde of speculators who put huge valuations on businesses that were almost certain to offer modest or no value. "It was as if some virus, racing wildly among investment professionals as well as amateurs, induced hallucinations in which the values of stocks in certain sectors became decoupled from the values of the businesses that underlay them."[21] Promoters were merchandising birdless bushes, putting money in their own pockets along the way. "[A] pin lies in wait," wrote Buffett of this bubble.[22]

So, what do you do in these circumstances?

First, don't participate in the insanity; don't attempt to pick the winners from a vast collection of unproven businesses. Buffett and Munger insist that they are not smart enough to figure out which young firms will succeed. They restrict themselves only to those cases in which they have reasonable confidence as to how many birds are in the bush and when they will emerge.

This does not mean they can precisely predict future cash flows – hence their insistence on building in a margin of safety by keeping their estimates at the conservative end.

Furthermore, they only look at industries that are subject to few surprises – and certainly those where conceivable surprises will not wreck the business. "Even so, we make many mistakes: I'm the fellow, remember, who thought he understood the future economics of trading stamps, textiles, shoes and second-tier department stores."[23]

Thus, when the stock market was going through a wild time with excess enthusiasm, Buffett and Munger looked to bushes elsewhere – places where entire businesses were available to buy. Even so, given the generally high prices for businesses during this period, they were not expecting to achieve anything more than "reasonable returns"[24] from any such purchase. It would be far better for them to be buying when capital markets were constrained and when business owners were pessimistic; but that is not the environment they were faced with at the beginning of the 21st century, so they had to adapt to the times.

Given the expectation of a US stock market offering low future returns because it was so highly priced right from the start, how is it that Buffett and Munger achieved extraordinary returns? Answering that question is the focus of this book.

First, they held on to wonderful companies bought in the previous third of a century, led by excellent managers and in good strategic positions. Second, they found some brilliant companies selling at reasonable prices in the aftermath of the bubble. It is those discoveries, the rationales behind the investments and outcomes that we'll look at in this book.

What this book covers

We start with **MidAmerican Energy**, later renamed **Berkshire Hathaway Energy**. At the time, Buffett observers scratched their heads when they saw him buying a utility of all things, with neither exceptional balance-sheet strength nor high returns on equity. After all, it was constrained by regulators allowing only 10–12% per annum on money invested in much of its business. But Buffett could see a way of making it pay. And indeed it has, increasing its value by at least 18 times the $5 billion paid. These days, annual earnings are around $2–4 billion.

This is also a story of three remarkable people, each of whom was to have a profound impact on Berkshire Hathaway. Greg Abel, a Canadian, joined MidAmerican as a 29-year-old accountant in 1992 to sort out its systems. He quickly proved to be an adept manager of people with a keen strategic mind and rose through the ranks accordingly. He is now CEO of Berkshire Hathaway and has been named as Buffett's successor with respect to the non-insurance operating business.

Walter Scott Jr, a childhood friend of Buffett, went on to become CEO of fabled Omaha construction company Peter Kiewit Sons' Inc. Later, he gave wise counsel as a board member of Berkshire. Scott had spotted MidAmerican's potential nine years before Berkshire bought into it and was instrumental in guiding its future.

David Sokol, as a young man in 1991, took hold of a troubled small energy producer – the forerunner of MidAmerican – and guided it for two decades, applying his special brand of astute management, shrewd acquisitions and even shrewder post-merger integration. After buying MidAmerican, Buffett thought so highly of Sokol that he called on him to restore the fortunes of a couple of other Berkshire business, Johns Manville and NetJets. He became Buffett's 'Mr Fixit'.

CORT, the largest furniture rental company in America, is one of those investments that didn't work out so well for Buffett. Despite being the biggest player in the country and being led by an excellent team of managers, it suffered from operating in an industry that afforded little to no pricing power. There is a high degree of rivalry in the sector, low barriers to entry and plenty of alternatives to renting furniture. The business boat that the managers were rowing was not one of the best.

Moody's was a brilliant Buffett investment: thus far, the shares he bought have risen twentyfold. It is one of three leading global credit rating firms. These oligopolists maintain very good margins and returns on capital employed because an issuer of, say, a corporate bond generally feels compelled to employ the services of at least one of them to assess its ability to repay the debt. Moody's is an example of a 'moat' business, meaning that it had a great deal of protection for its economic franchise 'castle'. It's extraordinarily difficulty for a potential new entrant to build the requisite capability, reputation and name recognition to serve the same market. This is also an example of that very rare thing: an 'inevitable' – companies that dominate their fields for an investment lifetime. They have such enormous competitive strengths that they will still be great companies 25 or 30 years from now.

H&R Block has a strong economic franchise, as the dominant name for calculating and submitting Americans' annual tax returns. The key feature of H&R Block on which Buffett focused was the power of customer recognition: it had a very significant 'share of mind' as the largest player in the business, with a presence in just about every town and 16 million regular clients. If Americans thought about the chore of doing a tax return, they most likely also thought about H&R Block. Buffett has almost tripled Berkshire's money devoted to this investment so far.

Shaw Industries is the world's biggest floor covering manufacturer. During the first few years under Berkshire's ownership, it produced high profits and return on capital employed, taking advantage of its lowest-cost producer status. But when the Great Recession struck in 2008, profits were hard hit. The company eventually recovered, but doubt persists as to whether the $2.42 billion paid for it in 2001 was within a reasonable range. Did such a sum allow for a good margin of safety?

Star Furniture was the third company mentioned to Buffett when he asked Irv Blumkin of Nebraska Furniture Mart, "Are there any more like you at home?" – meaning excellently run furniture stores that dominated their regions. Berkshire had bought the second on the list, R. C. Willey, in 1995; and, after bagging Star, he sought to complete the trio by acquiring outstanding retailer, **Jordan's Furniture** – a New England chain with the highest sales per square foot for any US furniture store and a legendary reputation for brilliant advertising and in-store entertainment. This was accomplished in 2000.

Buffett also likes to collect the best in jewellery retailing. He had already bought Borsheims and Helzberg Diamond Shops, and it was Bob Helzberg who persuaded Buffett that **Ben Bridge Jeweler** was great at what it did and would be a perfect fit for Berkshire Hathaway. Its culture of prudent growth, reputation for integrity and highly competent managers were right up Buffett's street. On the other side, Helzberg told the Bridge family that Buffett was a quality guy to do business with, and that Berkshire had proven to be a wonderful home for dozens of other family-owned businesses dealing with similar dilemmas to those faced by the Bridge family.

Justin Boot, the world's largest cowboy boot maker, and **Acme Brick**, the most recognised brand of brick in the US (and the biggest seller), came as a package to Berkshire as the two parts of a famous Fort Worth, Texas, firm. Buffett was delighted to bring both of them into the fold. Justin Boot had the Old West heritage (dating back to 1879) that boot buyers love, as well as a reputation for quality; and there was an increasing trend for non-riders to wear boots of a certain style. Acme Brick has strong economic franchise castles surrounded by 250-mile moats around its plants, because it becomes too costly to transport bricks at greater distances.

The **Benjamin Moore** case study describes a rare instance of Warren Buffett becoming so annoyed with the direction of a company that he sacked the chief executive. He was concerned that reputations were about to be trashed – Benjamin Moore's and his own. While that story is interesting, it should not distract us from the overall success of this $1 billion investment. Benjamin Moore makes premium-quality paints and can charge premium prices, producing large amounts of cash for Berkshire Hathaway.

CTB International makes boring, utilitarian products for bargain-hunting farmers (for rearing chickens and pigs, and for moving and storing grain – it uses plenty of galvanised steel). It's not exactly an industry that sets the pulse racing; there is very slow technological change and no real excitement. But CTB is a low-cost producer making decent profits, and Buffett was able to buy it at a PER of only ten. It took less than eight years for CTB to return everything Berkshire had paid for it and since then, it has pumped out cash for Buffett to invest elsewhere. It just goes to show that an intense focus on a single market segment can bring great rewards.

How this book is structured

The book is organised into 12 case studies. You can dip in to learn about particular deals that pique your interest if you wish, but I would encourage you to read it chronologically to achieve an understanding of how Buffett developed as an investor.

Investment 1

MIDAMERICAN (RENAMED BERKSHIRE HATHAWAY ENERGY IN 2014)

Summary of the deal

Deal	MidAmerican/Berkshire Hathaway Energy
Time	2000–2006 + 2024
Price paid	$5bn + $1bn
Quantity	Initially: 76% of the equity Today: 100%
Sale price	Still held
Profit	Profits after tax generated and reinvested in first 25 years: $42bn. Earnings after tax are now $2bn–$4bn pa.
Berkshire Hathaway in 2000	Share price: $40,800–$80,000 Book value: $61.724bn Per share book value: $40,442

The small company that grew into MidAmerican Energy was in danger of complete failure when a brilliant management team took over in 1991. They built it into a $5.8 billion company that Warren Buffett was glad to be able to buy into.[25] That $5.8 billion is now valued at around $90 billion; and billions of dollars still flow in each year from electricity production, from the distribution of natural gas and from wind turbines and nuclear power stations.

Back in 1999, the announcement of the deal took many of us by surprise. We had grown used to seeing Buffett invest in net current asset value (NCAV) investments – that is, Benjamin Graham-type investments with strong balance sheets (although there were far fewer of them in the latter part of the 20th century due to prices being high and Berkshire's sheer size, meaning that it needed larger deals to move the needle). And we were used to seeing Buffett – strongly influenced by Charlie Munger – buying larger businesses with robust economic franchises producing enduring high rates of return on capital employed. In 1999, to our shock, he announced he was going to buy a utility, of all things, with neither exceptional balance-sheet strength nor high returns on equity. Furthermore, MidAmerican was constrained in most areas of its business by regulators allowing only 10%–12% per annum on money invested.

We scratched our heads as we parsed Buffett's words on the subject to understand his logic. It slowly dawned on us that he hadn't lost his marbles: the deal made perfect sense. When you have billions to invest, you will be unable to find NCAV companies in anything like the volume needed; and when both the stock market and the private market for businesses are in an extraordinary bubble – with buyers often paying 30, 40 or even 50 times annual earnings for good economic franchise businesses – you cannot go on investing as before.

Sure, he could invest the billions in government bonds, waiting for the equity market to calm down – but where's the fun in that?

So, Buffett looked around for businesses that had been rejected by the market as boring or slow-moving, just as millions of speculators rushed into the 'industries of tomorrow', investing in everything from telecommunications companies and Internet infrastructure firms to the dotcoms willing to sell you anything online. Those were the places to be, according to the excited ones; not the steady-as-you-go utilities doing the same thing this year as they did two years ago. And why buy into a firm where returns were capped at 10%–12% – it isn't going to grow much from there, is it?

Buffett thought differently. Compared with puffed-up valuations elsewhere which heightened the risk of a large negative return when the bubble burst, a virtually certain 10%–12% income was fine. Especially if you could keep repeating the trick by ploughing back profits – or even sending across fresh capital from Berkshire as it flowed in from insurance and other businesses.

That said, it's interesting to note that for the first 25 years of Berkshire's control, MidAmerican paid not a cent in dividends on common stock and made no share buybacks. This was unusual, as most Berkshire subsidiaries were channelling large amounts towards Omaha for investment elsewhere. Buffett thought that the opportunities to reinvest in MidAmerican were so great that it made more sense to tell managers to keep going: to invest to create yet more long-term value. No doubt, one day it would be cash generative for Berkshire; but only when the return on the marginal dollar was poor relative to other companies that Berkshire could apply it to.

A tale of four Berkshire people

The MidAmerican deal brought together four people who were each to make a tremendous contribution to the development of Berkshire Hathaway. Remarkably, three of them were born in Omaha, attending local schools. The fourth – Canadian Greg Abel – is now CEO of Berkshire Hathaway. He is very wealthy to boot – not bad for someone who joined the MidAmerican Energy business (then called CalEnergy) as a 29-year-old accountant in 1992 to sort out its internal accounting.

Walter Scott Jr was born into a working-class Omaha family in 1931, the year after Buffett, and they became friends in their teenage years. I'm not sure if that was before or after they were chasing after the same girl, Carolyn Falk. Scott won her over and eventually married her; "Unfortunately, the best man won," Buffett would joke years later.[26] But that did not prevent a lifetime of affection, respect and admiration between the two men.

Scott spent the majority of his career working for fabled Omaha construction company Peter Kiewit Sons' Inc. He rose to CEO and chairman in his 40s and occupied an office on the floor below Buffett's in Kiewit Plaza. They saw each other frequently – a relationship nurtured by other bonds between the two families. Scott also contributed his wise counsel as a board member of Berkshire from 1988.

Scott had spotted the potential of MidAmerican nine years before Berkshire bought into it (he had been prompted to look at it by our fourth person, David Sokol), and he was subsequently instrumental in guiding its fortunes. "You cannot find a better model for a citizen than Walter Scott," Buffett told the *Omaha World-Herald* in 2021, in response to the news of Scott's death. "He was basically a builder, whether he was building Kiewit and physical things or building his vision of Omaha or Nebraska. He was nonstop." During his lifetime he amassed a family net worth of around $4 billion, using it for many good causes.

Sokol took hold of a troubled small energy producer as a young man in 1991 and guided it for two decades, applying his special brand of clever, rational management to day-to-day operations, shrewd acquisitions and even shrewder post-merger streamlining. When he joined, the market capitalisation was under $250 million; by the time he had finished, the company was making six to seven times that in after-tax profits year in, year out. Buffett thought so highly of Sokol that he called on him to go in and restore the fortunes of a couple of other Berkshire business, Johns Manville and NetJets (see Vol 3), when they were floundering. He became Buffett's 'Mr Fixit'. It was even rumoured that he might succeed Buffett himself – at least with regard to the non-insurance operations.

Of course, the remaining musketeer is Warren himself.

The origins of MidAmerican Energy

The first thing to note is that the original MidAmerican Energy was a really boring company, doing little more than generating electricity in Iowa. Year after year, this heavily regulated business churned out profits, but it was not exactly dynamic.

The really interesting company, with the energetic managers, was the one that in 1998 bought MidAmerican, promptly adopted that name for itself and then moved its headquarters to Iowa. That company was CalEnergy, run by Sokol and Abel. We can learn much from the steps taken by Sokol and his team to grow first CalEnergy and then the expanded organisation once MidAmerican was absorbed.

The story begins back in 1971, when Charles T Condy created California Energy Co as a small consulting firm offering advice to geothermal power production companies. Then the energy crisis struck. As oil prices soared, the US put more emphasis on developing alternatives. This led to the passage of legislation in the late 1970s which incentivised utilities to buy some power from small independent producers.[27]

Condy seized this opportunity by moving into the production of electricity using steam from geothermal pipes. Thus began a decade of pumping in $625 million of shareholders'[28] and debtholders' money to drill 98 wells and install nine turbine generators in the Mojave Desert. Losses accumulated until finally, in 1989, the nine sites could produce 240 megawatts (MW) – enough for around 240,000 households – to sell to Southern California Edison under a 30-year contract.[29] Thus, the speculative loss-maker turned into a $10.3 million profit-maker in 1989.

Condy was looking to repeat the trick of profitably generating power from natural steam elsewhere in California and the Pacific Northwest, and then beyond. But there was a problem: cash was low, debts high. While net assets were a mere $42 million, liabilities were $260 million.

And suspicions arose that the ship was not being run tightly – for example, Bloomberg reported that Condy was spending $2.5 million per year on a Falcon 20 jet, a Bentley and 15 other luxury cars for top executives;[30] and the company was involved in numerous 'legal brawls'. Short sellers came calling and the shares fell. This is where Scott and Sokol enter the story.

Scott and Sokol take control

In the late 1980s, Walter Scott – the second most renowned business leader in Omaha – saw limited opportunities to grow Kiewit's construction and mining operations: interest rates were high and potential clients were postponing projects. Furthermore, the cyclical slumps in these sectors made for a rollercoaster ride.

So, he started to add energy and telecommunications to the portfolio. "The issue was that we made more money than we could utilise within the contracting business. I was put into a position of finding good projects and rationally utilizing the company's capital," recalled Scott.³¹

Energy diversification was to be achieved through CalEnergy. Explained Scott:

> I decided to get into the energy business without any preconceived ideas about what was involved or how complicated it might be; the only thing I knew about the energy business was that it seemed potentially lucrative, so it was worth looking into.³²

It was a 36-year-old Sokol who pitched the idea of buying into CalEnergy to Scott in 1991.

Back in 1984, Sokol – a civil engineering graduate from the University of Nebraska, Omaha – had been asked, aged 27, to run startup biomass company Ogden Projects:

> I could not have been more excited to have the opportunity to start a business from the ground up ... Ogden Products, Inc, and the parent was Ogden Corporation which provided venture capital ... Soon, we went from a dozen employees to more than a thousand ... creating considerable value for Ogden Corporation.³³

The waste-to-energy plant organisation Sokol created became a public company on the NYSE valued at over $1 billion in less than six years – very impressive.

Right at the beginning of the journey building Ogden Projects, Sokol met Scott. The first energy plant, in Tulsa, had a very limited budget and the bank would only provide financing if the build contractor was creditworthy. Kiewit's solid reputation was naturally attractive, so Sokol called Kiewit HQ in Omaha and asked to speak with the CEO: "Luckily, I was put through."³⁴

Investment 1. MidAmerican (renamed Berkshire Hathaway Energy in 2014)

Sokol and Scott met the next day and a deal was completed ten days later. Said Sokol:

> I told Walter the honest truth that I had limited capital for the project, and that I wasn't trying to be arrogant, but I needed a firm price and a firm completion date. Walter said he wasn't sure if he could get the project done with the amount I offered but that he was willing to try.[35]

They made a 'gentleman's agreement' whereby if the project was under budget, Kiewit would pay half the difference back to Ogden; but if it came in over budget, Scott would "take care of it". They also sealed another deal with that handshake: if Ogden decided to build any more plants, Kiewit would be first-choice contractor.

When the project completed under budget and ahead of schedule, Sokol was mightily pleased to receive an envelope containing a cheque from Scott, confirming that he was dealing with a man of integrity. They built 11 more plants together. Sokol said that Scott represented all of the business virtues he believed in: "[T]o value hard work and know you'll be recognised in time; to be a man of your word; and to do what's right, not only what's profitable … his word is stronger than any contract."[36]

Fast-forward to a few months after the 1989 initial public offering (IPO) and Sokol found himself at a loose end after quitting the Ogden group in October 1990. His resignation was due partly to tensions with older, and perhaps less successful, managers whom this bright young tyro seemed to rub up the wrong way (he was often described as "hard-charging" or "demanding") – partly because Sokol refused, as a board member of Ogden Corporation, to vote in favour of "several ill-conceived acquisitions";[37] and partly because it had become clear to Sokol that nepotism was overruling business logic and competence, as highlighted by the chairman's son being lined up to take over as boss.

Scott learned of Sokol's sudden departure and called him in New York to ask if he was still keen to work in the energy field. Sokol's prompt response was that his interest was "strong". An excited Scott yelled: "So get back here to Omaha, and let's get something started!"[38] In February

1991, Sokol spotted the opportunity in CalEnergy after its stock fell to $7.25, giving it a market capitalisation of about $240 million.

They moved fast, with Kiewit injecting $29 million into CalEnergy by buying 4 million newly created shares of common stock at $7.25 in February 1991 and a further $50 million by way of convertible preferred stock (paying 8.125%). Kiewit also took options to buy 6 million more in common stock at $10.50. The following year, it purchased additional common stock for $23 million. In total, it pumped in $80 million by way of common stock and $50 million through preferred stock. By 1993, if the options were exercised and the preferred stock converted, Kiewit would own approximately 37% of CalEnergy.

Scott saw this investment as a bargain:

> The parent corporation [CalEnergy] was broke but had a great project, and because of banking requirements, even though they had a very profitable product, they had to let it go. Under those circumstances, we were able to take it over, and that initial foray into energy has led to many further engagements.[39]

Holding the whip hand, Scott was able to insist on the appointment of three Kiewit representatives to the board of CalEnergy, including himself. He was also able to make Sokol president and CEO, with the 53-year-old Condy remaining as chairman.

The Sokol effect

The Omaha "farm boy", as Sokol was labelled by Maria Shao of Bloomberg, got to work quickly. Even Shao was impressed:

> [T]he nation's largest independent purveyor of geothermal energy is putting its house in order. A no-nonsense whiz kid, 34-year-old Nebraska farm boy David L. Sokol ... has laid off 25% of employees, eliminated perks, and settled the fight with partners.[40]

The markets liked it: by June, the common stock had moved to over $12.

The company still only produced and sold 297 MW of electricity in 1991, but it had explored other electricity production possibilities – not least through the purchase of leases to 450,000 areas of geothermal development in the western US. One of Sokol's first acts to control costs was to move corporate headquarters from expensive San Francisco Bay to the cheap outskirts of Omaha (perhaps he hired lots of farm boys?).

CalEnergy's resurgence was soon a talking point in boardrooms across the country and other companies began to eye up "whiz kid" Sokol for their own turnaround programmes. It wasn't long before he was made an offer that he couldn't refuse. In January 1992, Sokol was lured to JWP Inc in New York. But the move was a terrible mistake: he quickly discovered that the chief financial officer (CFO), along with three senior accountants, had been deliberately reporting false numbers for years. It was a mess and Sokol felt he had been misled. He turned over all the information he had on the fraud to the board in October and promptly resigned.

Scott had been holding the fort back at CalEnergy as chairman and CEO but was keen to get Sokol back. Finally, in April 1993, Sokol was again appointed as president and CEO.

Greg Abel saves the day

Fortunately, in Sokol's absence, Scott was able to draw on the talents of a recent recruit to the accounting department: 29-year-old Greg Abel. After graduating from the University of Alberta with a commerce degree in 1984, this self-effacing, industrious, hockey-loving Canadian spent seven years working as an accountant for PricewaterhouseCoopers – first in Edmonton, then San Francisco. One of his clients was CalEnergy.

"Greg had a very easy going way about him and never got agitated," said John Sylvia, the former CFO who hired him. "He had a knack for being able to see where something was in the present, where it needed to be in the future and what needed to be done to get there."[41]

Friends at the time – and today – describe him as being fiercely intelligent and extraordinarily efficient, but also humble and soft spoken, avoiding the limelight as much as possible.

When Sokol returned to CalEnergy, the reaction at HQ was not one of unalloyed joy. He was perceived by some as too intense and hard-driving, and many employees simply couldn't hack it. "He's just so demanding ... people get exhausted,"[42] said Thomas Mason, who later became CalEnergy's president. But Abel was different: nothing seemed to disturb his equilibrium. Sokol freely admits that his success at CalEnergy was very much a team effort, and he was particularly grateful to have Abel at his side as his "business partner".[43]

Sokol said of Abel:

> The business-friend relationship normally comes into conflict. I think the reason that Greg and I can work it out is because we separate our two roles clearly ... we make sure we don't slack off and expect less of each other because we are friends. Instead we hold ourselves to much higher standards ... We think as a team and often solicit disagreement, recognising that it can be very beneficial in making better decisions.[44]

The energy industry transformation

The next few years were spent constructing an energy giant through both organic growth and acquisitions. By 1998, Sokol, Abel and Scott had taken CalEnergy from a 297 MW firm in 1991 to a 10,000 MW giant (enough to serve around 8–10 million households), with over 4,000 employees and net income of $127 million (see Figure 1.1).

Investment 1. MidAmerican (renamed Berkshire Hathaway Energy in 2014)

Figure 1.1 CalEnergy – phenomenal growth

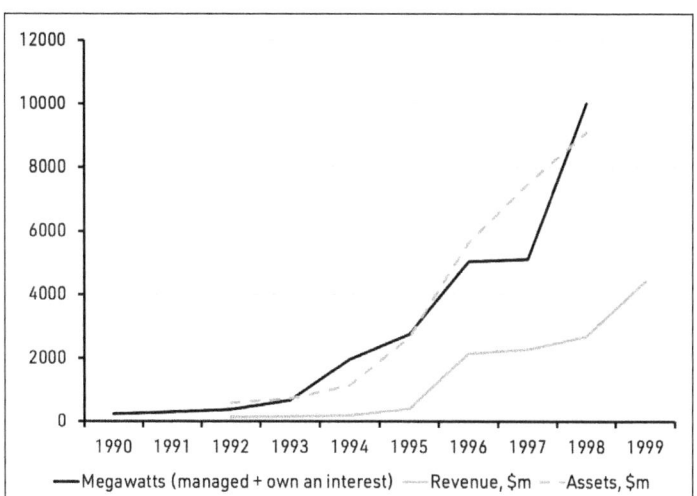

Source: CalEnergy Annual Reports 1996–1998.

In the early days, one factor behind CalEnergy's rapid growth was the ability to come up with ideas for new projects which were financed to a large degree through joint ventures with Kiewit. In 1993, for example, they launched power projects in the Philippines and Indonesia (two geothermal fields), with each party providing 50% of the equity. CalEnergy managed them and Kiewit was the "preferred construction contractor".[45] They also diversified outside of geothermal in 1993 with the construction of a natural gas facility in Yuma, Arizona. Alongside these self-propelled projects, the team went shopping for good companies (see Table 1.1).

Table 1.1 CalEnergy acquisitions 1995–1996

Date	Corporation	Cost	Type	Capacity of acquired firm
January 1995	Magma	$958m	Power producer: geothermal. The group became the largest geothermal generator in the world.	Operating: 228 MW Ownership: 154 MW
August 1996	Falcon Seaboard Resources	$226m	Power producer using natural gas (NY, Texas, Pennsylvania) + gas transmission pipeline.	Ownership: 520 MW
December 1996	Northern Electric, UK	70% for $840m. The other 30%, then owned by Peter Kiewit Sons' Inc, was bought by CalEnergy in 1998.	UK electricity and gas distributor (network of power lines, underground cables, substation, etc.; receives a small percentage of electricity costs from suppliers) and supplier (households and businesses pay suppliers that provide electricity to the distribution system, which they often purchase from generators/producers). It also had a small generating plant and four gas-producing fields in North Sea.	5 MW + 15.4% interest in a 1,875 MW gas-fired power station

Investment 1. MidAmerican (renamed Berkshire Hathaway Energy in 2014)

The Northern Electric acquisition was pivotal. Not only was the company large (revenues of $1.6 billion compared with CalEnergy's $0.54 billion; assets of $2 billion compared with CalEnergy's $3.7 billion); it also afforded deliberate exposure to a deregulated market, where monopoly power had been ended six years previously with the break-up of the all-encompassing energy companies, which had not only generated electricity but also distributed over cables (distribution/transmission) and interacted with consumers (supply). The lessons learned in the UK, the thinking went, could be applied when, sooner or later, the US power market was deregulated and de-monopolised across swathes of the country.

The acquisition of Iowa-based MidAmerican in March 1999 was largely motivated by the opportunities anticipated by Sokol and his team presented by "deregulation becoming a reality in America".[46] They were confident that their team would be ahead of the game thanks to their learnings from Northern Electric's systems, management, modes of operation and market price behaviour.

The Northern Electric acquisition also allowed CalEnergy to gain exposure to the full spectrum of energy services, serving as a springboard for growth in four areas: generation, distribution, supply and gas pipelines. MidAmerican's 1998 Annual Report stated:

> Since the U.K. progressively deregulated its electricity and gas supply sectors, the Company believes that its Northern management team has the knowledge and skills to compete in a competitive supply market. By virtue of its ownership of Northern, the Company also possesses the sophisticated billing and proprietary information systems that are believed by the Company to be critically important components of the skill and technology base necessary to compete effectively in a restructured environment … The Company believes that the electricity industry in the U.S. will also progressively restructure over the next three to five years and will largely follow the regulatory model established in the U.K. (with incentive based rates or price caps).

Bringing Northern Electric on board was so important that Sokol asked Abel, his right-hand man, both to assist with the acquisition and to run the company thereafter. So, with three children under seven, Abel and his wife moved to England. They were not to reside in the US again until 1999, this time with Abel as company president of MidAmerican Energy. Sokol described Abel thus:

> [H]is broader business acumen and unequalled understanding of operations enabled him to rise rapidly to our company's presidency. He is a great communicator, highly perceptive and a pleasure to partner with. His friendship has been unparalleled during my own periods of crisis over these past 15 years. We think alike in many ways, and we feel free to challenge each other until we agree on a course of action. I learn from Greg every day.[47]

The old way and the deregulated way of producing and selling electricity in the US

The opportunities presented by deregulation – and the clever positioning of the company to exploit these opportunities, both before and after acquisition by Berkshire – are so important to the success of this investment that I want to spend a few moments looking at the difference between the old way of producing and selling electricity and the new way.

If the UK experience was anything to go by, many US producers, distributors and suppliers realised by the mid-1990s that, sooner or later, they would be faced with competition for the first time. They would also have to cope with falling electricity prices charged to consumers and their business lives would become more complex. This new environment required skills that were often beyond the incumbents. No longer would US utility companies be vertically integrated local monopolies bundling generation, distribution and supply. These services, in many parts of the country, would be delivered by separate companies, which would be forced to compete for business based on value and price.

Consumers would have a choice of supplier: they could stay with their local utility or opt to buy from one competing for their custom. In some places, instead of a monopoly generator, a power exchange was established to operate as a wholesale pool through which both independents and the old utility producers sold the power generated. The exchange set the clearing price based on supply and demand. As expected, many of the legacy power stations turned out to be inefficient and were closed down, creating opportunities for other producers.

There were some limits to deregulation. For example, because large parts of the distribution/transmission business are natural monopolies, it would be pointless to have two or three networks of pylons. Thus, much of the industry was destined to remain under regulatory constraints. But instead of taking electricity from a single source to push through their cables, the distributors had to open up, accepting power from many generators.

The supply businesses – those firms in direct contact with the end user – were destined to provide electricity in their franchised areas but also had the freedom to supply customers in other markets. This created opportunities for newbies ranging from oil and gas companies to supermarket groups to enter the electricity market as suppliers and marketers. No generation by these firms is required, because that can be bought from the pool.

CalEnergy/MidAmerican saw its advantages as follows:

- **Cost advantage**: "Because the lack of competition has not provided incentives for upgrades, many utility companies are operating older, technologically outdated power plants at relatively high cost. CalEnergy has continuously invested in new, advanced facilities and technological improvements to existing facilities, allowing us to generate electricity at a lower, more competitive price."[48]

- **Knowledge advantage**: "Our experience in countries that already have undergone privatisation prepares us to do business in other markets where private power is just beginning … Northern Electric purchases almost all [its] electricity from other generating concerns."[49]

- **Diversification advantage**: "Our acquisition of three natural gas-fired cogeneration plants in New York, Texas and Pennsylvania along with the construction of our gas-fired Viking facility in the UK and our hydroelectric plant in the Philippines … continues

CalEnergy's geographical and fuel diversification."[50] Diversification into adjacent industries such as gas pipelines reduced risk further.

- **Financial firepower**: This element really took off after Berkshire Hathaway pumped in billions of equity capital and $1.7 billion of debt capital. Furthermore, being part of the AAA-rated Berkshire, with its diversified cash flows, brought the ability to borrow externally at very good rates. As well as massive organic investment, such as billions into wind turbines, MidAmerican bought more large companies.

- **Acquisition integration**: Because the team set out to acquire energy companies, and because it was so well led and experienced in post-acquisition integration, it was able to avoid or ameliorate many of the common pitfalls of mergers, such as culture clashes or misunderstanding of the acquired business.

Kiewit cashes in its chips, but Scott wants more

In January 1998, CalEnergy bought back 20.23 million of its shares owned by Kiewit – approximately 30% of CalEnergy's stock. To complete Kiewit's cashout, CalEnergy also bought Kiewit's 30% stake in Northern Electric and its interests in the Philippines and Indonesia. In all, CalEnergy paid $1.16 billion.

The agreement to complete this transaction was inked on 11 September 1997. Interestingly, a few days later, on 17 October, Scott[51] bought 2 million shares at $37.875 in CalEnergy. At that time, he was chairman and CEO of Peter Kiewit Sons' Inc but was set to relinquish executive responsibilities early in 1998. Thus, in 'retirement' at 67, Scott became the largest individual shareholder in CalEnergy.

To assist with paying such a large amount to Kiewit, CalEnergy placed 15.1 million common stock at $37.875 to raise a total of $550 million in October. After these transactions, CalEnergy's market capitalisation stood at $2.35 billion.

The original MidAmerican

MidAmerican Energy was a generator of electric power (4,378 MW) for customers in Iowa, with small footholds in neighbouring Nebraska, Illinois and South Dakota. As well as generating electricity, the company distributed it directly to customers – a classic vertically integrated regulated utility. It also had a substantial natural gas business, supplying 618,600 customers. Strangely, it owned a small railcar business, investments in telecommunications companies and "a portfolio of passive investments".[52]

The formative event was in 1995, when the gas and electric supplier for southeast Iowa merged with the main provider for central and western Iowa, coming up with the name 'MidAmerican' for the combined company. Its service area covered two-thirds of the state. By 1997, revenues had grown to reach $1.9 billion and net income was $135 million, so it was of a comparable size to CalEnergy.

The directors of MidAmerican welcomed the advances of Sokol and Abel in Summer 1998, and by August they had entered into an agreement to merge, which closed in March 1999. Cash totalling $2.42 billion (a 36% premium to early August trading) was paid for all the shares of the original MidAmerican, which thus became a wholly owned subsidiary. It wasn't long before the parent adopted the name of its newest family member and by the end of 1999, the parent had reincorporated in the state of Iowa, making Des Moines its HQ to this day.

The company had become a giant with annual revenues of about $4.6 billion and assets of $11 billion, serving 3.3 million retail customers.

Time to go private

Sokol became increasingly disillusioned with running a listed company when there was so much irrational investor behaviour going around. It didn't help that CalEnergy/MidAmerican had some bad luck which disappointed shareholders. First, in 1998, the Indonesian government renounced major contracts on two large geothermal projects nearing completion, resulting in $87 million being written off.

Second, in 1999, the British energy regulator decided to cut the revenue of Northern Electric. The stock fell another 21% in the first ten months of 1999 on top of the 15% drop since its 1997 high of $40 – and this at the time of a raging bull market. The low stock price meant that the company had to turn down a number of acquisition opportunities because it had such a weak currency to offer.

Meanwhile, the bull market mood had pushed up other utility companies: the fast dealmakers, the storytellers, such as Enron. Month after month, they could announce new acquisitions and, quarter after quarter, rising earnings; they were rewarded with high price-earnings ratios (PERs) as excitement about growth abounded. However, we discovered later that many were cooking the books.

Sokol was advised by brokers to "announce more deals" if he wanted the company to be viewed positively on Wall Street. Being a rational, practical manager with much experience in the difficulties of merger integration, he replied that the company was doing all the business it could handle. "Ah!" exclaimed the deal-helping brokers, "You don't have to make *good* deals. What you need is deal *velocity*."[53] He was even told that "peers, including Enron, were making two or three deals per month";[54] but, said Sokol, "We were only making one or two a year."[55]

Resentment was stoked further when it became obvious that the market didn't want to accept reality. The actions of the Indonesian government were not confined to CalEnergy; a number of companies had experienced the same treatment. While Sokol regarded honesty and openness as a touchstone of communication with Wall Street, he was shocked when advisers urged him to hide the bad news because neither analysts nor investors wanted to hear it. "[C]over it up with positive announcements about new deals,"[56] he was told.

Sokol opted for candour. After all, he reasoned, if a number of utility firms were announcing much the same thing that day, the market response regarding any one firm would be muted. Far from it. The other companies embraced the counsel of obfuscation and were rewarded with reasonably robust share prices, while CalEnergy's price got hammered.

Sokol understood that a utility company's credibility with regulators is boosted when it can offer a long-term vision rather than being continually buffeted by the need to maintain rising quarterly earnings: "I began to grow weary of the excessive focus public equity markets place upon quarterly earnings … analysts' unrealistic focus on short term-performance can cause management to make poor long-term decisions. By the fall of 1999, I had concluded that the public market had been rewarding bad behaviour by many of our competitors, Enron being an obvious example. I was hopeful that we could find a way to go private."[57]

There was also the terrible strain and grief that arose from the tragic death of Sokol's son, David Jr, 13 days after his 18th birthday on 11 June 1999, after a three-and-a-half-year fight with cancer. Sokol said that his son "exemplified courage, kindness, tenacity and compassion in everything he did. He taught me to … see the good in every person … about strength of will and courage".[58]

Sokol was no longer sure that he wanted to run a public company, so he told the board in Summer 1999 that he could either step down, making way for Abel, or take it private.

The board agreed that the company should go private via a leveraged buyout, through which the managers would become significant owners and the company would be loaded with debt. Plans were put in train; but it quickly became apparent to Sokol that the investment bankers they spoke with wanted to break up the company, which "would hurt our employees".[59]

In a quandary, he phoned Scott for advice. Scott suggested that Berkshire Hathaway might make a good home for MidAmerican. Berkshire seemed like an excellent option to Sokol and Abel – due not only to Buffett and Munger's reputation for allowing managers to continue to run the show with their own teams, but also to the possibility of large injections of equity capital, allowing it to continue with its acquisition strategy to consolidate the energy industry.

Furthermore, Berkshire could supply debt finance directly and its triple-A rating would allow MidAmerican to go into the marketplace to borrow at low rates. The cherry on the cake was that Sokol and

Abel would be able to interact with Buffett and Munger – two of the most well-informed, engaged and rational businesspeople on the planet – and would never again have to explain themselves to some wet-behind-the-ears 20-something Wall Street analyst with a tenuous grasp of the business model.

But why would Berkshire Hathaway invest in a utility, of all things?

By then, Berkshire Hathaway was generating annual profits in the billions of dollars (see Table 1.2). (Don't be deceived by the underwriting loss in 1999 – this was an aberration due to the crisis at General Re. In most years, a large underwriting profit was made.)

Buffett and Munger had to invest that money. Ideally, they would find businesses similar to See's Candy, Scott Fetzer or Nebraska Furniture Mart – that is, businesses capable of producing very high rates of return on capital. But these were rare. And even if they could be found, they were likely to cost merely $100 million or so – less than one month's cash generation for Berkshire. Of course, when found, they were snapped up. But it was clear that to really move the needle, Berkshire needed to find companies worth billions turning out profits in the hundreds of millions.

Investment 1. MidAmerican (renamed Berkshire Hathaway Energy in 2014)

Table 1.2 Berkshire Hathaway – sources of reported earnings ($m)

($m)	Pre-tax Earnings		Berkshire's Share of Net Earnings (after taxes and minority interests)	
	1999	1998	1999	1998
Operating Earnings:				
Insurance Group:				
Underwriting – Reinsurance	$(1,440)	$(21)	$(927)	$(14)
Underwriting – GEICO	24	269	16	175
Underwriting – Other Primary	22	17	14	10
Net Investment Income	2,482	974	1,764	731
Buffalo News	55	53	34	32
Finance and Financial Products Businesses	125	205	86	133
Flight Services	225	181[1]	132	110[1]
Home Furnishings	79[2]	72	46[2]	41
International Dairy Queen	56	58	35	35
Jewelry	51	39	31	23
Scott Fetzer (excluding finance operation)	147	137	92	85
See's Candies	74	62	46	40

($m)	Pre-tax Earnings	Berkshire's Share of Net Earnings (after taxes and minority interests)
Shoe Group	17	23
Purchase-Accounting Adjustments	(33)	11
Interest Expense[3]	(739)	(648)
Shareholder-Designated Contributions	(109)	(70)
Other	(17)	(11)
Operating Earnings	33	20
Capital Gains from Investments	60[4]	45[4]
	1,899	1,277
	1,085	671
	1,365	886
	2,415	1,553
Total Earnings - All Entities	$4,314	$2,830
	$2,450	$1,557

(1) Includes Executive Jet from August 7, 1998 (2) Includes Jordan's Furniture from November 13, 1999. (3) Excludes interest expense of Finance Businesses. (4) Includes General Re operations for ten days in 1998.

Source: Berkshire Hathaway Annual Report 1999.

Investment 1. MidAmerican (renamed Berkshire Hathaway Energy in 2014)

When potential wholly owned high-return-on-equity companies were unobtainable, one possible outlet for cash was to buy more of the same equities already held, such as Coca-Cola or American Express. But, as explained in the introduction, the market was in the grip of irrational exuberance, resulting in the prospect of poor future returns:

> Right now, the prices of the fine businesses we already own are just not that attractive. In other words, we feel much better about the businesses than their stocks. That's why we haven't added to our present holdings. Nevertheless, we haven't yet scaled back our portfolio in a major way: If the choice is between a questionable business at a comfortable price or a comfortable business at a questionable price, we much prefer the latter. What really gets our attention, however, is a comfortable business at a comfortable price.[60]

Buffett had been considering deploying his growing cash pile in the utility industry for some time. Back in 1998, he gave a talk to MBA students at the University of Florida in which he said he had thought about investing in this area "a lot because you can put big money in it. I have even thought of buying entire businesses … the guy with very low-cost power has a huge advantage".[61]

Following the purchase of railway operator BNSF – another business requiring vast amounts of money in operations – Buffett explained his logic a little more in his 2009 letter to shareholders:

> In earlier days, Charlie and I shunned capital-intensive businesses such as public utilities. Indeed, the best businesses by far for owners continue to be those that have high returns on capital and that require little incremental investment to grow. We are fortunate to own a number of such businesses, and we would love to buy more. Anticipating, however, that Berkshire will generate ever-increasing amounts of cash, we are today quite willing to enter businesses that regularly require large capital expenditures. We expect only that these businesses have reasonable expectations of earning decent returns on the incremental sums they invest. If our expectations are met – and we believe that they will be – Berkshire's ever-growing collection

of good to great businesses should produce above-average, though certainly not spectacular, returns in the decades ahead.[62]

In 1999, most of MidAmerican's subsidiaries were still heavily regulated. Generally, they were permitted to achieve returns on equity in the low single digits (in the order of 10%–12% per annum). If they operated with billions of capital, the cash flowing to shareholders from these returns could be substantial. In Iowa, as an example, the rates were fixed to 2005, which allowed 12% return on equity. After that, any additional return would be shared with customers.

MidAmerican had particular attractions for Buffett. First, it was widely acknowledged to be a low-cost operator and could therefore keep rates low for customers, which impressed regulators – even those in parts of the country where MidAmerican had not yet set foot. The goodwill of regulators was, and is, vital to securing a competitive position in many states. Of course, its cost advantage would be enhanced further by the ability to pay low interest rates on borrowed funds as part of Berkshire Hathaway.

There was also the potential to add billions more to MidAmerican in future years because there were so many organic growth and acquisition opportunities as the industry restructured. This was good for Berkshire – not only because MidAmerican presented as an outlet for funds, but also because few competitors in the energy field would have such an ability to find cash for capital expenditures, giving MidAmerican an edge.

And Buffett was convinced that money put into the hands of MidAmerican's managers would be used well. On the announcement of the deal, he said of them: "If I only had two draft picks out of American business, Walter Scott and David Sokol are the ones I would choose for this industry."[63]

There were also two tax benefits. First, Berkshire Hathaway produced taxable profits in abundance, whereas MidAmerican often had tax credits that it could not immediately benefit from internally when profits were low. Second, MidAmerican was allowed to accelerate depreciation (high writing-down allowances) on fixed assets, thus reducing cash flowing out to pay taxes in the short run. Taxes would eventually fall due, but in the meantime there was a stock of cash caused by deferred taxes. This cash could be used to earn a return.

The deal

In September 1999, Scott was in California for a conference – also attended by Buffett – when he received a telephone call from Sokol asking his advice on what to do with the company. Warren's sister, Bertie, has a house in Carmel near San Francisco and she threw a party – a casual gathering for her brother and a few close friends, naturally including Scott.

At the party, "Walter pulled me aside and asked if he could speak with me for a minute in another room,"[64] Buffett recalled:

> He talked about this public-utility company called MidAmerican that he was into, which wasn't going anywhere. They had tried to explain the business to Wall Street, but analysts didn't like it because they were looking for companies like AES or Calpine that had what they called 'deal velocity'. Walter said they were thinking of taking MidAmerican private and asked if I would be interested. I said yes.[65]

When Buffett returned to Omaha, he read some of MidAmerican's public reports. Within a few days, Sokol, Scott and Buffett met for breakfast, followed by another short meeting which concluded with Buffett saying: "[At] an appropriate price, we would indeed like to make a deal."[66] (At one point, Sokol handed over what he called "Energy 101" – a one-and-a-half-inch-thick presentation explaining the basics of the energy business, which Buffett has never opened.)

A press release was issued on 25 October to say that an agreement to do a deal had been reached, in which Buffett explained: "We buy good companies with outstanding management and good growth potential at a fair price, and we're willing to wait longer than some investors for that potential to be realized. This investment is right in our sweet spot."[67] The announcement also stated that while company HQ would remain in Des Moines (with Abel in charge of operations), the office of the chairman and CEO (Sokol) would stay in Omaha, focusing on strategic planning, mergers and acquisitions and global development.

The press release continued:

> No management changes are planned, no employee reductions will result from the transaction and the Company's name will stay 'MidAmerican'. It will be business as usual, with advantages that did not exist before. We will focus even harder on delivering high-quality service and the best possible value to customers, using leading-edge technology. As we prosper, so should our communities. This is a great deal for all concerned.[68]

MidAmerican shares immediately rose from around $27.25 to nearer the deal price of $35.05. "Why the odd figure of $35.05?" asked Buffett rhetorically in his 2007 letter to shareholders:

> I originally decided the business was worth $35.00 per share to Berkshire. Now, I'm a 'one-price' guy (remember See's?) and for several days the investment bankers representing MidAmerican had no luck in getting me to increase Berkshire's offer. But, finally, they caught me in a moment of weakness, and I caved, telling them I would go to $35.05. With that, I explained, they could tell their client they had wrung the last nickel out of me. At the time, it hurt.[69]

Of course, Buffett protests too much: per-share earnings were $2.59, giving a low PER of only 13.5 at a time when many companies were on multiples double or treble that.

The deal was not for Berkshire to acquire 100% of the equity. This was not possible, for two reasons. First, the Public Utility Holding Company Act of 1935 (PUHCA) stated that an unregulated corporation – as Berkshire was – could not have voting control of a regulated utility. Thus, Berkshire would hold only 9.7% of the common stock, limiting its votes: 900,942 shares were bought at $35.05, costing $31.6 million.

Second, Scott, Sokol and Abel each wanted to hold shares. Between them, they were to control 90.3% of the votes. Scott had about 86%, costing about $280 million; Sokol roughly 3% (around $10 million); and Abel approximately 1% (around $3 million).

Obviously, Berkshire wanted more than a 9.7% economic stake in the business. Furthermore, the old shareholders had to be paid a lot more than the $325 million or so handed over for the common stock. So,

Investment 1. MidAmerican (renamed Berkshire Hathaway Energy in 2014)

Berkshire also bought 34,563,395 shares of convertible preferred stock for $35.05 per share, costing $1.21 billion. With the two types of stock, Berkshire would have a 76% economic interest in MidAmerican.

The convertible preferred stock did not carry the right to vote generally with the common stock in the election of directors, but it did give Berkshire the right to elect 20% of MidAmerican's board – that is, Berkshire did not have managerial control, merely "significant influence".[70] Crucially, the convertible preferred stock had economic rights much the same as the common shares – for example:

- the preferred holders participated in dividends and other distributions to common shareholders as if the stock were common shares;
- the preferred stock was convertible into common shares on a one-for-one basis, as adjusted for splits, combinations, reclassifications and other capital changes; and
- upon liquidation, the preferred holders ranked equally with the shareholders of common stock.

Thus, Berkshire Hathaway's 2002 Annual Report stated: "[T]he convertible preferred stock is, in substance, a substantially identical subordinate interest to a share of common stock and economically equivalent to common stock."

Very importantly, the preferred stock could be converted into common stock if the government modified or repealed the PUHCA (which it did in 2005). Were that law to change, Berkshire could therefore end up with both an economic and a voting interest of 76%.

A third injection of cash also came from Berkshire: it bought from MidAmerican $455 million in fixed-income securities paying an annual 11% yield.

The deal closed on 14 March 2000. But that was not the end of the Berkshire money flowing to MidAmerican. In 2002, Berkshire bought another $402 million of preferred stock (an additional 6.7 million shares of convertible preferred stock – or "common-equivalent", as Buffett called it – at $60), taking its economic interest to over 80%. Also purchased were another $1.273 billion of the 11% bonds (see Table 1.3).

Table 1.3 Purchases of MidAmerican shares by Berkshire Hathaway

Date	Common stock purchases	Convertible preferred stock purchases	Fixed interest securities ('non-transferable trust preferred')	Berkshire's percentage of shareholder votes (fully diluted)	Berkshire's percentage of economic interest (fully diluted)	Other investors
March 2000	900,942 shares for $35.05 = $31.6m	34,563,395 shares for $35.05 = $1.211bn	$455m	9.7%	76%	Walter Scott: $280m 86% of voting interest David Sokol: roughly $10m, or 3% Greg Abel: roughly $3m, 1%
March 2002		6.7m shares for $60 each = $402m	$1.273bn	9.7%	80.2%	
2003			$150m redeemed	9.7%	80.5%	19.5% of stock owned by: Sokol, Abel and Scott (who controls approx 88% of the voting interest)
2004			$100m redeemed	9.7%	80.5%	

Investment 1. MidAmerican (renamed Berkshire Hathaway Energy in 2014)

Date	Common stock purchases	Convertible preferred stock purchases	Fixed interest securities ('non-transferable trust preferred')	Berkshire's percentage of shareholder votes (fully diluted)	Berkshire's percentage of economic interest (fully diluted)	Other investors
2005				9.7%	80.5%	Scott controls approx 86% of the voting interest.
2006	23,268,793 shares at $145 per share = $3.37bn	All convertible preferred converted to voting common stock			86.6%	Scott controls 11% of the voting interest.
Total paid for common stock	$3.4bn	$1.6bn				
2007					87.4%	
2008					87.4%	
2009					89.5%	
2010					89.8%	
2011					89.8%	

Date	Common stock purchases	Convertible preferred stock purchases	Fixed interest securities ('non-transferable trust preferred')	Berkshire's percentage of shareholder votes (fully diluted)	Berkshire's percentage of economic interest (fully diluted)	Other investors
2012					89.8%	
2013					89.8%	
2014					89.9%	
2015					89.9%	
2016					90.0%	
2017					90.2%	
2018					90.9%	
2019					91.0%	
2020					91.1%	
2021					91.1%	
2022					92.0%	
2023					92.0%	
2024					100%	

Source: Berkshire Hathaway annual reports.

The biggest event of all was the repeal of the PUHCA in 2005. On 9 February 2006, Berkshire converted its MidAmerican preferred stock, one for one, into voting common shares, giving it an economic and a voting interest of 80.5% (this is after allowing for executive options outstanding – until they were exercised, Berkshire's voting interest was 83.4%).

PacifiCorp was acquired in 2006 and, as a very large regulated electric utility (serving customers in six western states), it came with a hefty price tag: approximately $5.1 billion in cash. To pay for it, $1.7 billion in long-term debt and other securities was issued and MidAmerican turned to Berkshire to raise a further $3.37 billion through the sale of yet more common stock, taking Berkshire's ownership percentage to 86.6% when fully diluted (allowing for executive share options).

Note the valuation of each share: $145 – quite an advance from $35.05 in only six years; but then, it had increased its earnings per share from $2.59 to $15.78 by 2007. Buffett wrote in 2007: "And yes, I'm glad I wilted and offered the extra nickel."[71]

What happened after the deal

First, there were no changes in managerial personnel or corporate culture. Buffett and Munger do not see the point of buying a company if managerial change is necessary; it must come with good management in the first place. Shortly after buying into MidAmerican, Buffett explained – no doubt with Sokol, Scott and Abel in mind – that one indicator of good managers is that they care about who they sell the business to:

> [W]hen this emotional attachment exists, it signals that important qualities will likely be found within the business: honest accounting, pride of product, respect for customers, and a loyal group of associates having a strong sense of direction. The reverse is apt to be true, also. When an owner auctions off his business, exhibiting a total lack of interest in what follows, you will frequently find that it has been dressed up for sale, particularly when the seller is a "financial owner." And if owners behave with little regard for their business and its people,

their conduct will often contaminate attitudes and practices throughout the company. When a business masterpiece has been created by a lifetime—or several lifetimes—of unstinting care and exceptional talent, it should be important to the owner what corporation is entrusted to carry on its history. Charlie and I believe Berkshire provides an almost unique home. We take our obligations to the people who created a business very seriously, and Berkshire's ownership structure ensures that we can fulfil our promises.[72]

As far as reporting was concerned, Buffett explained to Sokol and Abel that his rule was that managers were free to talk about what was going on as much or as little as they wished. He said that in each of Berkshire's companies, the managers were doing a first-class job of running their operations in their own individual style and they did not need help from him. In a *Vanity Fair* interview, he added that his hands-off approach helped Berkshire to gain an enviable reputation among managers/owners who were thinking of selling their businesses, making Buffett "buyer of first resort". He added: "There are things where I've had to get involved, but I've usually done it through other people."[73]

Second, Sokol's and Abel's morale was boosted. Buffett liked what they were doing. It was an approach akin to that of Berkshire Hathaway: hunting for quality assets that were undervalued. Sokol and Abel were constantly looking at potential targets – and there were a lot of them. Long before the chance to acquire a company arose, they analysed it and worked out a plan, focusing on how to go about integrating the firm into the group should it ever become available. With this detailed preparation, they could act very quickly if the opportunity presented itself.

Sokol said that Abel was great to have at his side when making key business decisions of this kind because he could identify potential targets and get stuck into the detail of the analysis – so much so that he often ended up with a more in-depth knowledge of the business than many directors. He also excelled at assembling, managing and motivating teams.

Furthermore, they were now able to interact with two of the world's finest business minds. Said Sokol ten years after the deal:

> [S]elling MidAmerican to Berkshire Hathaway is the best decision I have ever made in my career. Buffett … has both breadth and depth of knowledge. He understands all sectors of business, and understands the logic behind each. Sometimes he sounds like he does not know much about technical issues of a sector because he isn't actively engaged in it. But he actually knows a lot because he reads so much, and has the ability to put all of his research and information together to come to rational decisions … What I have learned from Warren is that one should never bring emotion to a decision. Business decisions should always be based on facts, data, and circumstances … you have to be disciplined enough not to swing at every pitch![74]

Sokol, in his biography, wrote that Buffett provides a perfect haven for businesses that wanted to grow sensibly, creating a climate for business managers akin to playing in the Pro Bowl, but where individual performance takes a back seat to team performance:

> There are no most valuable player awards, just the satisfaction of being among the best in the world. Warren is a kind and considerate man who genuinely cares about people. He is as soundly based in the fundamentals of business as any human in history. All of us at MidAmerican are honoured to be part of Berkshire Hathaway.[75]

Third, there was an astounding expansion of the business. MidAmerican started 2000 with four 'platforms':

- **MidAmerican Energy**: Pretty well the original MidAmerican (without CalEnergy), with 89% of its sales in Iowa, serving nearly 700,000 electric customers.

- **Northern Electric**: A UK-based electricity company with over 1.6 million customers.

- **CalEnergy Generative**: An electricity producer in the US and other countries.

- **HomeServices**: At the time, the second-largest residential real estate brokerage firm in the US. It seems so out of place in an energy utility company, but it remains there to this day (still in second place). MidAmerican bought it in 1998 as a way of gaining access to new home buyers in need of utilities – a 'cross-selling' move. As well as brokerage services, it offered mortgage origination, title services, insurance, warranties and maintenance in 12 states. It was mostly Midwestern focused back in 2000, with 1,670 employees plus 6,600 associates (independent contractors). In the 2020s, it has over 40,000 real estate agents and more than 50,000 franchisees working in two-thirds of US states; and in a good year, it makes over $380 million after tax – so it's a substantial company in its own right. Ron Peltier, who built up the business through acquisitions and organic growth, sent financial reports directly to Buffett on the sixth of each month. What he said of Buffett is illuminating, especially considering how many companies are in the Berkshire family: "If you talk with him, he could probably cite you chapter and verse of our past year."[76]

By the beginning of 2025, MidAmerican – today known as Berkshire Hathaway Energy (BHE), following a rebrand in 2014 – had, through organic growth and acquisition, become a $128 billion asset company employing more than 24,000 people and adding assets through capital expenditure at a rate of $7–$9 billion per year.

Its cumulative profit after tax attributable to Berkshire was $42 billion over those 25 years (see Figure 1.2). Yet Berkshire has not taken anything out because Buffett wants the firm to add to its asset base to generate even higher profits in future, as "the industry offers owners the opportunity to deploy large sums at fair returns".[77] At least, that was his attitude until 2023, when he expressed his annoyance at the high likely cost of payouts for forest fires, particularly in California, caused by overhead powerlines; the response of regulators to those complaints is awaited.

Figure 1.3 shows the very high capital expenditure level maintained throughout; and Figure 1.4 shows the growth in total assets flowing from that investment.

Investment 1. MidAmerican (renamed Berkshire Hathaway Energy in 2014)

Figure 1.2 Berkshire's earnings from MidAmerican/BHE, after taxes and minority interests ($m). Total $42 billion

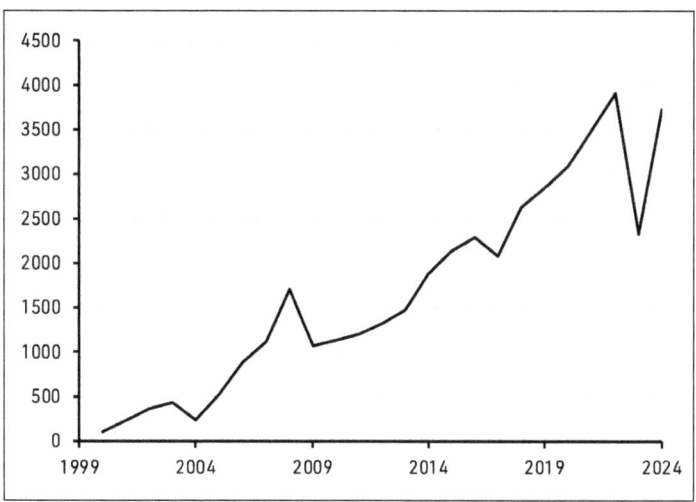

Source: Berkshire Hathaway annual reports.

Figure 1.3 MidAmerican/BHE capital expenditure has been much higher than profits ($m)

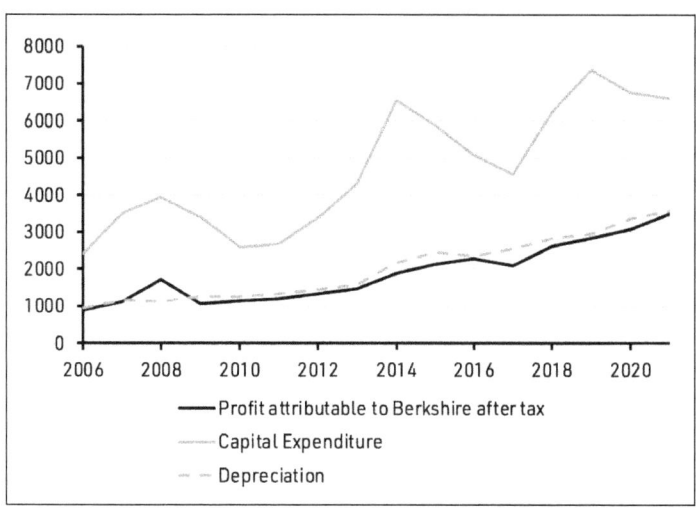

Source: Berkshire Hathaway annual reports.

Figure 1.4 MidAmerican/BHE assets ($m)

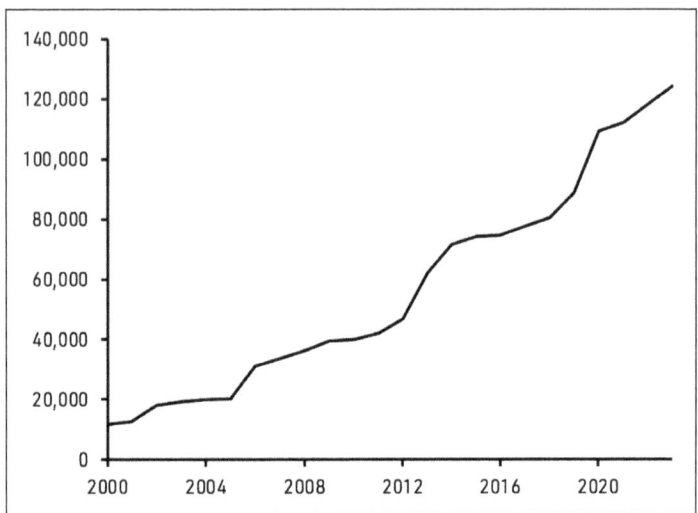

Source: Berkshire Hathaway annual reports.

Growing by leaps and bounds

In 2001, UK-based Yorkshire Electricity, with its 2.1 million customers, was added to Northern Electric, whose own customer base stood at 1.6 million. Another big leap was taken the following year when MidAmerican bought two natural gas pipelines. The Kern River pipeline, running from Wyoming to Southern California, cost $450 million. It was then undergoing a $1.2 billion expansion to double throughput so as to carry enough gas to generate electricity for ten million homes. The Northern Natural Gas route ran from Texas to the upper Midwest (16,600 miles) and cost MidAmerican $928 million. The two together transported about 8% of all gas used in the US.

Yet another key development was the aforementioned Pacificorp acquisition in March 2006 for $5.1 billion in cash. This added 1.6 million electricity customers in six western states (revenue $3.3 billion), with Oregon and Utah providing the most business. Pacificorp was in need of significant capital investment and Berkshire had capital inflows looking for a home.

Investment 1. MidAmerican (renamed Berkshire Hathaway Energy in 2014)

Sokol and Abel started investing in wind energy in 2004 and just four years later, almost 20% of Iowa's total capacity was wind-based. By 2016, wind accounted for 55% of all megawatt-hours sold to Iowa retail customers. Around that time, so many projects had been launched that it was anticipated wind energy would cover the annual needs of all Iowa customers (24.6 gigawatts (GW)) by 2021. This emphasis on renewable energy had a second-order effect in Iowa as it attracted large high-tech installations – both because of its low prices for electricity (which data centres use in huge quantities) and because most tech CEOs are enthusiastic about using renewable energy.

MidAmerican started a similar programme of wind power growth at Pacificorp as soon as it was acquired. But not everything was positive at the new company. "Arriving at PacifiCorp, we found 'wind' of a different sort: The company had 98 committees that met frequently. Now there are 28," wrote Buffett in 2008.[78]

By 2022, MidAmerican – now BHE – had over 3,400 turbines in operation in Iowa and had invested $13.6 billion in wind production there. In addition, BHE invested $16.5 billion in other wind, solar and geothermal energy projects that it operates itself, and financed an additional $6.9 billion for other operators. It has retired 18 coal generation units, cutting greenhouse gas (GHG) emissions by 35% since 2005.[79] According to its 2023 Annual Report:

> BHE plans to continue investing in renewable and other low-carbon generation and storage in the future and to cease coal operations at an additional 15 coal generation units between 2025 and 2030 in a reliable and cost-effective manner, thereby achieving a 50% reduction in GHG emissions from 2005 levels in 2030.

BHE also plans to retire all remaining coal units by 2049 and all natural gas units by 2050, enabling it to achieve net-zero GHG emissions. The proportion of energy derived from different generation methods is shown in Figure 1.5.

Figure 1.5 BHE net owned electricity generation capacity (GW) by type in 2023. Total: 34.8 GW

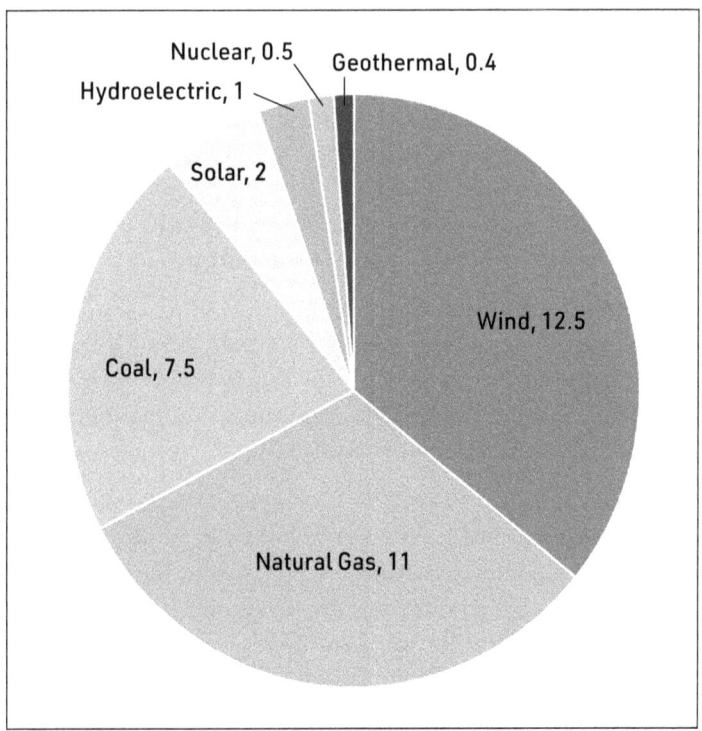

Source: Berkshire Hathaway Annual Report 2023.

The year 2006 saw the start of a massive commitment to renew and extend much of the grid that transports electricity throughout the west. This needed to be done – not least to connect up scattered renewable energy production sites. The company accepted that the task would not be complete until 2030 and would cost $18 billion:

> BHE's decision to proceed, it should be noted, was based upon its trust in America's political, economic and judicial systems. Billions of dollars needed to be invested before meaningful revenue would flow. Transmission lines had to cross the borders of states and other jurisdictions, each with its own rules and constituencies. BHE would also need to deal with hundreds

of landowners and execute complicated contracts with both the suppliers that generated renewable power and the far-away utilities that would distribute the electricity to their customers … we are today searching for other projects of similar size to take on … Whatever the obstacles, BHE will be a leader in delivering ever-cleaner energy.[80]

In 2008, MidAmerican went after Constellation Energy. Despite being outbid, it still walked away with $917 million as a result of a profit on preferred stock already bought and another $175 million in the form of a break fee.

In December 2013, NV Energy was bought for $5.6 billion. The company supplies electricity to about 88% of Nevada's population (1.2 million electricity and 0.2 million retail natural gas customers). AltaLink – an electric transmission system serving 85% of Alberta's population – was acquired the following year for $2.7 billion.

Natural gas transmission and storage business Dominion Energy was added to the other pipe businesses in 2020 for approximately $2.5 billion. It brought a further 5,400 miles of pipeline and 420 billion cubic feet of natural gas storage capacity, as well as partial ownership (25%) of a liquefied natural gas export, import and storage facility (Cove Point); a further 50% share of that was acquired for $3.3 billion in 2023.

According to Sokol, one of the reasons why the company has succeeded in identifying and integrating acquired firms when many others fail is because it does all the hard work before deciding whether to offer to buy:

> [W]e have made 18 acquisitions in the past 12 years … In virtually every case, we have met or exceeded our initial expectations of value … Equally important is that we have chosen not to pursue more than 115 potential acquisitions during the same time frame because they did not appear to us, after evaluation, to represent a value-enhancing opportunity. Without question, history has shown that some of our best decisions are those that kept us from making overpriced acquisitions.[81]

Figure 1.6 shows the profits produced from BHE's different streams and Table 1.3 offers further detail.

Figure 1.6 Earnings from MidAmerican/BHE energy divisions ($m)

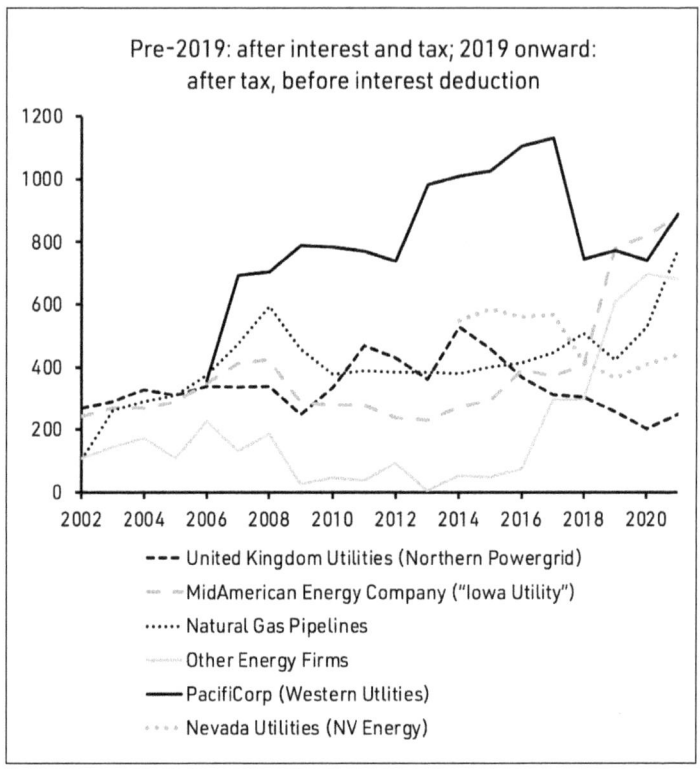

Source: Berkshire Hathaway annual reports.

Investment 1. MidAmerican (renamed Berkshire Hathaway Energy in 2014)

Table 1.3 Business units of MidAmerican/BHE earnings, 2002–2024

	Home Services ($m)	UK utilities (Northern Electric, Northern Powergrid), ($m)	MidAmerican Energy Company ('Iowa Utility') ($m)	Natural gas pipelines ($m)	Other ($m)	PacifiCorp (Western utilities), ($m)	Nevada utilities (NV Energy) Earnings $m	Canadian Transmission Utility ($m)	Renewable projects ($m)
2002	70	267	241	104	108				
2003	113	289	269	261	144				
2004	130	326	268	288	172				
2005	148	308	288	309	107				
2006	74	338	348	376	226	356			
2007	42	337	412	473	130	692			
2008	−45	339	425	595	186	703			
2009	43	248	285	457	25	788			
2010	42	333	279	378	47	783			
2011	39	469	279	388	36	771			
2012	82	429	236	383	91	737			
2013	139	362	230	385	4	982			50
2014	139	527	270	379	54	1,010	549	16	194
2015	191	460	292	401	49	1,026	586	170	175

	Home Services ($m)	UK utilities (Northern Electric, Northern Powergrid) ($m)	MidAmerican Energy Company ('Iowa Utility') ($m)	Natural gas pipelines ($m)	Other ($m)	PacifiCorp (Western utilities) ($m)	Nevada utilities (NV Energy) Earnings $m	Canadian Transmission Utility ($m)	Renewable projects ($m)
2016	225	367	392	413	73	1,105	559	147	157
2017	220	311	372	446	296	1,131	567		
2018	204	304	407	507	296	745	417		
2019	160	256	781	422	608	773	365		
2020	375	201	818	528	697	741	410		
2021	387	247	883	774	680	889	439		
Reclassification								Reclassification	
2022	100			1,040	1,356			US utilities: 2,295	
2023	13			1,079	1,024			US utilities: 906	
2024	−107			1,232	1,334			US utilities: 1,961	

Note: For 2002–2018, the numbers are before interest and tax deduction. For 2019 onwards, the figures are after tax but before interest charged to corporate centre.

Source: Berkshire Hathaway annual reports.

If it were publicly traded, BHE would be the second-largest utility in the US ranked by market value. But because it is private and backed by a company with a long planning horizon – Buffett is famous for repeatedly saying: "Our favourite holding period is forever" – it can discuss with regulators a vision for decades ahead. Berkshire's reputation for high integrity, its AAA balance sheet and its long history of delivering for utility customers mean that BHE is the owner of choice for regulated assets – and will be for years to come.

What happened to our leading characters?

David Sokol

In April 2008, aged 51, Sokol stepped down as CEO of MidAmerican but remained chairman, with Abel taking on the CEO role. This left Sokol free to develop his career beyond MidAmerican – at the time, he was referred to in the press as a potential successor to Buffett.

Later in 2008, Sokol was instrumental in persuading Buffett to invest $232 million in BYD (8.2%). The story goes that Munger was a great admirer of BYD's founder, Wang Chuanfu, thinking he would achieve great things with his battery and car business. Munger's enthusiasm intrigued Buffett because he was rarely so effusive in his praise. But a second opinion can be useful, so before committing, Buffett sent Sokol to take a closer look. On his return, Sokol said that Wang was amazing and Buffett should meet him: "Many good entrepreneurs can go from zero to a couple of million in revenues and a couple of hundred people. He's got over 100,000 people. Few can do that."[82]

Of course, BYD was to become the largest electric vehicle manufacturer in the world and those shares increased to $10 billion – a phenomenal return on $232 million. Sokol joined BYD's board in 2009.

In 2009, Sokol was again called on by Buffett to sort out a problem at another subsidiary by becoming CEO of NetJets (see Volume 3, Investment 9). However, in March 2011, Sokol resigned from Berkshire,[83] telling Buffett that for some time he had wanted to do something on his own. This was after it was revealed that Sokol had bought shares in Lubrizol just weeks before suggesting to Buffett that it would be a good company for Berkshire to buy. Sokol could not know for sure how Buffett would react to this suggestion – in particular, whether he would or would not buy. He also made plain to Buffett from the outset that he had bought some stock in Lubrizol.[84] But many people thought the gain he made when Berkshire did offer to buy the company was accompanied by a failure to disclose all relevant information to Buffett, going against Berkshire's ethical standards and harming the reputation not only of Sokol, but also of Berkshire (the Securities and Exchange Commission investigated the case but did not bring charges).

Sokol then said he wanted to build his own 'mini-Berkshire' and develop his philanthropic ventures. He set up Teton Capital to manage his family business investments. This holding company oversees investments in the banking, manufacturing, consumer products, energy, real estate and technology sectors. He also joined the board of directors of the Horatio Alger Association of Distinguished Americans – a non-profit educational organisation which honours contemporary citizens who serve as role models and also provides scholarship assistance.

Greg Abel

From 2008, Abel grew MidAmerican into one of the top three energy utility companies in the US, with over 5 million customers and valued (by Barron's)[85] at $90 billion (about 12% of Berkshire's market capitalisation). Following that success, in 2018, Abel was elected to the board of Berkshire Hathaway and was appointed as vice chairman – non-insurance operations. Then, in 2025 he was appointed CEO with Buffett retaining the Chairman's role.

In June 2022, Berkshire Hathaway acquired all of the BHE common stock held by Abel, for $870 million; and the 2022 Annual Report stated:

> If for any reason the services of our key personnel, particularly Mr. Buffett, were to become unavailable, there could be a material adverse effect on our operations. Should a replacement for Mr. Buffett be needed currently, Berkshire's Board of Directors has agreed that Mr. Abel should replace Mr. Buffett.

In 2024, all remaining outstanding shares in BHE were purchased by Berkshire for just over $1 billion.

Abel's increased workload does not seem to have affected his calm demeanour, even temper, knack for rational analysis and ability to get the job done with quiet efficiency. It's just that he now has a bigger canvas on which to paint his masterpieces.

Walter Scott

Scott served as a board member of Buffett's Berkshire Hathaway conglomerate from 1988 until his death in September 2021, aged 90. To add to his portfolio of interests, Scott took on the role of chairman at Level 3 Communications after it was spun out of Peter Kiewit and Sons in 1998. The company built fibre-optic networks to carry Internet traffic. Traded on Nasdaq, it reached a market value of more than $40 billion in the late 1990s but then struggled to make a profit from the billions it had spent on its fibre-optic network. Its stock plunged and it was ultimately acquired by CenturyLink in 2017.

In 2010, Buffett, Bill Gates and Melinda French Gates established the Giving Pledge movement – a group of billionaire philanthropists who have committed to give the majority of their wealth to charitable causes, either during their lifetimes or in their wills. At the outset, in August 2010, 40 of America's wealthiest people made this commitment. Today, the movement's 242 pledgers come from 29 countries.[86]

In June 2010, Buffett appealed to Scott to join, which he did. By the time of his death, Scott had a net worth of over $4 billion, mostly still in the form of BHE stock. Scott vowed to donate nearly all of his wealth to good causes. Helping young people and contributing to his community were his two main philanthropic goals, he stated in his pledge letter. "My children were taken care of long ago – what they make of their lives is now their own responsibility," Scott said to the *World-Herald*. "Ultimately, nearly everything will go to the foundation, with the hopes it will benefit my hometown for many generations to come."

Even before his death, Scott was generous. For example, he sent $64 million to his *alma mater*, Colorado State University, where he had earned his degree in civil engineering in 1953. There is now a Walter Scott, Jr College of Engineering at the university. Scott and his wife also gave large sums to the University of Nebraska at Omaha, especially the Medical Center. Sections of the Joslyn Art Museum and the Holland Performing Arts Center in Omaha are also named in honour of the Scotts; as is an aquarium at Henry Doorly Zoo in his beloved Omaha.

Learning points

- **In investing, you do not have to stick forever to one approach**. When Berkshire Hathaway was small, it made sense to hold a collection of tiny NCAV investments, plus a few strong economic franchise businesses. As it grew, an increasing proportion of its capital went to wonderful companies selling at a fair price, rather than those cheap relative to balance sheet or historical earnings. But when the cash to be allocated became much greater than the opportunities available in the NCAV and economic franchise arenas, the marginal dollar was sent to earn an acceptable return in utilities. Of course, this can be spiced up by buying into utilities when they are cheap, when others are selling them off.

- **Putting your trust in a few people who seem worthy of that trust is a good way to make money in business (and, more widely, a good way to live)**. Buffett said that all major decisions at MidAmerican were unanimous, in that the four key people agreed. And Buffett completely trusted the other three to make all of the other decisions without him. That level of trust and freedom is often reciprocated with great loyalty, effort and a desire to 'make Warren proud'.

- **Merging one company with another is very difficult to get right**. Having senior managers who acknowledge the difficulties, who limit the number of deals so that each has sufficient attention and who carefully plan post-merger integration is vital. Sokol, Scott and Abel knew the pitfalls and thus emphasised careful planning and imposed strict rejection criteria for many merger opportunities that did not offer assured shareholder value.

- **Be a 'buyer of first resort'.** Over time, Buffett built a reputation for being a 'good owner' – he placed great faith in the extant managers; gave them freedom to grow the business if good returns were available on each extra dollar committed; praised their efforts; was supportive with fresh injections of capital if justified; and was a font of wisdom on business matters. This reputation encouraged many company owners and CEOs to prefer Berkshire Hathaway as their home, rather than be controlled by uncaring, interfering, ill-informed Wall Street financiers.

Investment 2

CORT BUSINESS SERVICES

Summary of the deal

Deal	CORT Business Services
Time	2000
Price paid	$386m
Quantity	Wesco, 80.1% owned by Berkshire, bought 100% of CORT. In 2011, Berkshire bought the other 19.9% of Wesco.
Sale price	Still held
Profit	The data is patchy, but average annual profits after tax for the first 11 years were $12.4m, then rose to around $39m in mid-2010s, but fell thereafter. So, in its best year, CORT generated a return of 10% on the amount paid; in its worst, it lost money.
Berkshire Hathaway in 2000	Share price: $40,800–$80,000 Book value: $61.72bn Per share book value: $40,442

Investment 2. CORT Business Services

This was not one of Warren Buffett's best deals. CORT is in the business of buying furniture and other things needed for an office or home and then renting it to people or businesses wanting to use it for a limited time, typically nine months. After about three years of the furniture being used by a series of organisations or families, it is cleaned up and sold in one of CORT's stores – usually for slightly more than the purchase price.

It's a sound business model that fulfils a social need. And in all the years since 2000, except those in deep recession, it has been profitable. Another positive is that CORT is the biggest 'rent-to-rent' firm in the US, offering a wide selection of furniture across the country. Furthermore, it was led by an excellent management team with vast experience: the CEO, for example, had started with the company in his mid-20s, back in 1972. They knew what they were doing and they did it at low cost.

And yet – and this is where we can get some insight into the importance of industry structure when analysing a company – CORT produced low profits relative to the $386 million paid for it because its pricing power was constrained. Despite being the biggest 'rent-to-rent' firm, with the most recognised brand, it had numerous direct competitors in most cities and other places. It couldn't get customers to pay a significant premium over the cost of providing its service because they could generally turn to an alternative provider.

And this was a relatively easy sector to enter. Sure, some capital was required to buy the furniture, but it didn't need tens of millions. So, even if CORT bought up competitors to try to gain a pricing advantage, it wouldn't be long before a 'mom-and-pop' startup entered the market with lower rental prices.

CORT also came under pressure through indirect competition. Running through the minds of many customers were the alternative options of rent-to-own and outright buy. If the players in these substitute product markets decided to compete hard with each other for each customer dollar, they would affect CORT's potential to raise its prices.

Of course, there was a price – its intrinsic value – that could be paid for CORT in 2000 that would take into account its pressured competitive position. But in my view, that price was not as high as $386 million. But then, I do have the benefit of hindsight: I've seen (most of) the profit numbers since 2000.

Growth, with some bumps

CORT Furniture Rental began in 1972 as an offshoot of Mohasco Corporation. Mohasco's main business was Mohawk Carpets, the largest US carpet manufacturer, which saw potential in manufacturing furniture as well as carpets. Thus, from 1963, it went on an acquisition spree of US furniture makers.

By 1972, Mohasco recognised that it was frequently producing a surplus of furniture, so it set up CORT Furniture Rental, bought five regional furniture rental companies and merged them into one. With this strategic move, Mohasco's excess output could be rented by people who only needed to equip a place for a limited time, such as those temporarily moving into an area and taking a short-term apartment lease, newlyweds or those recently separated. The company's showrooms displayed a variety of 'furniture groups' with different styles and prices, ranging from the essentials bundle for a one-bedroom apartment (e.g., bed, dresser, lamps, table) to more upmarket and extensive packages. A young Paul Arnold – later to become Berkshire's key person at CORT – joined the company in 1972, fresh out of law school.

While the initial focus was on households, it quickly became apparent that a much larger potential market was corporate furnishings: companies that needed to furnish an office quickly and without the capital commitment of buying desks, chairs, cabinets and so on. An additional argument for renting rather than buying was that the monthly payments made to CORT were 100% tax deductible.

By 1986, CORT's revenue had reached $84 million, accounting for one-tenth of Mohasco's sales. It has a bumper year in 1987, making it the fastest-growing member of the group, with revenues of $93 million.[87]

In 1988, Mohasco was the subject of an unwanted takeover bid. To find an alternative and 'friendlier' buyer, it opened itself up to being acquired. The winning bid (out of 16 offers) was MHS Holding, an entity organised by Citicorp Venture Capital (CVC). It subsequently geared up the company with over $300 million of debt, but at least it permitted the old management team to continue.

To service the debt, CORT was sold a year later for $150 million. The buyer was a management group financed by CVC. Now CORT itself was burdened with enormous debt and little cash. As a result, the company struggled.

Arnold – who by 1992 had worked his way up to the position of president and CEO – took the tough decision to close some showrooms and cut costs wherever he could. But losses continued: $6 million lost on revenue of $106.5 million in 1992.

The position was clearly unsustainable, so CVC created another company – New CORT Holdings – to acquire all the shares in CORT Furniture Rental for $82.2 million. Crucially, the interest rate was much more bearable and there was cash to grow again.

Part of the growth strategy was to acquire other furniture rental companies. At first, CORT bought several small firms; but in 1993, it went much bigger by acquiring a major competitor in Texas with revenues of $41.5 million, lifting the group top line to $128.6 million.

November 1995 was a landmark month for the company as it went public on the NYSE at $12, changing its name to CORT Business Services Corporation. The following year, it sold $32 million more shares (at $18.75 a share), allowing it to repay almost half its debt and CVC to take out cash. But CVC still held a 45% equity stake in the company.

More large company purchases followed as CORT spread across the US. By then, 80% of revenues came from corporate customers. Even multinationals such as Warner Bros and Exxon valued the ability to quickly obtain and make use of furniture in offices for a few months without further commitment. Teams on special/temporary assignment often needed quick setups; as did groups of consultants on secondment and company training camps.

But now, office furniture accounted for only one-third of the corporate revenue. The other two-thirds came from companies paying for apartment furniture for people sent on temporary assignment or relocating to another part of the country. CORT even went so far as to supply crockery, appliances, towels and toothpaste.

The lease terms could be for three, six or 12 months (the average length turned out to be nine months), with the business model predicated on retrieving the initial cost over the first ten months. After each rental, the items were thoroughly cleaned. Generally, after three years of use, they would be sold through CORT's furniture rental clearance centres (it had 86 of these by 2000, alongside its 118 showrooms). Because CORT had such good buying power, with $80 million of purchases annually, it could usually sell items on at prices averaging about 8% more than what it had paid three years – and three to five rental customers – previously.

A developing business around this time was the supply of furniture for trade shows and conventions, assisted by the acquisition of yet another three established firms.

With 1997's revenues growing to $287 million, CORT had become the largest player in the industry and was perceived as a company really going somewhere: its shares had risen from $20.75 at the beginning of the year to $38.87 by October. Wrote Jerry Knight in the *Washington Post*:

> On its way to becoming a hot stock, Cort over a quarter of a century walked through the hot coals of just about every financial fad of the late 20th century. Cort was rolled up, vertically integrated, spun off, overleveraged, junk bonded and LBO'd before it was IPO'd.[88]

CORT still had $50 million of junk bonds outstanding, carrying a 12% interest rate. The thinking was that it was able to service this because its performance was regarded as "highly predictable, minimising the possibility of surprises that spook investors".[89] The reliability of its earnings would be severely tested in recessions in the next couple of decades – when losses appeared – and during the Covid-19 pandemic, when activity declined dramatically.

But at the time, these difficulties were all in the dim and distant future. In 1997, the managers and investors were full of confidence, looking to scale up across the nation. CFO Frances Ann Ziemniak told the *Washington Post* in 1997 that "acquisitions are part of our strategy". She continued: "[T]here a lot of mom-and-pops out there doing between $1 million and maybe $8 million a year, and a few bigger ones."[90]

By the end of 1998, CORT had grown its salesforce to 900 people working out of 119 showrooms in 32 states and the District of Columbia. It also had 83 clearance centres. In all, it had about 2,700 employees (106 at HQ, 1,500 in warehouse and distribution, and just under 200 in regional administration).

Despite its 20 or so acquisitions since January 1993, Arnold was hungry for more. The growth model adopted was generally to buy lease portfolios – that is, the rental contracts and furniture. It also retained sales personnel "with strong local customer relationships";[91] but it did not acquire showrooms, distribution facilities or clearance centres in markets where it already had operations. However, in geographical areas new to the company, it would often opt to take the real estate too. Occasionally, it bought larger regional companies to provide critical mass in new markets and/or increase market share in existing markets.

An attempted management buyout

CORT was doing well, with after-tax profits rising to $23.4 million in 1998 – up from $15.9 million in 1996 – when, in March 1999, Arnold put together a management buyout (MBO) in partnership with Bruckmann, Rosser, Sherrill & Co – a private equity firm established by a trio of alumni from none other than CVC (is this the fourth time CVC was involved in a leveraged buyout in connection with CORT?). The price offered was $24 per share in cash plus $2.50 in liquidation value of a new series of preferred stock. This $26.50 (making a total of $347 million) was almost 60% more than the stock was selling for.

Preston G Athey – manager of T. Rowe Price's Small-Cap Value Fund, which owned 10.4% of CORT, making it the second-largest shareholder after CVC (44%) – was opposed to the leveraged MBO, arguing that the price was too low given the enterprise's long-term value, and that it had been trading at $45 in 1998.

In response, CORT managers with Bruckmann *et al.* increased their offer to $28 in August. A few days later, Brook Furniture Rental – a rival which had been eyeing CORT for 14 years – stepped in with a $28 offer. This was rejected by the directors. Also in August, an independent proxy advisory firm declared the offer at $28 "inadequate".

There was so little support from public shareholders that the directors decided to cancel the buyout in November. That decision was reinforced by the difficulty they would have experienced selling the required junk bonds given the weakness in that market.

The deal

Meanwhile, Bruce Cort – who, despite his surname, was unconnected to CORT – had been watching these turbulent events at the company. He had a tenuous connection with Buffett, as an airline broker who, back in 1986, had sold a jet to Berkshire Hathaway. Cort thought that CORT would be a good fit for Berkshire and, on 23 November 1999, sent a one-page fax to suggest the idea to Kiewit Plaza HQ, together with a *Washington Post* article detailing the failed MBO.

Buffett was intrigued and immediately printed out CORT's Securities and Exchange Commission filings and "liked what he saw".[92] Later that day, he told Cort that he did have "a possible interest" and asked if he could arrange a meeting with Arnold. Six days later, Buffett, Arnold and Cort met in Omaha and discussed the company and its recent history. Buffett was impressed both with the financials of CORT and with Arnold: "I knew at once that we had the right ingredients for a purchase: a fine though unglamorous business, an outstanding manager, and a price (going by that on the failed deal) that made sense."[93]

Arnold relished obtaining a good price for his shareholders and looked forward to being in a permanent home presided over by a couple of gentlemen who could supply capital for expansion without the need to leverage the company. And he could duck out of all the hassle that comes with an NYSE listing. He said: "[T]his transaction delivers significant value to our shareholders as they receive a substantial premium over the current price level of our shares. It is also an outstanding vote of confidence in CORT's strategy, long-term growth potential and its people. Wesco and its parent, Berkshire Hathaway, are perfect partners for CORT as they share our management philosophy and values, as well as our vision for what we can become."[94]

They didn't hang around: six weeks later, the deal was announced to the market at $28 per share in cash. The announcement was made by Wesco, Berkshire's 80.1% subsidiary (see Volume 1, Investment 22 for more on Wesco) – which, by 2000, had become a holding company principally engaged in property and casualty insurance, with a substantial float of money to invest.

CORT's board of directors met at their Fairfax, Virginia HQ and unanimously approved the agreement and recommended that CORT shareholders tender their shares. CVC had already agreed to tender its 44% holding and Arnold was willing to sell his 1.6%.

Charlie Munger, as chairman of Wesco, welcomed the firm to his group: "CORT is a classic example of a fine company that can be even better as a result of the strength and stability that result from inclusion in the Berkshire group of companies."[95] Buffett added that he thought CORT was a "best in class" business and that he was certain this would be a great relationship. The tender offer was wrapped up on 18 February 2000.

Disappointment

Things started positively: CORT reported a good profit for 1999, at $50.8 million pre-tax and $30 million after tax, on a turnover of $295 million in rental income plus another $59 million in furniture sales. So, the one-year PER at the buying price was $386 million/$30 million = 12.9 – less than half the average PER in the stock market (at 30), which was then in the throes of a giant bubble.

The acquired balance sheet looked relatively good too, with $209 million of furniture and $107 million of other tangible assets. Liabilities amounted to $172 million, so CORT had net tangible assets of $144 million.

Arnold was lauded as a star executive by Munger in Wesco's 1999 Annual Report. He stated that Arnold was to continue as CEO with no interference from Wesco HQ: "We would be crazy to second-guess a man with his record in business. We are absolutely delighted to have Paul and CORT within Wesco and hope to see a considerable expansion of CORT's business and earnings in future years."[96]

Sales rose in 2000 – as did profits, to $33.4 million after tax – so all was looking good.[97] Buffett and Munger were full of praise for Arnold and his team. But black clouds loomed on the horizon after the stock market fell from its March 2000 high. Munger wrote in early 2001: "[C]ommencing late last year, and continuing to date, new business coming into CORT has declined sharply … its management attributes this to reduced industry demand caused by a weakening economy."[98] Nevertheless, Munger maintained that CORT was recession-proof and optimistically supported raising the employee count to 3,000. He believed "that CORT's operations will remain profitable in any likely recession-related decline in the rent-to-rent segment of the furniture business".[99]

But Munger also acknowledged one key negative factor:

> The rent-to-rent segment of the furniture rental industry is highly competitive. There are several large regional as well as a number of smaller regional and local rent-to-rent furniture companies. In addition, numerous retailers offer residential and office furniture under rent-to-own arrangements.[100]

For me, this is the crux of the issue; but then, I have the benefit of hindsight. This was a business boat in which, no matter how hard the managers rowed, it was difficult to maintain a satisfactory speed – there were simply too many direct competitors and suppliers of substitute services in the adjacent rent-to-own segment.

CORT was very good, with a great command of all the competitive factors, which arguably made it the best in the industry: good furniture condition, a large selection, flexible terms of rental agreement, speed of delivery, deposit requirements and customer service. But for all that, it had limited pricing power because customers had alternative suppliers: in many areas, there were numerous competitors to CORT.

The branding might have helped a little in raising the monthly charge, but customers remained very price sensitive.

As economic optimism petered out, CORT's sales and profits just got worse (see Figure 2.1). People moved for temporary assignments less often; there were fewer startups looking for furniture to rent, fewer expansions of established firms into new offices and fewer trade show exhibitors. It turned out that CORT was vulnerable to recession after all.

Figure 2.1 CORT profits after tax ($m), February 2000–December 2004

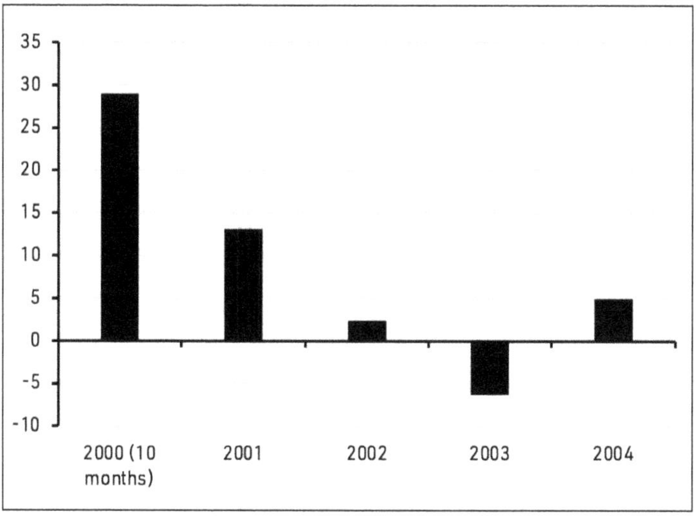

Source: Wesco annual reports.

Munger refused to be pessimistic, seeing opportunity in the economic downswing: "We happily tolerate a poor part of the business cycle when we turn it to our advantage by expanding business through cash acquisition at sound prices."[101] CORT spent a total of $57 million on several small acquisitions in 2002 and 2003. Despite buying additional activity, overall group revenue fell from $395 million in 2001 to $360 million in 2003 as the post-dot-com mood and the 9/11 Twin Towers attack depressed demand.

Four years on, Munger was perhaps at least regretting the timing of the purchase: "[O]bviously, when we purchased CORT we were poor predictors of near-term industry-wide prospects of the 'rent-to-rent' sector of the furniture business."[102] But he continued to believe in CORT's long-term prospects, as signalled by his applauding the $24 million pumped into a home-grown Internet-based finder of apartments, which also allowed customers to select furniture rentals.

A revival

Finally, green shoots of economic recovery appeared in late 2004, so CORT was set to enjoy four years of reasonably good profits (see Figure 2.2). But these didn't get anywhere near the $33.4 million seen in 2000. Even CORT's 2006 net income of $26.9 million was a mere 7% return on the $386 million paid for the company more than six years before. CORT added yet more businesses, spending $3 million in 2004, which secured its position as the largest – and only national – provider of rental furniture in the rent-to-rent segment. And in January 2008, it stepped outside the US for the first time by adding Roomservice Group in the UK for a mere $5,500.

Figure 2.2 CORT profit after tax ($m), 2005–2010

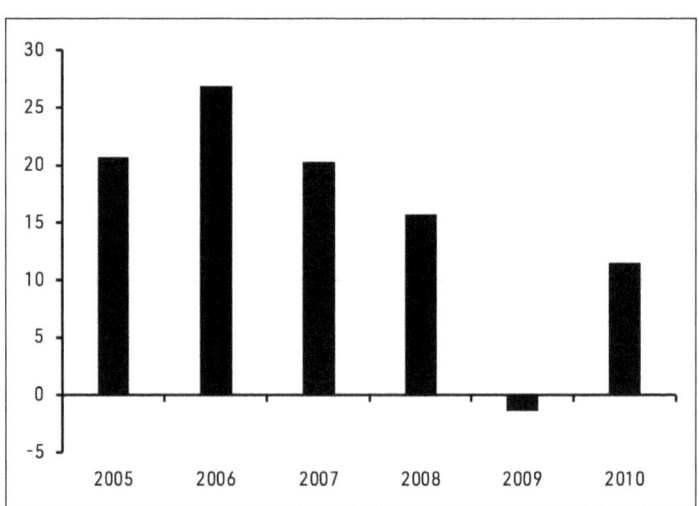

Source: Wesco annual reports.

Around this time, CORT was hit by the financial crisis of 2007–2008 and the Great Recession that followed. Despite bringing a few more companies into the fold, there were still plenty of rivals around. In 2007, Munger again stated that the rent-to-rent segment of the furniture rental industry was highly competitive, with "several large regional competitors, as well as a number of smaller regional and local rent-to-rent competitors".[103] The company fell into losses in 2009, with Munger admitting that "business has been melting away faster than CORT can fix it".[104] So it trimmed its workforce to 2,074.

The (fairly) good years

The 2010s were good years for CORT. It seemed that at last, the price of $386 million could – if you squinted – be justified. The profits shown in Figure 2.3 are before the deduction of tax, unlike the previous charts: Wesco became fully owned by Berkshire Hathaway in 2011 and thus ceased providing annual reports, so we do not have the after-tax profit numbers. But even if we knock off around one-third for tax, annual earnings of $20–$40 million make it to the 'just-about respectable' mark – and Berkshire shareholders had to wait a decade to get to this point.

Arnold retired in 2012, after 40 years with the company. His endeavours had grown the organisation through more than 40 acquisitions to become the industry leader, serving millions of families and 80% of Fortune 500 companies. CORT was also the largest tradeshow and event furnishings company in the US, and had the largest global network of partner firms in over 70 countries. Arnold was succeeded as CEO by Jeff Pederson, who had served as CORT's CFO from 2004 to 2006 and as president since 2006.[105]

Figure 2.3 CORT profit before tax ($m), 2011–2016

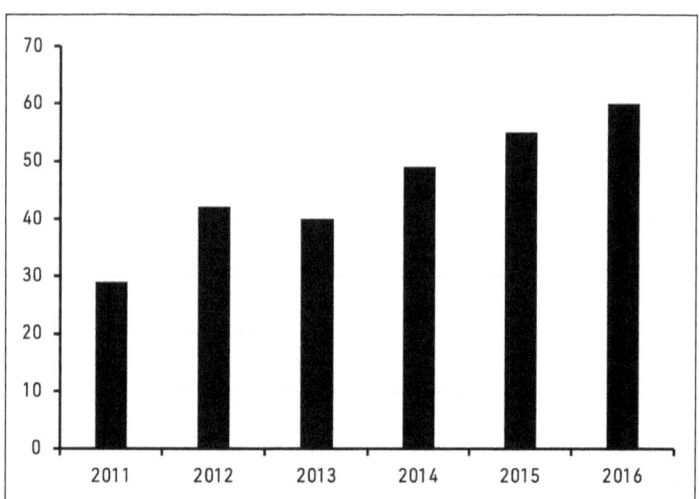

Source: Berkshire Hathaway annual reports.

After 2016, Berkshire's annual reports did not reveal CORT's profit numbers; they were simply too small to deserve separate reporting. However, we can glean hints from Buffett's narrative – the situation did not improve, even before Covid-19 hammered profits as offices were closed:

- 2017: "Lower earnings from CORT." The number of employees fell from 3,002 to 2,487 over the year.
- 2018: No comment made.
- 2019: "Revenues increased"; no comment on profits.
- 2020: "Decline in earnings." Covid-19 had a big impact.
- 2021: "Lower earnings."
- 2022: No comment made, but employee numbers reached a new low of 1,966.
- 2023: No comment made.

Arnold, now in his late 70s, keeps active and is currently a non-executive director of H&E Equipment Services, a $2 billion company which rents out construction equipment.

Learning points

- **Barriers to entry can help maintain good pricing.** CORT has struggled to erect barriers against new entrants to its markets. Its branding, national presence and extensive range provide a little bit of pricing power, but this is nothing like what the 'share of mind' of Coca-Cola, Disney or See's Candy can do for a product.

- **Quality of managers is crucial, but not sufficient.** CORT had some of the best managers, but the business boat they rowed was far from the best. Arguably they had the best furniture rental business in the world, but that wasn't enough to generate satisfactory returns on $386 million.

- **Very few businesses are recession-proof.** Munger was convinced that furniture rental would glide through recessions. It did not. Fewer offices were being set up, fewer people were on temporary assignment and in need of apartment furniture for a few months and so on. If you think a business is recession-proof, test your thinking by asking whether the product or service is an absolute necessity or is bought only after basic needs are satisfied and people are feeling optimistic and expanding.

Investment 3

MOODY'S

Summary of the deal

Deal	Moody's
Time	Bought: Q1 2000 Sold 48.6% of holding 2009–2013 Remaining 51.4% still held
Price paid	$499m
Quantity	24m pre-split shares (about 15% of Moody's) (after the May 2005 2:1 split: 48m)
Sale price and current value	The sold shares raised an estimated $656m. Market value of those still held: $10bn
Profit	Estimated $10.2m; twentyfold so far
Berkshire Hathaway in 2000	Share price: $40,800–$80,000 Book value: $61.72bn Per share book value: $40,442

Moody's is one of three leading global credit rating firms, the other two being Standard & Poor's and Fitch. Between them, these three commanded in 2000 – and still command – over 90% of the market for credit ratings of bonds and other financial instruments. The oligopolists maintain very good margins and returns on capital employed because an issuer of, say, a corporate bond generally feels compelled to employ the services of at least one of them to assess the ability to repay the debt – that is, the relative risk of default compared with other bonds. In the absence of such a credit rating, the seller of the bond will normally find it difficult to attract investors to buy at a good price – that is, it will end up paying a higher interest rate on the debt.

The world of rating systems

A debt rating depends on the likelihood of payments of interest and capital not being made (i.e., default), and on the extent to which the lender is protected in the event of default on the loan contract (i.e., the recoverability of debt).

The rating agencies say that they do not, in the strictest sense, give an opinion on the likelihood of default, but merely evaluate relative creditworthiness or relative likelihood of default. And because rating scales are relative, default rates fluctuate over time. Thus, a group of middle-rated bonds is expected to be consistent in having a lower rate of default than a group of lower-rated bonds; but it will not, year after year, have a default rate of, say, 2.5%.

The highest rating is Aaa (Moody's), AAA (S&P) or AAA (Fitch) – pronounced 'triple-A'. This rating indicates very high quality, with an extremely strong capacity to repay interest and principal. Single A indicates a strong capacity to pay interest and capital, but some degree of susceptibility to impairment as economic events unfold. Baa (Moody's) or BBB (S&P and Fitch) indicates adequate debt service capacity but vulnerability to adverse economic conditions or changing circumstances.

Debt rated B or Caa has predominantly speculative characteristics and thus a high credit risk. The lowest rating is C (Moody's) or D

(Fitch and S&P), which typically indicates that the firm is in default, with little prospect for recovery of principal or interest. Moody's adds 1, 2 or 3 to the generic category to indicate a finer gradation of risk.

Ratings of Baa3 (Moody's) or BBB (S&P and Fitch) or above are regarded as 'investment-grade debt'. This is important because many institutional investors are permitted to invest in investment-grade bonds only (see Exhibit 3.1). Bonds rated below this are called 'non-investment grade', 'high-yield' or 'junk' bonds.

Exhibit 3.1 Moody's rating scale

Investment-grade bonds – highest to lowest	Non-investment grade bonds – highest to lowest
Aaa	Ba1
Aa1	Ba2
Aa2	Ba3
Aa3	B1
A1	B2
A2	B3
A3	Caa1
Baa1	Caa2
Baa2	Caa3
Baa3	Ca
	C

In addition to ratings on bonds still with many years until redemption, Moody's has a short-term ratings system (see Exhibit 3.2). These ratings indicate an individual issuer's capacity to repay all short-term obligations, not a specific short-term debt. Once Moody's has given its short-term rating, it applies to all of the issuer's senior, unsecured obligations with an original maturity of less than one year (e.g., commercial paper or medium-term note programmes) and applies to a variety of currencies of issue or markets of issue (e.g., London, New York).

Exhibit 3.2 Moody's short-term rating definitions

P-1: Prime-1 Superior ability to repay

P-2: Prime-2 Strong ability to repay

P-3: Prime-3 Acceptable ability to repay

NP: Not Prime – does not fall within any Prime rating categories

Beyond that, Moody's assesses bank financial strength (see Exhibit 3.3)

Exhibit 3.3 Bank financial strength ratings

A) Superior intrinsic financial strength (highly valuable and defensible business franchises, strong financial fundamentals, predictable and stable operating environment).

B) Strong intrinsic financial strength (valuable and defensible business franchises, good financial fundamentals, predictable and stable operating environment).

C) Adequate intrinsic financial strength (more limited but still valuable business franchises, acceptable financial fundamentals, predictable and stable operating environment; or good financial fundamentals within a less predictable and stable operating environment).

D) Modest intrinsic financial strength (possibly requiring some outside support at times. Limited by one or more of a weak business franchise, deficient financial fundamentals and unpredictable and unstable operating environment).

E) Very modest intrinsic financial strength, with high likelihood of periodic outside support or eventual need for outside assistance.

In addition, Moody's provides bank deposit ratings, insurance company financial strength ratings, money market and bond fund ratings. Also, it was – and is – a major research publisher, including in-depth research on major issuers, industry studies, economics, special comments and credit opinion handbooks.

In 2000, Moody's employed approximately 1,400 employees, maintaining offices in 14 countries. As well as ratings and credit research on corporations and their bonds, it assessed and rated government issuers in approximately 100 countries. Its customers included investors, depositors, creditors, investment banks, commercial banks, other financial intermediaries and a wide range of corporate and governmental issuers of securities.

At the time Berkshire Hathaway bought its shares, Moody's had ratings on approximately 100,000 corporate issuances – including industrial corporations, financial institutions, governmental entities and structured finance (e.g., mortgage bond) issuers – and more than 68,000 public finance obligations. Back then, the ratings were disseminated to the public through a variety of print and electronic media; but these days, electronic communication dominates.

In 2024, Moody's covered:

- 100 sovereign nations issuing debt;
- 12,000 company issuers;
- 29,000 public finance issuers (e.g., local authorities); and
- 96,000 structured finance obligations.

It now employs over 3,000 people worldwide.

A quality company

Warren Buffett was attracted to Moody's because it is a 'moat' business. Buffett explained what he meant by a 'moat' at Berkshire's 1995 shareholder meeting:

> We're trying to find a business with a wide and long-lasting moat around it, protecting a terrific economic castle with an honest lord in charge of the castle.
>
> And in essence, that's what business is all about. I mean, you want to be the lord of the castle, yourself. In which case, you don't worry about that last factor.
>
> What we're trying to find is a business that, for one reason or another – it can be because it's the low-cost producer in some area, it can be because it has a natural franchise because of

capabilities, it could be because of its position in the consumers' mind, it can be because of a technological advantage, or any kind of reason at all – has this moat around it.

All moats are subject to attack in a capitalistic system, so everybody is going to try to figure out how to get to it.

And most moats aren't worth a damn in capitalism. That's the nature of it. And it's a constructive thing that's the case.

But we are trying to figure out … why is that castle still standing? And what's going to keep it standing or cause it not to be standing five, ten, 20 years from now? What are the key factors? And how permanent are they? How much do they depend on the genius of the lord in the castle?

And then, if we feel good about the moat, we try to figure out whether, if the lord is going to try to take it all for himself, whether he's likely to do something stupid with the proceeds, et cetera.

Following Charlie Munger's death in late 2023, just 33 days before his 100th birthday, Buffett recalled how Munger had told him flat-out in 1965 that he had made a dumb decision in buying control of Berkshire, "But, he assured me, since I had already made the move, he would tell me how to correct my mistake."[106] At the time, Munger had no financial interest in Buffett's investment partnership and did not expect to ever own any shares in Berkshire; they were just friends, accustomed to having frank conversations.

Munger offered the following advice:

> Warren, forget about ever buying another company like Berkshire. But now that you control Berkshire, add to it wonderful businesses purchased at fair prices and give up buying fair businesses at wonderful prices. In other words, abandon everything you learned from your hero, Ben Graham. It works, but only when practiced at small scale.[107]

Moody's fell into the category of a wonderful company. And, if bought for a fair price relative to proven earnings, Berkshire Hathaway could look forward to steadily rising earnings per share because as economies and companies grew, it seemed likely that there would be an increasing volume of bonds coming to market needing a rating.

Given the industry's high barriers to entry because of the exceptional reputation of the three incumbents, there was a virtual guarantee that Moody's would continue to attract clients eager to gain a reliable and credibly independent credit rating. The moat surrounding Moody's franchise is the extraordinary difficulty that a new entrant would have in building the required capability, reputation and name recognition to serve the same market.

A closely related concept is the 'inevitable'. 'Inevitables' are companies that will dominate their fields for an investment lifetime. They have such enormous competitive strengths that they will still be great companies 25 or 30 years from now. Inevitables are to be found in industries that are unlikely to experience major change – a fast-changing industry precludes the possibility of reaching a conclusion as to the probability of a company dominating its sector three decades hence.

Imagine that you are going on a ten-year mission to Mars and while you are gone, you are unable to alter your portfolio. If you could make only one investment now, what would you look for?

Answer: it would have to be in an industry on a steady growth path and where the company leading the industry will remain the leader. Coca-Cola or Kellogg comes to mind – as does Moody's.

Market leadership does not equate to inevitable status. General Motors, Kodak, Intel, Nokia and Sears enjoyed periods when they seemed invincible. "For every inevitable, there are dozens of Imposters, companies now riding high but vulnerable to competitive attack."[108]

Do not expect to come up with a long list of inevitables. Buffett and Munger said that they would never be able to create a list as long as 20. Also note that many on their list were never bought because to do so would mean over-paying. So, it's possible even for inevitables to be bad buys – always remember to ask: "What's the price?"

The creation of Moody's

John Moody, a keen 32-year old investor, published his first *Moody's Manual of Industrial and Miscellaneous Securities* in 1900. This provided investors with summary descriptions of companies along with basic statistics on their shares and bonds. It also covered financial institutions and government agencies. It was an instant hit, selling out after two months. Clearly, it was worthwhile for him to bring out annual editions. By 1903, it was firmly established as the go-to publication for data on hundreds of organisations and securities – its title shortened to *Moody's Manual* by most users.

The stock market crashed in 1907, at a time when Moody's company was poorly capitalised. Things were so bad that he had to sell the business. But in 1909, he returned with a new publication – one that did more than just bring data together: it also provided some analysis, not least of which was the innovative idea of bond safety ratings on a scale of Aaa to E. This more detailed work initially focused exclusively on railway companies – 1,300 bonds in total. Said Moody in 1950:

> In the Spring of 1909 I brought out the first edition of [Moody's Analyses of Railroad Investments] ... which attempted to analyze railroad reports and rate their bond issues. While it raised a storm of opposition, not to mention ridicule ... it took hold with dealers and investment houses ... and long before 1914 it was a recognized authority and 'Moody's Ratings' had become an important factor in the bond trading and bond selling field.[109]

The annual volumes sold well – to investors, financial institutions, public libraries and university libraries. They were even published in London to help those investing in US railroads. By 1911, the manual was 4,000 pages long; and by 1913, the scope of the publication had expanded to include industrial companies and utilities in several volumes. In 1919, US state and local government bonds were rated; and from 1924, the publication covered all issues on the US bond market.

The Great Depression in the 1930s created a challenge for bond raters because a goodly proportion of US corporations went bust and their bonds lost all value. Nonetheless, Moody's persisted in publishing its ratings and other analysis. And, to the credit of its analysts, few of the bonds highly rated by Moody's missed payments.

Moody's Manuals were so well established by 1950 that they were Buffett's primary source for summary information on companies. For example, when he was a student at Columbia University, he discovered by looking in *Moody's* that Benjamin Graham's investment fund owned 55% of a small insurance company called GEICO (see Volume 1, Investment 2 and Volume 2, Investment 1). Using *Moody's*, he was able to quickly check whether this company was worth further investigation. Presented there were profit components and balance-sheet items.

The young Buffett spent hundreds of hours reading *Moody's Manuals* looking for bargain shares. He later said: "I went through the Moody's Manuals page by page. Ten thousand pages in the Moody's Industrial, Transportation, Banks and Finance Manuals – twice. I actually looked at every business – although I didn't look very hard at some."[110]

In April 1952, Buffett married Susan Thompson in Omaha. Aunt Alice (who was to become one of the first investment 'partners' a few years later) lent the newlyweds her car for the honeymoon. Before they set off, Buffett loaded the backseat with – you've guessed it – *Moody's Manuals*.

As his father's five-person brokerage in Omaha subscribed to *Moody's*, Buffett had access to the manuals when he worked there in the early 1950s:

> I found a little company called Genessee Valley Gas near Rochester [New York]. It had 22,000 shares out. It was a public utility that was earning about $5 per share, and the nice thing about it was you could buy it at $5 per share.[111]

No wonder Buffett has such fond memories of using *Moody's Manuals*. There were no brokerage reports for such a tiny company – but, he said: "[A]ll you had to do was turn the page. It worked out so well I actually went through the book a second time."[112]

"I found Western Insurance in Fort Scott, Kansas. The price range in Moody's financial manual … was $12–$20. Earnings were $16 a share. I ran an ad in the Fort Scott paper to buy that stock."[113]

Buffett also discovered a New Bedford-based bus company by the name of Union Street Railway, selling for about $45 when it had $120 in cash and no liabilities. "Nobody is going to tell you about the Union Street Railway [or] Genessee Valley Gas … [sometimes] you find something that shouts at you."[114]

Between 1954 and 1956, Buffett was paid a salary to spend his days going through the manuals alongside Walter Schloss – another of the 'peasants' at tiny Graham-Newman. "We would look up stuff and read. We would go through Standard & Poor's or a Moody's Manual and look at companies selling below working capital. There were a lot then," recalled Schloss.[115]

As a 24-year-old working in New York, Buffett was able to take things one step further: he often went down to Moody's or Standard & Poor's offices:

> I was the only one who ever showed up at those places. They never even asked if I was a customer. I would get these files that dated back 40 or 50 years. They didn't have copy machines, so I'd sit there and scribble all these little notes, this figure and that figure.[116]

In February 1958, Moody died at the age of 89; and within four years, Moody's Corporation was bought by credit reporting and information collection giant Dun & Bradstreet Corporation (D&B).

A year later, another wing of D&B investigated a fledgling investment partnership in Omaha. The Buffett Partnership was described as:

> Volume steady. Condition sound … maintains a prompt local pay record … had a net worth of $9.4m consisting of cash resources, income-producing securities and other investments. A sound condition continues … employs one … rents office space on eighth floor … premises orderly.[117]

For its first few decades, Moody's business model was to charge investors a subscription to obtain the information. But by the 1970s, it was clear that issuers of bonds were greatly advantaged if they ensured that their bonds were rated, so Moody's figured it could charge the issuers substantial sums. Financial regulators didn't want just anybody issuing ratings, so they approved only a handful of firms with the requisite capability to do bond ratings, thus ensuring an oligopoly and boosting Moody's pricing power – if you want a rating for the bond you are about to issue, you've got to pay up.

In the late 1990s, it was apparent that Moody's was doing far better than its parent and the feeling among shareholders was that they would benefit if they held shares in the two operating businesses independently, each focused on its own distinct core businesses. While Moody's was focused on bonds, D&B provided much more wide-ranging analysis on tens of millions of companies, with particular attention on their creditworthiness, regardless of whether they were bond issuers. Thus, it analysed small and medium-sized firms in addition to large ones. A $1 million company might consult D&B to decide whether to grant trade credit to another $1 million company, for example. It might also ask D&B for a list of potential customers that it could approach or for information on supplier firms – say, on risk of failure.

The directors agreed to split and made the announcement in December 1999. The separation was completed on 30 September 2000 by creating a new quoted company for the D&B business while continuing with the old company, which was quickly renamed Moody's Corporation. In anticipation of the split, Buffett bought $499 million of D&B's shares in February 2000 (24 million shares).

The separation was accomplished through a tax-free distribution to shareholders of D&B of all the shares of a newly formed 'new D&B'. So, just to be clear: investors that did nothing still held shares in the 'old D&B', which was renamed Moody's, and were also given their rightful proportion of the 'new D&B', which is the D&B we know today. Buffett sold all the spun-off (new D&B) shares held by Berkshire Hathaway over the following four years.

Buffett's approach to buying

In 2010, Buffett was asked: "What kind of due diligence did you and your staff do when you first purchased Dun & Bradstreet?" He responded that he didn't have any staff – it was just him:

> I do all my own analysis. And basically it was an evaluation of both Dun & Bradstreet and Moody's, of the economics of their business. And I never met with anybody. Dun & Bradstreet had a very good business, and Moody's had an even better business. And basically, the single-most important decision in evaluating a business is pricing power. If you've got the power to raise prices without losing business to a competitor, you've got a very good business. And if you have to have a prayer session before raising the price by a tenth of a cent, then you've got a terrible business. I've been in both, and I know the difference.[118]

Interestingly, Buffett said that he knew nothing about the management of Moody's:

> I've also said many times in reports and elsewhere that when a management with reputation for brilliance gets hooked up with a business with a reputation for bad economics, it's the reputation of the business that remains intact. If you've got a good enough business, if you have a monopoly newspaper, if you have a network television station – I'm talking of the past – your idiot nephew could run it. And if you've got a really good business, it doesn't make any difference. It makes some difference maybe in capital allocation or something of the sort, but the extraordinary business does not require good management.[119]

He hastened to add that he wasn't implying that Moody's had bad management; simply that he didn't know them. Even after a decade of being the largest shareholder, he found it difficult to comment on the quality of the managers: "It's hard to evaluate when you have a business that has that much pricing power. I mean, they have done very well in terms of huge returns on tangible assets, almost infinite."[120]

What did Buffett buy?

This section offers a few of Moody's numbers to try to gain insight into the value of the business at the time of buying. Market capitalisation was $20.79 × 161.7 million shares outstanding = $3.36 billion.[121] With such a large market capitalisation, it is surprising to find that revenue in 2000 was just $602 million – up only slightly from 1999, when it was $564 million.

The key factor here is that a lot of that revenue drops through to the bottom line (see Figure 3.1). Net profit was 26% of revenue in 2000. Another notable feature is the growth rate in net income, which doubled in five years.

Figure 3.1 Moody's net income ($m), 1996–2000

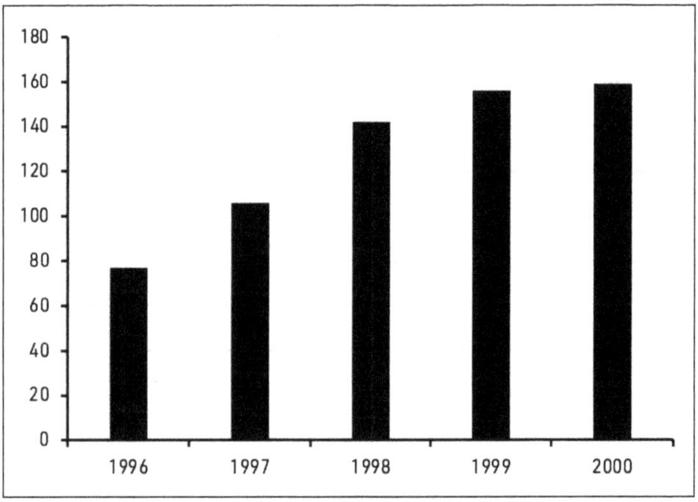

Source: Moody's Corporation Annual Report 2000 (Moody's presented these numbers as though the Moody's wing of D&B were a separate entity all the way through this period).

And this pattern of growth is reflected in the earnings per share numbers (see Figure 3.2). At Buffett's buy price of $20.79, the historical PER paid is $20.79/$0.98 = 21. To pay such a high multiple, Buffett must have anticipated fast earnings growth. And he was right, as we will see later.

Figure 3.2 Moody's earnings per share ($), 1996–2000

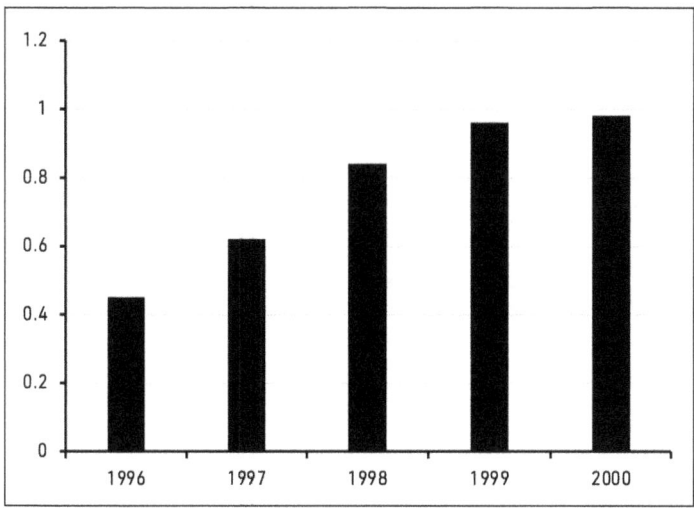

Source: Moody's Corporation 2000 Annual Report (Moody's presented these numbers as though the Moody's wing of D&B were a separate entity all the way through this period).

This was certainly not a Graham-type investment. It lacked the requisite balance-sheet safety – it had a net liability balance sheet (see Figure 3.3). Buffett, and the company, were relying on the qualitative factors around the strength of the economic franchise.

Figure 3.3 Moody's total assets and shareholders' equity ($m), 1996–2000

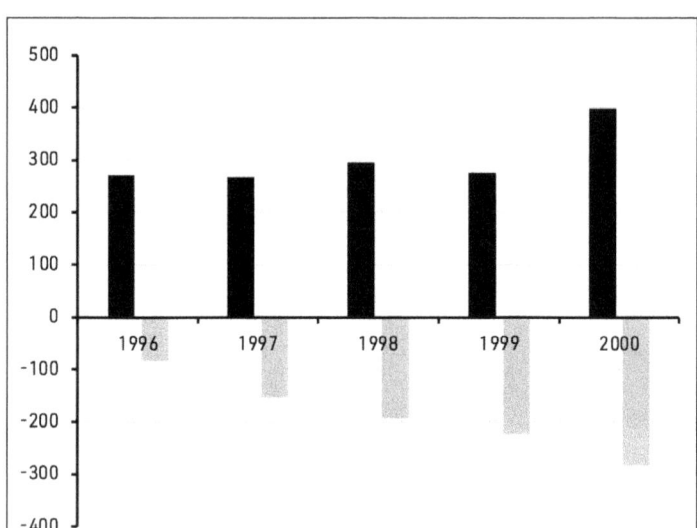

Source: Moody's Corporation 2000 Annual Report (Moody's presented these numbers as though the Moody's wing of D&B were a separate entity all the way through this period).

Table 3.1 is an attempt to construct an owner earnings analysis as though we were back in 2000 – but there isn't much data to go on, so treat it with caution. (At a minimum, I normally look at ten years of data to estimate owner earnings, but this is not possible for Moody's given its separation from D&B as late as 2000.)

With owner earnings, we are trying to determine the earnings that, in future, would be left for shareholders after the managers have used sufficient cash to pay for expenditure to maintain the strength of the economic franchise (e.g., additional capital items, additional working capital, marketing spend, R&D and staff training), to maintain unit volume and to invest in all value-generating projects available.

Depending on the circumstances, the owner earnings figure may be the same for every future year or on a steadily rising (or falling) trend.

Naturally, owner earnings are impossible to obtain with any degree of precision because many of the input numbers are merely educated guesses about the *future*. The only evidence we have available is past data, so we start with that and then use qualitative analysis to judge whether to simply project forward the past pattern or modify the previous trend for future-orientated thinking. Despite this imprecision, it remains an important method for thinking through valuations.

We use what the company *actually* invested in new working capital items and in new fixed capital items, and what it spent on marketing, R&D, staff training and so on, already deducted from the income statement. In Moody's case, the split from D&B caused distortions in working capital reporting, so this element is ignored (in any case, for this service business, working capital is not a major element of additional cash use).

What the analysis really requires is the amount *necessary* to maintain the quality of the economic franchise and the unit volume, and to invest in value-generating projects. To start with, we make the bold assumption that what was spent by the managers was also the necessary amount.

When we move to forward-looking analysis to attempt to value the firm, we need to make another bold assumption on the real amount needed to invest in new working capital, fixed capital items and so on in the future. The historical analysis helps us to make that judgement.

Table 3.1 Moody's 'owner earnings' in the past

$m	2000	1999	1998	1997
Profit after interest and tax deduction	159	156	142	106
Add back non-cash items such as depreciation, goodwill and other amortisation	17	13	15	16
Totals to: Amount available for distribution to shareholders before considering the need to spend on fixed capital items and working capital to maintain the company's economic franchise and unit volume and invest in value-generating projects	176	169	157	122
Deduct fixed capital expenditure other than for property; and deduct additional cash invested in working capital – in Moody's case, the split from D&B caused distortions in working capital reporting, so this element is ignored. The figures shown are actual expenditures and are therefore a rough proxy for the 'necessary' expenditures to maintain franchise, etc.	−14	−13	−12	−12*
'Owner earnings'	162	156	145	110

* Estimated capital expenditure for 1997 (not presented in Moody's 2000 Annual Report, the earliest available).

Source: Moody's 2000 Annual Report.

The average annual 'owner earnings' in the past was $143 million over the four years we have. If we conservatively assume that all future years will produce the same as in the period 1997–2000, an estimate of intrinsic value could be put forward for further thought:

Intrinsic value = Owner earnings next year denoted as a perpetuity ÷ Required rate of return for this risk class of asset

Investment 3. Moody's

If we use the risk-free rate – as represented by the US government ten-year bond – as our 'required rate of return', we find that in October 2000, this was 5.6%.

Using this as the 'discount rate', intrinsic value = $143 million ÷ 0.056 = $2.55 billion.

Arguably, we should use a higher discount rate because ownership of equity in Moody's comes with greater risk than ownership of US government bonds. The extra return on an averagely risky US share in the 101 years up to the end of 2000 was 5% per year greater than that on ten-year government bonds.[122]

Adding the equity risk premium of 5% to the risk-free rate of 5.6%, we obtain a required rate of return of 10.6%. An estimate of intrinsic value allowing for equity risk this way is $1.35 billion:

Intrinsic value = $143 million ÷ 0.106 = $1.35 billion

Buffett bought when the market capitalisation was $3.36 billion, so clearly he was allowing for something else in his valuation.

That factor is growth in owner earnings year on year over the decades to come. We will look at the actual earnings reported later. For now, let's jump to an assumption that Moody's owner earnings rise by 4.3% in every year after 2000 (I chose this because this is the actual rise in average annual nominal gross domestic product 2000–2024).

Intrinsic value estimate = Next year's owner earnings ÷ (Required rate of return minus growth rate)

Intrinsic value estimate = ($143 million x 1.043) ÷ (0.106 – 0.043) = $2.37 billion

The estimate of $2.37 billion is still short of what Buffett willingly paid – which indicates, perhaps, that he anticipated a faster rate of growth in owner earnings than 4.3%.

At 8% growth, for example, the intrinsic value estimate rises to $5.94 billion:

Intrinsic value estimate = ($143 million x 1.08) ÷ (0.106 – 0.08) = $5.94 billion

This seems an appropriate point to look at the actual reported net income – it's a bit of a leap to use accounting net income as a substitute for owner earnings, but it will give us some idea of the growth rate experienced.

Figure 3.4 Moody's net income ($m), 2000-2023

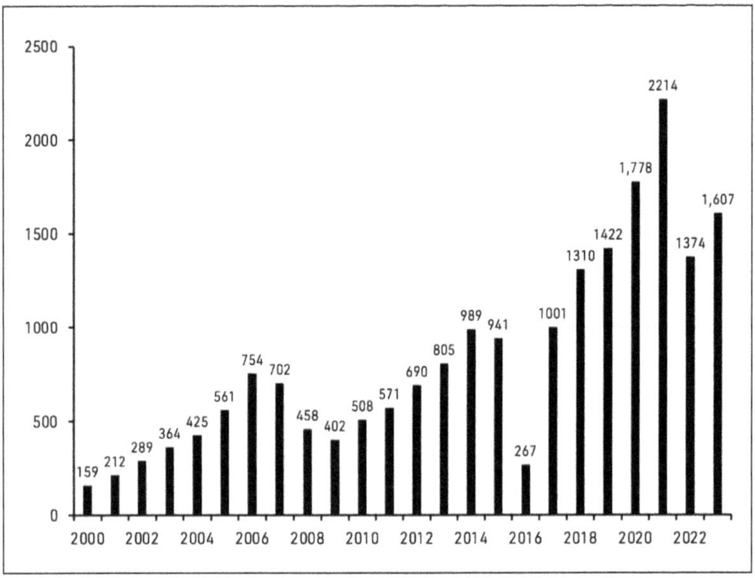

Year	Net Income ($m)
2000	159
2001	212
2002	289
2003	364
2004	425
2005	561
2006	754
2007	702
2008	458
2009	402
2010	508
2011	571
2012	690
2013	805
2014	989
2015	941
2016	267
2017	1001
2018	1310
2019	1422
2020	1,778
2021	2214
2022	1374
2023	1,607

Source: Moody's Corporation annual reports.

Figure 3.4 shows a tenfold rise in net income over 24 years – that is, an average annual growth rate of 10.6%. This is much faster than anything we have allowed for in the intrinsic value calculations above. If we knew then what we know now about growth in net income, we would be willing to pay multiples of the $3.36 billion Moody's was valued at in 2000. Buffett could see this glorious future – or at least something like it.

Mr Market, on the other hand, couldn't perceive this and so offered a bargain on a PER of 21. This is another example where the division into 'growth' stocks and 'value' stocks makes no sense – both rely on discounting future cash flow and a high PER can be justified as offering good value if intrinsic value is much more than market price.

To check that net earnings are not too distant from owner earnings, the numbers for 2021–2023 are provided in Table 3.2.

Table 3.2 Moody's owner earnings estimates 2021–2023

$m	2023	2022	2021
Profit after interest and tax deduction	1,607	1,374	2,214
Add back non-cash items such as depreciation, goodwill and other amortisation	373	331	257
Totals to: Amount available for distribution to shareholders before considering the need to spend on fixed capital items and working capital to maintain the company's economic franchise and unit volume and invest in value-generating projects.	1,980	1,705	2,471
Deduct fixed capital expenditure other than property and additional cash invested in working capital. The figures shown are actual expenditures and are therefore a rough proxy for the 'necessary' expenditures to maintain franchise etc.	-88	-658	-341
Owner earnings	1,892	1,047	2,130

Source: Moody's Corporation annual reports.

The owner earnings numbers are in the same ballpark as reported net income, which allows for some confidence in saying that both net income and owner earnings have risen about tenfold.

What happened after buying?

First, Buffett did not interfere. He said in 2010 that he had never been in Moody's office or initiated a call to it.[123] During the next decade, on three or four occasions, the CEO or an investor relations person stopped by in Omaha:

> [T]hey think they have to do that. I have no interest in it basically, and I never requested a meeting. It was part of what they thought investor relations were all about. And we don't

believe much in that ... If I thought they needed me, I wouldn't have bought the stock.[124]

It seems they did not need Buffett's input: the price of Moody's stock doubled by the end of 2001 as net income soared to $212 million in 2001. And this was the pattern set for the next few years: by 2006, net income was $754 million – a 374% increase on 2000. The stock rose over sixfold during the same period (see Figures 3.5 and 3.6) (the shares were split 2:1 in May 2005).

Figure 3.5 Moody's share price (in pre-split prices), December 2000–March 2005

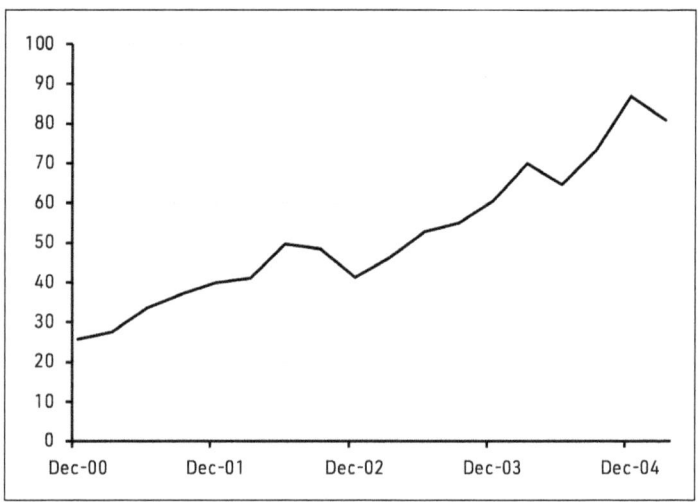

Source: Berkshire Hathaway 13-F filings with the SEC.

Figure 3.6 Moody's share price June 2005–March 2024, prices after the 2:1 share split

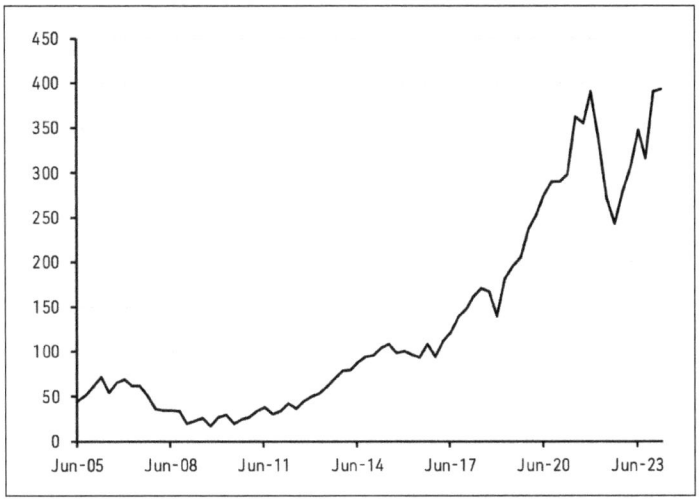

Source: Berkshire Hathaway 13-F filings with the SEC.

Much of the rise in earnings over the 2000–2006 period was due to Moody's selling services to those wishing to issue securitised bonds backed with subprime mortgages on US homes. The 'structured finance' business shown in Figure 3.7 is mostly subprime bond ratings, but also includes bonds secured against credit card receivables, commercial property and automobile loans.

Moody's 2001 Annual Report said:

> In its simplest form, in structured finance, corporations and financial firms sell assets, including mortgages, credit card receivables and auto loans, to companies which issue securities backed by the cash flows from (or market values of) the assets. Using structured finance, issuers can accelerate the rate at which these assets generate cash. Using a range of structuring techniques, issuers can also create securities with credit ratings higher than the rating of the company itself, tapping a wider array of investors and enhancing liquidity.

In some years, Moody's rated over 95% of such asset-backed securities issued in the US. (There is more on securitisation in the chapter on H&R Block, which was a big arranger of such bonds at this time.)

Figure 3.7 Moody's revenue from operating segments ($m), 2000–2006

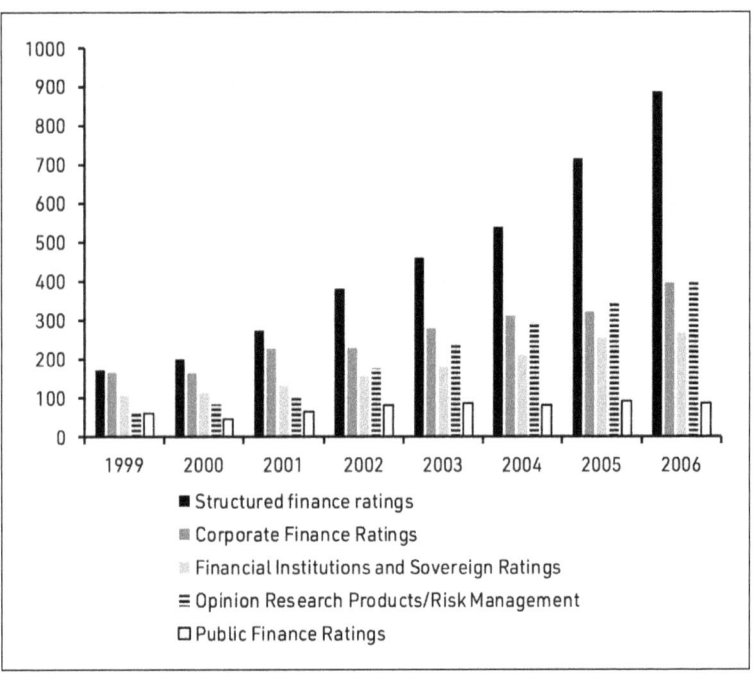

Source: Moody's annual reports.

But in 2007, the party was brought to an abrupt halt. Moody's 2007 Annual Report noted that the company:

> confronted significant challenges in 2007 as credit problems that began in the U.S. housing sector affected important parts of our ratings business globally. The severity and protracted nature of market dislocations that grew from the initial credit problems confirm that the challenges of 2007 will persist.

By the end of the following year, things were really bad: amid falling profits, the directors stated in the 2008 Annual Report that:

> challenges not only persisted but also deepened and widened, breaching previously safe havens of the global economy. By the fourth quarter of 2008 we were witnessing worldwide paralysis in the global credit markets ... Revenue contracted by approximately $500m and net income by $235m.

At one point, the shares fell to under $16 – 80% below the 2007 price.

Even worse was that Moody's reputation was now under attack. In the boom years for subprime mortgage securitised bonds, Moody's – along with other rating agencies – had granted high credit ratings to many of the bonds which were now in default. People had relied on Moody's to guide them on the likelihood of losing money; they had selected 'safe' investments, but it turned out that these were high risk. Many holders of these bonds went bust, including some storied banks. Others had to be bailed out by governments.

Accusations flew that Moody's had a conflict of interest when it came to rating many of these bonds because it was paid by the promoters to provide an opinion on an issue. It was said that if an issuer thought that Moody's would give a poor rating, it would take its business to another rating agency; therefore, the critics claimed, the typical Moody's analyst came under pressure to grant a generous rating.

Moody's responded to these voices in its 2008 Annual Report:

> Policymakers and private sector commentators have suggested changes in rating agency business models, additional levels of oversight and/or competition as mechanisms for improving performance. Often embedded in these suggestions are unchallenged assumptions about 'structural' conflicts and the nature of competition in the credit rating industry. At the heart of this debate, however, there is a tacit consensus that credit rating agencies perform an indispensable market function by assessing the risks of securities for the investing public. A critical starting point in evaluating proposed changes for the credit rating industry is to acknowledge that the only parties likely to pay for ratings—whether issuers, investors or

government agents—are those interested in particular ratings. Parties naturally want ratings that are most beneficial to their interests, and their wishes often conflict with the 'right' rating as independently determined by the agency. As a result, attempts to persuade rating agencies about their opinions can and do come from all types of market participants. Managing potential conflicts of interest is a necessary aspect of the rating business, and rating agencies must continuously manage those pressures appropriately and transparently … Moody's has long held that healthy competition among rating agencies on the basis of quality is in the best interest of financial markets.

In response to the criticism, Moody's promised better oversight where potential conflicts might arise to determine whether they were being effectively, demonstrably and transparently managed. It said that this might require direct third-party oversight of potential conflicts or periodic reviews of customer concentration levels. It also accepted that there would henceforth be additional scrutiny from regulators.

Why didn't Buffett get ahead of the game and sell before the financial crisis?

Soon after the 2008 Annual Report was published, Buffett began selling one-half of Berkshire's holdings (see Table 3.3). But he sold at much lower prices than were obtainable in 2006. He kicked himself for being too late. So why did he miss the opportunity? Answering this question leads us on a journey through the history of bubbles and why they are so difficult to spot when they are in the inflation stage, even for someone with Buffett's experience.

Table 3.3 Moody's shares sold by Berkshire, out of 48 million (prices after the 2:1 share split)

Quarter period	Number of shares sold (m)	Average of stock price at beginning and end of quarter ($)	Rough estimate of amount raised (m)
Q4 2009	16.186	21.8	353
Q1 2010	1.030	28.3	29
Q3 2010	1.910	22.5	43
Q4 2010	0.459	25.8	12
Q2 2013	3.494	57.1	200
Q4 2013	0.251	74.4	19
Total	**23.33**		**656**

Source: Berkshire Hathaway 13-F filings with the SEC.

At the 2010 inquiry into the financial crisis, Buffett was asked whether credit ratings and their apparent failure to predict accurately credit quality had caused or contributed to the crisis. He stated his belief that the failure of ratings agencies had added to the problem but that there were far more fundamental foundations:

> It didn't cause it, but there were a vast number of things that contributed to it. The basic cause, you know, is embedded partly in psychology and partly in reality in a growing and finally pervasive belief that house prices couldn't go down and everyone succumbed – virtually everybody succumbed to that. But that's the only way you get a bubble is when basically a very high percentage of the population buys into some originally sound premise and – it's quite interesting how that develops – originally sound premise that becomes distorted as time passes and people forget the original sound premise and start focusing solely on the price action … the media investors, the mortgage bankers, the American public, me, my neighbour, rating agencies, Congress – you name it – people overwhelmingly

came to believe that house prices could not fall significantly. And since it was the biggest asset class in the country and it was the easiest class to borrow against, it created probably the biggest bubble in our history.[125]

Long before the crash, Buffett had identified the housing market as a source of potential trouble. For example, at the 2006 Berkshire shareholders' meeting, he said that residential brokerage business HomeServices was seeing "a slowdown every place", and that this was most dramatic in what had previously been the hottest parts of the country, "where you've had the biggest bubble". These tended to be areas where people had a greater tendency to buy for investment or speculation, rather than personal use. They bought on the assumption that the ease of selling real estate experienced in the early stages of the boom would continue.

But the situation worsened very quickly. What often happens in a property bubble is that prices get so high that families find homes unaffordable precisely at a time when suppliers have increased the volume available to buy. "You can get real discontinuities in a market like that, where all of a sudden people realize that the whole supply-demand situation has changed," Buffett told us in 2006.[126] His reading of the situation then was that there would be "significant downward adjustments" from the peak.

Four years later, a chastened Buffett acknowledged that while he had been somewhat aware of trouble brewing, the sheer scale of it came as a shock: "[I]f I had seen what was coming, I would have behaved differently, including selling Moody's. So I was wrong."[127] He made an error in judgement in not selling when prices were riding high – like so many at that time.

In his 2010 reflections, Buffett defended himself for missing the chance to sell Moody's. He pointed out that, regardless of the prevailing economic background, there were very few businesses with the competitive position enjoyed by Moody's and Standard & Poor's:

> Anybody coming in and offering to cut their price in half had no chance of success. And there's not many businesses where someone can come in and offer to cut the price in half and

somebody doesn't think about shifting. But that's the nature of the ratings business. And it's a naturally obtained one. It's assisted by the fact that the two of them became a standard for regulators and all of that, so it's been assisted by the governmental actions over time.[128]

By September 2008, Buffett was referring to the financial crisis as an economic Pearl Harbor. He hadn't fully realised until then the degree to which the financial system problems would spill over into the wider economy – but who had?

A wider consideration of bubbles

Graham taught Buffett that you can get in a whole lot more trouble with a sound premise than with a false premise. Buffett illustrated what Graham had meant with the premise that common stocks do better than bonds. This idea took hold following the publication of a book by Edgar Lawrence Smith in 1924. He tested the idea that bonds would overperform during deflation and common stocks would overperform during inflation. But after studying many periods, his investigations showed that his original hypothesis was wrong. He found that common stock always overperformed. As Buffett explained:

> [H]e started thinking about that and why was that. Well, it was because there was a retained earnings factor … the dividend yield on stocks was the same as the yield on bonds, and on top of it, you had retained earnings. So they overperformed.[129]

This premise took hold to such an extent that it contributed greatly to the 1929 bubble. People simplistically took the premise as the only determinant of performance – they started to think that stocks were always wonderful regardless of the price paid. Then they got hooked on the 'price action': prices rise, which incites others to join the party in the hope of more price rises, which attracts others – and so on in a self-reinforcing spiral.

When it came to the US housing market in the early part of the 21st century, we start with the sound premise that houses will become worth more over time due to inflation, economic growth and population increases. Furthermore, most people want to own a home; and because you can borrow money on houses while believing that they will go up in value, you buy one as soon as you can:

> So this sound premise that it's a good idea to buy a house this year because it's probably going to cost more next year and you're going to want a home, and the fact that you can finance it gets distorted over time if housing prices are going up 10% a year and inflation is a couple percent a year.[130]

So far, so good. But now comes trouble. At some point, the price action takes over and people want to make money owning houses. They buy two houses, five houses. And they want to buy with as low a deposit as possible. What does it matter if you run into a little difficulty making the interest payments? The real estate will rise in price to cover that.

But who is dumb enough to lend to these speculators? Well, the suppliers of mortgage finance have also observed rising prices and have come to a similar conclusion that houses will be worth more over time. So even if they have to take possession of the asset, it will be okay: they can sell it for far more than the loan.

Another example: the Internet. It changed our lives, leading to improved productivity and economic growth. That was a good premise in the late 1990s; it made sense. But, says Buffett:

> it didn't mean that every company was worth $50 billion that could dream up a prospectus ... For some reason, it gets to a critical mass, a critical point is that where the price action alone starts dominating people's minds. And when your neighbour has made a lot of money by buying Internet stocks; and your wife says that, 'You're smarter than he is and he's richer than you are, so why aren't you doing it?'[131]

There was a particularly insane bubble in the Dutch Republic in the 1630s. People liked tulips, as they do today. The premise that people would always be attracted to tulips – particularly unusual ones – made sense. But the fashion for growing and displaying tulips took off and the price of bulbs rose. People became speculators in bulbs, buying in the expectation of selling at a high price later and pushing up prices. Some eventually reached ten times the annual income of a typical worker.

Buffett refers to a "pathology of bubbles", saying: "[W]hen a crowd is rushing in one direction, going the other direction is very hard. And usually, the people that do that become discredited by the price action."[132] You might have been absolutely right to go around shouting the truth like Cassandra in 2005 and 2006 – and yet house prices kept rising. Similarly serious voices, such as Alan Greenspan at the Federal Reserve and Professor Robert Shiller, spoke of an irrational exuberance in 1996; but there were still almost four years of share price rises to go as speculators got more excited.

> When people think there's easy money available, they're not inclined to change. Particularly if somebody said a month or two ago, 'Watch out for this easy money,' and then their neighbours made some more money in the ensuing month or two, it's just – it's overwhelming.[133]

Investing, speculation and gambling

After the subprime bubble burst, Buffett had time to refresh in his mind the difference between investing, speculation and gambling. He concluded that the key element is the intent of the person making the transaction. In 2010, he expressed his simplification of Graham's definition of an 'investment operation'. Graham had said that an investment operation has four elements in the mind of the individual taking the decision:

- **A willingness to undertake thorough analysis of what might be bought**: Study the facts of the underlying business – assets, profits, debt, competitive position, quality of managers and so on.
- **A desire to ensure the safety of the capital devoted**: Margin of safety means that your estimated intrinsic value range is significantly higher than market price.
- **A desire for a satisfactory rate of return**: Do not try to shoot the lights out on investments, trying to beat the market through

over-optimism and greed for the fast buck. There lie speculation, risk and leverage.

- **A willingness to diversify**: An investment might be justified as a part of a group of stocks, but not on its own. However, beware of excess diversification to the point where you don't understand what you are buying due to the inability to conduct a thorough analysis of everything in your portfolio.[134]

Buffett defined an 'investment operation' as:

> one where you look to the asset itself to determine your decision to lay out some money now to get some more money back later on. So you look to the apartment house, you look to the stock, you look to the farm, in terms of what that will produce. And you don't really care whether there is a quote on it at all. You are basically committing some funds now to get more funds later on, through the operation of the asset.[135]

Buffett's emphasis on the unimportance of liquidity is significant. He is genuinely willing to hold shares in a thoroughly analysed company and look to the future returns coming from its operating activity and not to the daily price quote. He has said time and again that he would not be bothered in the slightest if Wall Street stock trading ceased for a few years (except for the opportunity Mr Market gives to buy bargains).

Buffett's definition of 'speculation' again lies in the mind of the person, who this time is "focused on the price action of the stock"[136] due to some factor such as expectations of next quarter's earnings or the sector being flavour of the month. Here is a test of whether you are speculating: do you care whether the markets are open?

Buffett defined 'gambling' as "engaging in a transaction which doesn't need to be part of the system".[137] For example, bets on a football game are not part of the system – that is, the game of football does not depend on whether I bet or not. A bet is an artificial transaction that has no need to exist within an economic framework.

In contrast, those who buy/sell wheat futures are part of the economic system. They might be speculators or investors. Either way, they assist because farmers have to grow and sell wheat. When they plant it, they don't know what the price will be later on. So, they need activity on the other side – that is, farmers value either a forward/futures commitment from someone else to purchase or the ability to hedge in the financial markets themselves. Thus, through risk reduction, they are encouraged to produce food. There is a need for a futures transaction to exist within an economic framework.

Moody's emerges from crisis

In the decade after the financial crisis, Moody's had a fight on its hands trying to persuade regulators and courts that its analysts were indeed independently minded and of the highest integrity. The courts did not always see the company's past behaviour in the same way as the senior managers and it was forced to enter into a number of legal settlements over structured finance ratings, including the following:

- In 2012, Moody's settled with stockholders, the Louisiana Municipal Police Employees Retirement System and other investors. The litigation had asserted various claims related to Moody's ratings of mortgage-backed and structured securities before the financial crisis, alleging that the company had permitted itself to be pressured to move away from its normal focus on ratings accuracy, honesty and integrity.

- Fourteen plaintiffs reached an agreement with Moody's in 2013 to settle lawsuits claiming that they concealed risks in two mortgage-related deals that collapsed during the financial crisis. Investors accused Moody's of collaborating with banks in arranging high ratings, even though much of the underlying collateral was low-quality or subprime mortgage debt.

- In late January 2017, Moody's paid out $864 million after the US Department of Justice, the attorneys general of 21 states and the District of Columbia sued the company over its conduct in the lead-up to the financial crisis. "The settlement resolves allegations arising from Moody's role in providing credit ratings for Residential Mortgage-Backed Securities (RMBS) [and other derivatives]. Moody's failed to adhere to its own credit rating standards and fell short on its pledge of transparency in the run-up to the Great Recession," said Principal Deputy Associate Attorney General Bill

Baer. 'Today's settlement contains not only a significant penalty and factual admissions of its conduct, but also a commitment by Moody's to new and continued compliance measures designed to ensure the integrity of credit ratings going forward.'[138] The settlement caused the profit reported in 2016 to fall all the way to $267 million from $941 million the year before (see Figure 3.4).

Naturally, Moody's moved resources away from structured finance ratings (see Figure 3.8).

Figure 3.8 Moody's revenue from operating segments ($m), 2007–2014

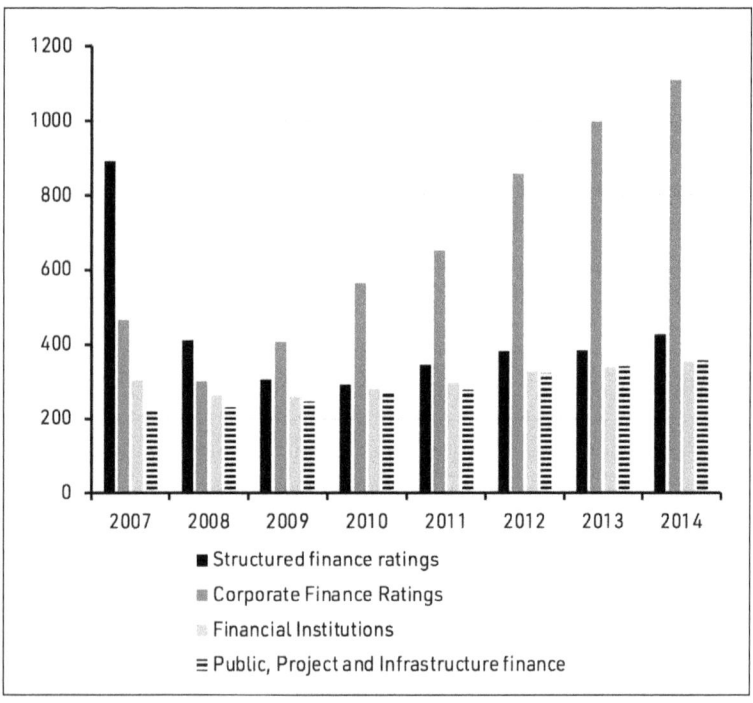

Source: Moody's annual reports.

Bond markets gradually recovered and Moody's was again able to use its reputation and oligopolistic position to charge good fees for its ratings. As volumes were restored, profits bounded ahead. Shareholders only had to wait until 2013 for profits to exceed the previous record and the share price to move back above its 2007 level. From there, the stock rose fivefold over the next eight years. Now, that is the power of a moat!

Despite Berkshire Hathaway selling almost half the 15% stake it bought, because Moody's has pursued a regular share buyback policy, the roughly 7.5% of Moody's retained has become 13.5% of the issued shares today, making Berkshire by far the largest shareholder.

Learning points

- **Moat businesses can be great investments if you buy at the right price**. A wide and dangerous moat means that there are sustainable barriers preventing, or at least inhibiting, potential rivals from entering the market and thus damaging the castle – that is, the economic franchise formed by the strong strategic position of the firm which affords good pricing power.

- **An 'inevitable' is a company that will dominate its field for an investment lifetime**. These companies are not found in fast-changing industries. Expect to find fewer than 20 in a lifetime. Always remember to ask the price.

- **Graham's focus on safe financial structure firms selling cheap does work**. But there are few larger companies around that fit his criteria.

- **Buying wonderful businesses at fair prices can be a good investment strategy**. This is true even if the PER appears high (Moody's was on a PER of 21) and the balance sheet looks poor (Moody's had negative net assets).

- **Real investors look under a lot of stones to find gems**. Buffett spent hundreds of hours reading *Moody's Manuals* to find his bargains.

- **Even Buffett can fail to sell out before a crash**. He misjudged the severity of the problems in housing and the financial sector.

- **You can get into a whole lot more trouble with a sound premise than with a false premise**. A sensible thesis can be taken too far, such as that stocks outperform bonds; or that houses are good leveraged investments; or that highly priced Internet stocks will do well. What the wise do in the beginning the foolish do in the end. People start to love the price action more than fundamentals.

- **The definition of an 'investment operation'**: You look to the asset itself – not market price action – to determine your decision to lay some money out now to get some money back later on. This requires:
  - thorough analysis;
  - margin of safety;
  - satisfactory return ambition; and
  - sensible diversification.
- **The definition of 'speculation'**: In this case, the mind of the person is focused on price action, not fundamentals.
- **The definition of 'gambling'**: Engaging in a transaction which doesn't need to be part of an economic system.

Investment 4

H&R BLOCK

Summary of the deal

Deal	H&R Block
Time	Buying: Q2 2000–Q4 2001 Selling: Q4 2003–Q2 2007
Price paid	$255m
Quantity	15.999m shares (about 9%)
Sale price	Estimated $767.9m
Profit	Estimated $513m or 201%
Berkshire Hathaway in 2000	Share price: $40,800–$80,000 Book value: $61.72bn Per share book value: $40,442

This is one of Warren Buffett's greatest stock market investments, trebling the $255 million committed. The feature of H&R Block on which he focused most was the power of customer recognition: the company had a very significant 'share of mind' among typical Americans. For decades, H&R Block was the go-to if you needed help with calculating and submitting your annual tax return. It was the largest in the business, with a presence in just about every town and 16 million regular clients. When Americans thought about the chore of doing a tax return, they most likely also thought about H&R Block.

The tax side of the business was a sustainable engine, generating high returns on the capital employed. Building on its name recognition and its contacts with millions of households, the company created other revenue streams, from investment services to mortgages. The potential to cross-sell a range of financial products looked very interesting.

After Buffett bought, things looked very good and the shares zoomed away as profits climbed. However, the managers started to make mistakes – the worst of which was to plunge wholeheartedly into the subprime mortgage market, writing over $40 billion of business in one year just before the start of the financial crisis around 2007.

Buffett – well informed from his reading of six newspapers a day, his phenomenal memory and his conversations with knowledgeable people – was ahead of the curve here. He saw the storm coming and sold down the bulk of the holding in 2005 and 2006 at good prices.

Humble origins

Henry Bloch – the 'H' in H&R Block – was born eight years before Buffett, in Kansas City, an afternoon's drive from Omaha. After studying at the University of Kansas City and the University of Michigan in 1944, aged 22, he joined the Army Air Corp to serve as a navigator on 32 B-17 bombing flights over Germany. His courage earned him the Air Medal and three Oak Leaf Clusters.

In between missions, Henry (or 'Hank') corresponded with his two brothers, Leon and Richard, about starting a family business. "I didn't just want to be born, get a job and have that be the end of it," he recalled in 2014.[139]

This entrepreneurial drive was boosted when the Army sent Henry to Harvard Business School to study statistical control. There, he happened upon the transcript of a speech given by Professor Sumner Slichter, which highlighted that big business and labour had many resources that small businesses lacked. The professor emphasised that small businesses were the backbone of the country and needed greater support. "The future," he said, "would be in helping small business."

Henry could see gaps in markets that needed to be filled. He told his brothers that they should offer an array of services to small businesses. Full of ambition, Henry and Leon (Richard was busy at university) originally planned to offer 50, including bookkeeping, typing and window dressing. The two older brothers approached a wealthy aunt to see if she would be willing to inject $50,000 to help them start up, open a smart office and hire a large group of employees. "She did the most wonderful thing; she really made us," Henry recalled. "She said no."[140]

Instead of a big bang approach, the brothers were forced to create a very lean organisation limited by the aunt agreeing to put in only $5,000 – and even that was merely a loan (guaranteed by their father). This lean philosophy extended to the range of services offered: instead of the grand array, when they launched the business in 1946, Henry and Leon decided to concentrate on bookkeeping. "It seemed like our biggest competitor was the wives of the owners," said Henry.[141]

At first, business was very disappointing. It wasn't supporting the two of them, so Leon decided to go back to law school and Henry lived off his $50-per-month benefit paid to military veterans under the GI Bill.

Meanwhile, Richard was working in Kansas City in the municipal bond business. He was a determined entrepreneur too. When a boy, he found an old hand press in his uncle's attic and started a business as a printer. By 12, he had three automatic presses and was printing for a number of high schools. By 16, he was studying at Wharton, graduating with a degree in economics in 1945. On the side, he bought and sold second-hand cars to pay his way through college.

Henry's business eventually improved and he found himself needing help. There was only one response to an advertisement in the newspaper. It was from his mother. "She said, 'I know who you should hire—your brother, Dick.'"[142] And so it was that in 1954, Richard – the 'R' in H&R Block – became a partner.

The brothers did offer assistance with tax preparation, but this was merely a courtesy for their bookkeeping clients. Given the time, cost and tiny revenue in helping people file taxes shortly before the 1955 tax season, they decided to stop providing this service. However, client John White suggested that instead they build up this side of the business, starting with a display advertisement in the *Kansas City Star*. It just so happened that White worked at the newspaper as, yes, a display advertiser. The brothers first pooh-poohed the idea because they were too busy with their other work. Finally, they relented and allowed White to run an ad twice in January 1955. It showed a man behind an eight ball with the caption, "Taxes, $5."

On the Monday after the first ad was published, Henry was out visiting clients when he got a message urging him to call the office. Richard answered breathlessly, "Hank, get back here as quick as you can. We've got an office full of people!"[143] It turned out that their timing was perfect: first, many people had just received their annual government form asking for their Wage and Tax Statement (Form W-2); second, the Internal Revenue Service (IRS) in Kansas City had announced that it would discontinue its offer of free tax return preparation.

Until that point, the brothers had been trading as the United Business Company. But a Boston company had the same name and it contacted the Blochs asking them to change it. Henry had never really liked the mouthful of 'United Business Company', so they willingly rebranded as H&R Block in July 1955. The use of the 'K' was to avoid people mispronouncing 'Bloch'.

The next city to lose free IRS tax preparation services was New York, so Richard suggested opening there. In 1956, they opened seven more offices, more than tripling annual revenue to $65,000. Henry concentrated on developing central functions in Kansas City while Richard led the nationwide expansion; and by 1969, they were expanding internationally.

The New York branches needed the attention of either Henry or Richard on a constant basis, but neither brother wanted to uproot his family and move to New York. The decision was made to sell the New York operations. A pair of business partners wanted to buy, but they couldn't raise the full asking price. Instead, they agreed to pay the Blochs $10,000-plus future royalties – that is, they became franchisees using the H&R Block name, training and systems. Under the Blochs' franchise system, a franchisee gained the right to open a number of offices in a given area.

In January 1957, franchise operations were opened in Columbia, Missouri and Topeka. In 1958, H&R Block began operating in Des Moines, Oklahoma City and Little Rock. And so it went on – at such a rapid rate that by 1962, the company had 206 offices in 34 states and boasted an annual revenue stream of nearly $800,000. It was ready to go public, so it floated, offering 75,000 shares at $4.

In 1972, Henry first appeared in television commercials which helped to build the company into one of the most widely recognised brands in the country. He came across as a sincere man of high integrity, exhibiting those Midwestern values that engendered trust. By the late 1970s, H&R Block was preparing about 10% of the nation's returns, inexpensively and efficiently, from 8,600 offices.

The brothers were dealt a blow in 1978, when Richard – aged 52 at the time – was given just three months to live following a lung cancer diagnosis. Determined as ever, he refused to accept his fate and sought out the best in the cancer business, which turned out to be the MD Anderson Center, Houston. Two years of rigorous treatment led to remission. From that point forward, he and his wife Annette concentrated on funding cancer research. To assist with this, Richard sold his H&R Block shares in 1982. Despite being diagnosed with cancer again (this time of the colon) in the late 1980s, he was successfully treated again and died not of cancer, but of a heart attack in 2004 aged 78.

Diversification and synergy

H&R Block's managers had long recognised a problem: its thousands of offices were frantically busy for four months of the year in the "tax season" leading up to the April filing date;[144] but for the other eight months, they lost millions of dollars in overhead costs – in 1997, for example, there was an $83 million loss as they paid out overhead costs.

They tried various diversification strategies in the 1980s and early 1990s, from buying a personnel agency to running a business seminar company. They even entered the credit card business. Most of these ventures were sold off or abandoned. By the late 1990s, they recognised that their core customer was an individual on a modest income looking for good value. Why not create a "one-stop financial shopping mall" aimed at these people? After all, most financial service firms targeted higher-income individuals, neglecting those with more modest means. Moreover, they had at least 16 million[145] readily contactable clients who might be amenable to buying additional services from trusted H&R Block.

With that in mind, they started hiring financial planners to offer investment advice for fees ranging from $10 to $250. They also began offering mortgages. This business was boosted by the purchase of Option One Mortgage for $218 million in 1997. It had relationships with 5,000 mortgage brokers throughout the country (46 states), which attracted families to borrow against the security of their house – called 'mortgage origination'.[146] After the acquisition, H&R Block also offered Option One mortgages through its offices.

All these mortgages were 'non-conforming'. This type of loan became better known by another name – 'subprime' – after it gained notoriety following the 2008 crisis. The defining feature that made these loans non-conforming was that government-sponsored agencies, such as Fannie Mae and Freddie Mac, would not buy them.

Option One also purchased bunches of mortgages from other financial companies and regularly sold collections of mortgages in securitisations – that is, a special purpose vehicle issued bonds which paid interest and principal as mortgagees repaid their debt. This business began to boom in the early 2000s. The rapid growth of this business and the attendant drop in standards highlighted to Buffett and Munger the dangers of over-reaching in this market (as Buffett regularly said, "What the wise do in the beginning, the foolish do in the end"), which eventually persuaded them to sell down Berkshire Hathaway's stake in H&R Block before the financial crisis hit; but that story is for later.

The procedure for getting funds to those borrowing to buy a house was explained by H&R Block as follows:

> In the nonconforming loan business, a borrower will complete a loan application with a loan broker and the broker will distribute the application to one or more nonconforming lenders such as Option One. These lenders are generally selected

by the broker based upon level of fees received, response time and approval experience with similar borrowers. Upon receipt of a deal satisfactory to the broker, the borrower is required to pay a non-refundable fee for an appraisal and for processing the application. This fee goes to the lender. At closing, the borrower will receive the loan proceeds net of other fees such as broker origination fees and document preparation fees. The broker will close the loan using the broker's funds or funds loaned to the broker by the nonconforming lender [e.g. Option One] under a 'warehouse line'. When the statutory rescission period expires, the broker sells the loan to the lender at a prearranged premium.[147]

The securitisation element was also explained as follows:

In the securitization process, a subsidiary of ... [H&R] Block ... acquires loans ... and assigns them to a trust. The trust issues certificates that are secured by the home equity loans, receives principal and interest payments on the loans and makes payments on the asset-backed certificates [or bonds]. Block ... applies the net proceeds from the sale of the certificates primarily ... to repay indebtedness incurred to obtain funds for its acquisition of the loans ... Block ... completed their second and third securitizations of nonconforming mortgage loans during fiscal year 1998. A $215 million asset-backed security issue closed on July 29, 1997 and a $184 million issue closed on January 27, 1998.[148]

Another income stream was in its infancy in 1998: investment and financial planning services. In the year to April 1998, H&R Block test-marketed this idea in just four cities: "Independent licensed securities brokers offered retirement planning, financial planning and financial products, such as annuities, mutual funds and insurance products, at select H&R Block Premium offices."[149]

Another nascent business saw Henry return to his roots by offering accounting and other assistance to small businesses. H&R Block made a start in 1998 by acquiring tiny Donnelly Meiners, Jordan Kline – an accounting firm in Kansas City offering a panoply of services to clients.[150]

The credit card business was still there, but it was losing money – for example, losses totalled $3 million in 1996, $7 million in 1997 and $16 million in 1998.

Finally, a longstanding adjunct business was lending to clients until a refund from the government came through ('refund anticipation loans').

The boldness of the managerial team in developing new business areas was rewarded by the February 1998 sale of H&R Block's Compuserve subsidiary for $1.03 billion. Table 4.1 shows a doubling of profits between 1996 and 2000, with the main contributor being the tax preparation business, but the mortgage operations growing strongly.

H&R Block's April 1998 balance sheet was very strong, with $900 million in cash, $636 million in marketable securities and receivables of $793 million, plus an assortment of other, less liquid assets. Set against the asset total was a mere $893 million in debt and $669 million in other liabilities. While balance-sheet 'stockholders' equity' was $1.34 billion, the stock market valued the company at around $5 billion.

In the year to 30 April 1999, the company bought six more regional accounting firms and several smaller local accounting firms. Later that year, it went all-in on the strategy of building a nationwide small firm service business by buying McGladrey and Pullen, the seventh-largest US accounting and consulting firm, for $240 million. The business services division could now offer a comprehensive range of services in six metropolitan areas.

H&R Block also acquired more companies in the mortgage business. Option One was able to bulk sell or securitise $3.6 billion mortgages in a year and could service more than $6.5 billion of loans.

Meanwhile, financial services was beefed up through the acquisition of an investment firm which offered stocks, bonds, mutual funds and other securities and insurance products through a network of registered representatives.

Table 4.1 H&R Block profits 1996–2000

Year end: April	Net earnings from continuing operations (excluding Compuserve) ($m)	Earnings per share from continuing operations ($)	Operating earnings ($m)				
			US tax operations	International tax operations	Mortgage operations	Business services	Financial adviser services
1996	125	1.20	173	12	0.1		
1997	148	1.42	210	14	30		
1998	184	1.75	252	12	31		
1999	238	2.38	314	3	63	7	
2000	252	2.57	320	5	95	17	41

Source: H&R Block annual reports.

Also in 1999, the still loss-making credit card operation was jettisoned through a sale to a Californian bank.

In the last financial year before Buffett started buying shares – that ending 3 April 2000 – the company grew its tax business to 19.2 million taxpayers served from more than 10,000 offices (16.9 million clients in the US). Another 1.8 million tax clients availed of its online preparation services. For Americans who paid for tax preparation rather than doing it themselves, H&R Block was the preferred choice in one out of four cases; the company was by far the largest and most recognised in the country, with its 25.3% market share. Importantly, there was staunch customer loyalty, with 85% of clients saying they were very satisfied with its service and very high retention rates. The combination of brand recognition and millions of satisfied customers meant that H&R Block had a good 'share of mind' among Americans pondering whom to engage for tax services.

And its other divisions were growing rapidly too:

- The financial adviser division was greatly expanded by the purchase of Olde Discount Corporation, one of the country's largest discount brokers, on 1 December 1999 for $850 million. During the first five months of ownership, Olde contributed $66.8 million of pre-tax earnings and 73 of Olde's 181 offices were quickly converted to create a total of 93 new H&R Block financial centres offering financial planning and investment advice. All remaining H&R Block offices were to be similarly converted over the subsequent two years to create "year-round onestop financial services offices".[151] Additional services included trading and advice on stocks, bonds and mutual funds.

- Option One Mortgage was performing well, with pre-tax earnings of $95 million and $5.7 billion of loan originations.

- The business service division was renamed RSM McGladrey and grew to 100 offices throughout the US plus affiliations with 550 offices in 75 other countries.

The company not only was diverse in its product offerings but also saw opportunities to cross-market financial products and services.

There was a good record to show, with profits having doubled over five years. It had also produced a very respectable average annual return of 18.5% of stockholders' equity over those five years (see Figure 4.1).

Figure 4.1 H&R Block net earnings from continuing operations as a percentage of stockholders' equity at beginning of year

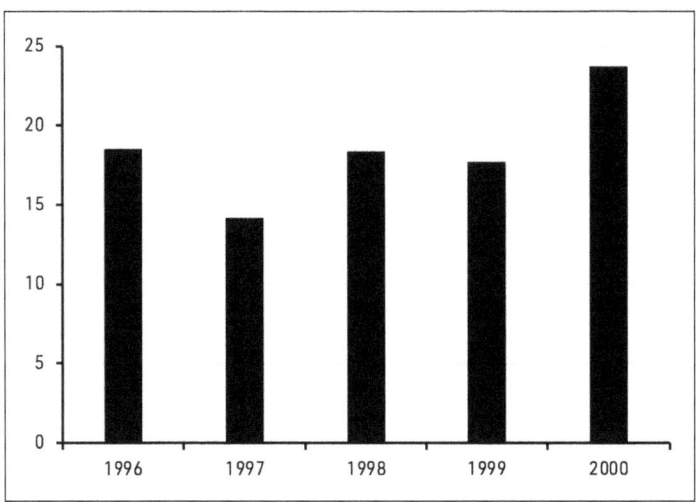

Source: H&R Block annual reports.

But despite all these positives, in early 2000 H&R Block's stock price fell (see Figure 4.2). There were operating issues, including:

> [c]hallenges in our U.S. tax operations and the new e-commerce initiative. We staffed to meet the increased tax client demand that traditionally occurs in April, however, the end-of-tax-season rush did not meet our expectations. Our new e-commerce operation experienced unexpected technical difficulties, which impacted our ability to generate revenue during key filing periods of the tax season. The result is that although our overall financial performance exceeded fiscal 1999, it did not achieve the earnings results we know we are capable of delivering and have delivered for the past three years ... In addition, we experienced a non-recurring loss on the sale of certain assets related to mortgage operations.[152]

Figure 4.2 H&R Block, stock price 1995–2000 (ignoring the 2:1 share splits in August 2001 and August 2005)

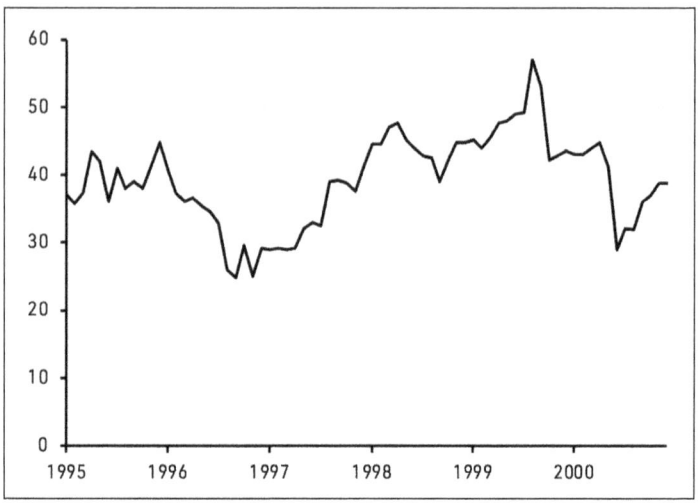

Source: Yahoo! Finance.

Another reason for the fall was that the prior high expectations of investors had pushed the shares to PERs of 23 or more. This optimism was predicated on continued rapid growth in earnings. But in the statement on the previous page, we see managers admitting to a failure to implement their strategies to perfection, resulting in only a tiny increase in earnings, from $2.38 per share in 1999 to $2.57 in 2000.

The group had also taken on debt to finance its acquisitions, raising it to $1.3 billion. This resulted in H&R Block's credit rating falling to BBB+.

But the most obvious reason for the share price decline was the bursting of the late-1990s stock market bubble. In the second quarter of 2000, the shares fell to the $29–$33 range, putting the company on a historical PER of under 13 on reported earnings. However, if earnings in 2000 are calculated before amortising acquired intangible assets, we come to $3.08 per diluted share, giving a PER of just ten or 11.

Investment 4. H&R Block

Buffett buys

This relatively low price presented an opportunity to Buffett. As well as price, he considered the sustainability and growth of earnings. First in his considerations was the share of mind the group already possessed in its core tax business; second, how that positive image might help attract customers to the other divisions. He said:

> Everyone knows H&R Block. You think of tax preparation, you think of H&R. How many people can name the number two? Not many. How much would it take to topple them? ... We were willing to buy the entire firm at 75% more than what we paid for the piece we bought.[153]

In the quarter ending 30 June 2000, Berkshire Hathaway bought 4.089 million in shares with a market value in June of $132.4 million. By December 2001, Berkshire had built up its stake to 15.999 million; an August 2001 2:1 share split meant that in 'old' share currency, that was 8 million shares. The clearest way to proceed is to convert the holdings of old shares into post-August 2001 shares – that is, double the share numbers Berkshire recorded in 2000 and early 2001, as done for Figure 4.3.

Figure 4.3 Berkshire Hathaway holdings in H&R Block recorded after the share split of August 2001, H&R Block stock price

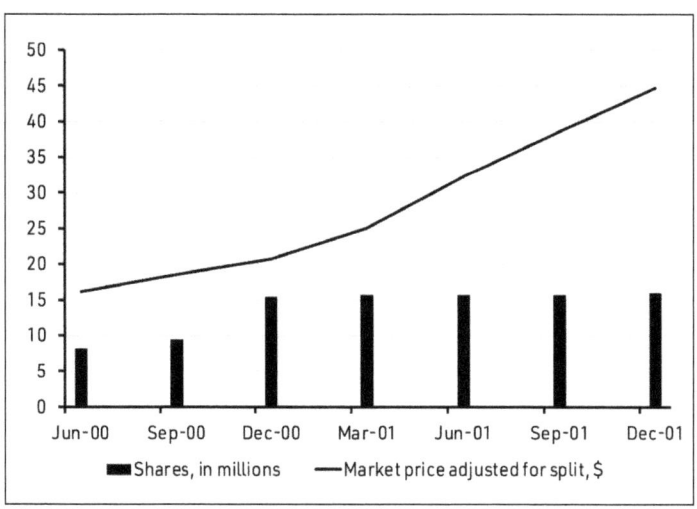

Source: Berkshire Hathaway 13-F filings with the SEC.

The total cost of the 16 million shares accumulated to December 2001 was $255 million. The average buying price was $15.94 in post-August 2001 shares (or $31.88 in pre-August 2001 split shares).

Remarkably, by the time Berkshire stopped buying in December 2001, H&R's shares had risen on the market to be priced at $715 million. Investor confidence in H&R Block grew. ABC News put it like this in April 2001:

> Many fund managers say the stock's still cheap. If the company does a better job running some of its nontax operations in its bid to become a full-service financial-services company, it may be worthwhile for investors to pull their heads up from their 1040 forms and check out this stock.[154]

At 77, Henry Bloch decided to depart while the prospects for the business were on the up; he retired from his role of chairman in late 2000. He had a 2.76% stake. Table 4.2 shows the overall net income of H&R Block over the five years after Berkshire started buying its shares, plus the operating earnings of its various divisions.

In 2001, the share price was lifted by news of numerous tax clients being attracted by the mortgage offers available – "[E]vidence that our strategy is working," wrote the directors in their 2001 report. Cross-selling with the financial services division was also picking up pace.

Meanwhile, clever marketing campaigns were paying off for the core tax business – which at the start of the year the managers thought faced a very tough recession, prompting them to cut costs – boosting revenues by 15.6% and pre-tax profits by 35.5%.

Table 4.2 H&R Block profits 2000–2004

Year end: April	Net earnings from continuing operations (excluding Compuserve) ($m)	Earnings per share from continuing operations ($) after a doubling of shares in issue due to a share split in August 2001	Operating earnings ($m)				
			US tax operations	International tax operations	Mortgage operations	Business services	Financial adviser services
2000	252	1.28	320	5	95	17	41
2001	277	1.50	434	6	138	16	9
2002	434	2.38	533	7	339	23	-55
2003	580	3.23	547	11	694	-14	-128
2004	704	3.98	628	11	678	19	-64

Source: H&R Block annual reports.

And the US subprime market was developing nicely as the concept of lending to people with less than pristine credit histories or limited income stability gained greater acceptance. Mortgage operations raised pre-tax earnings by 45% in 2001. After packaging the mortgages through special purpose vehicles, Option One earned additional income by 'servicing' those mortgages – that is, collecting payments from households and other interactions with families and then making payments to investors, tax authorities and insurers.

There was a dramatic boom in the loan servicing portfolio in 2001, which reached $18.2 billion – a 61% rise. "We think servicing is a great business. It brings good value to our shareholders, gives us a fairly predictable revenue stream, and keeps us in touch with our clients each month."[155] Servicing revenues increased 76.3% in 2001.

However, the financial adviser division was suffering from the stock market downturn as retail clients curtailed their use of stockbrokers – profits fell by 69%. Nonetheless, the directors remained optimistic:

> While disappointing, these results hardly speak to Financial Advisors' real value. It plays a central role in our company's strategy of serving clients' financial needs. We have begun to make strides in product development, the creation of effective cross-selling opportunities, and the incorporation of advice into our business. In the long run, we will create a business that is far less dependent on transaction fees and the impact of stock market volatility.[156]

Profits were also curtailed in the business services division, but this was put down to integration issues and there was great optimism concerning the opportunities to cross-sell financial products and services.

The good news from the largest divisions saw H&R Block's stock more than double during 2001. Buffett must have been feeling very pleased with his series of buy decisions. But by the end of 2001, shares were selling at a PER of $44.7/$1.50 = 29.8 – far too rich for Buffett's liking, so he stopped buying. On an earnings yield of merely 3.4%, it was pricing in too much perfection regarding future earnings growth.

Profits rise, the stock goes nowhere

In 2002 and 2003, the business made good progress; but because the shares were highly priced at the beginning of 2002, they flatlined for two years (see Figure 4.4).

Figure 4.4 The no-change-in-holdings period: H&R Block share price, 2002 and 2003 (Berkshire Hathaway holds 15,999 shares throughout)

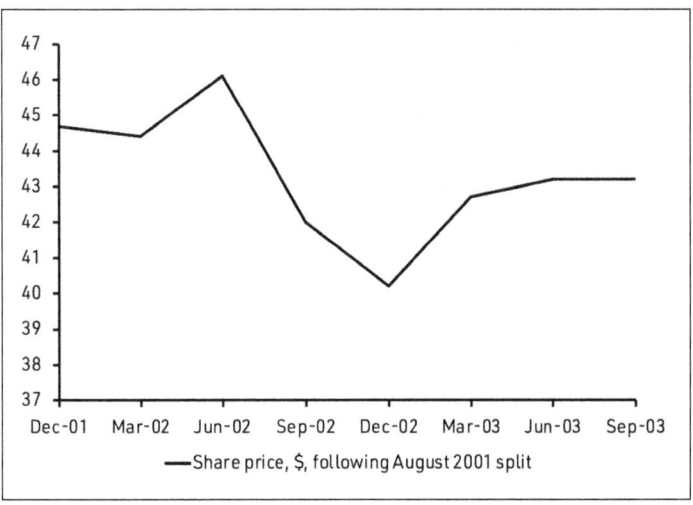

Source: Berkshire Hathaway 13-F filings with the SEC.

Option One was going great guns: in 2002, it almost doubled the quantity of mortgage originations to $11.5 billion and raised the servicing portfolio to $23.8 billion. As a consequence, profits more than doubled that year.

The business services division chugged along at a low level of profits in 2002, supplemented by four small acquisitions; but the financial adviser division made thumping great losses as it continued to suffer from declining retail investor activity.

This general pattern was confirmed the following year. The tax business grew profits pretty fast, with mortgages growing by leaps and bounds, while financial services lost money hand over fist. But now, business services joined the loss-making club. Buffett was getting a little nervous and refused to buy more despite the PER falling to the $43/$3.23 = 13.3 region. In fact, he sold off a few shares (0.38 million) in late 2003.

The mood was not improved by H&R Block setting aside $41.7 million for a lawsuit related to mis-selling of the refund anticipation loans. The hefty fees charged to clients, poor quality of information and questionable marketing got attorneys general in many parts of the US worked up. Many more lawsuits followed:

> Critics ... liken Block to a loan shark that preys upon low-income households, immigrants and financially unsophisticated people. They say Block doesn't do enough to make it clear that the refund advance is really a loan that must be repaid even if the Internal Revenue Service disputes the tax return or part of the money is siphoned away to pay for outstanding child support, student loans or other liens.[157]

Berkshire held onto the rest of its H&R Block stock through 2004. In H&R's 2004 Annual Report, the directors excitedly pointed at mortgage originations rising to over $23 billion and tax clients now topping 18 million. Income from mortgages at $678 million exceeded that from tax (at $628 million), having grown from less than $90 million just five years before. But the financial adviser division was awful, piling up yet more losses; and business services was producing very poor rates of return on the money poured into it.

There were some big questions to answer:

- How safe were the subprime mortgages written in the mid-2000s? The earlier ones might have made sense, with borrowers in reasonably good shape to repay. But now there was a whole ecosystem of fees, commissions and margins, everyone in the system hungry for more and more deals to feed on. Perhaps some of those people on benefits should never have been encouraged to apply for a mortgage?

- Was it now possible that house prices could fall in numerous property markets in the US at the same time (something thought impossible by true believers in subprime), thus wiping out

homeowner equity across the country and destroying the security for many securitised bonds?
- Would financial institutions be scared and run away from the sales teams pushing all this structured finance? Perhaps the whole edifice could collapse, with banks and a host of other institutions caught swimming naked as the tide went out?

These questions were starting to be raised in the specialised press. And anecdotal evidence was everywhere. For example, I remember watching TV news reporters interviewing those 'lucky' enough to have secured a place on the housing ladder despite their shaky credit history and/or insecure income.

Even H&R Block provided clues in its 2004 Annual Report, such as:

> Next year brings significant challenges. The expected increase in interest rates will test the quality of our organization and the ability of our associates to respond with agility to the rate changes. We expect somewhat lower margins as a result of the interest rate volatility that makes bond investors more cautious. Margins may improve after rates stabilize at a higher level.

There were even reasons to worry about the normally steadily growing tax business highlighted in the 2004 Annual Report:

> Our biggest disappointment was the decline in the number of retail tax clients, a 3% decrease. The U.S. tax business faces both short-term and long-term challenges. We've known for some time that our success in this market would attract competitors who believe they can duplicate at least part of what we offer our clients, notably speed of refund.

The selling period

With the share price still in the $50 area, Buffett sold significant blocks of shares throughout 2005 and 2006 (see Figure 4.5 and Table 4.3).

Figure 4.5 Number of H&R Block shares owned by Berkshire Hathaway and market price of shares (ignoring 2005 share split), September 2003–March 2007

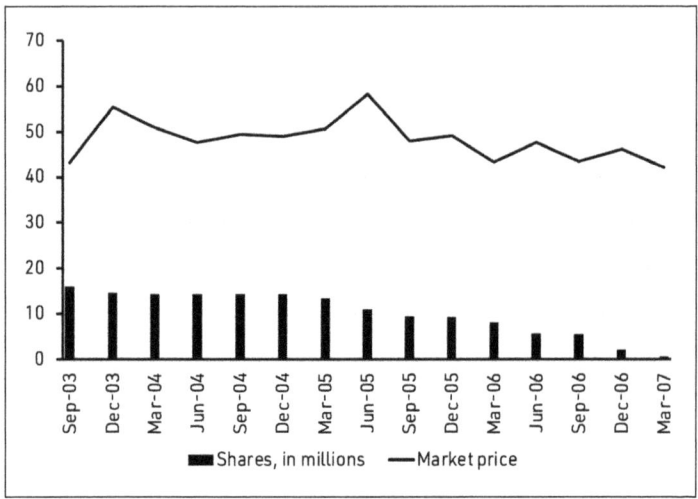

Source: Berkshire Hathaway 13-F filings with the SEC.

Table 4.3 Approximations of amounts raised by Berkshire Hathaway selling H&R Block shares (ignoring August 2005 share split for price and quantity)

Quarter	Share price (quarter beginning and quarter end price averaged) ($)	Number of shares sold in quarter (million)	Approximate amount raised ($ million)
Q4 2003	49.3	1.39	68.5
Q1 2004	53.2	0.26	13.8
Q1 2005	49.8	0.84	41.8
Q2 2005	54.5	2.59	141.2
Q3 2005	53.2	1.54	81.9
Q4 2005	48.6	0.11	5.3
Q1 2006	46.2	1.26	57.3
Q2 2006	45.5	2.31	106.0
Q3 2006	45.6	0.21	9.6
Q4 2006	44.8	3.43	153.7
Q1 2007	43.9	1.43	62.7
Q2 2007	41.5	0.63	26.1
TOTAL			767.9

Source: Berkshire Hathaway 13-F filings with the SEC.

Buffett was avidly reading H&R's reports looking out for further trouble – the annual numbers are summarised in Table 4.4.

Table 4.4 H&R Block profits 2004–2006

Year end: April	Net earnings ($m)	Earnings per share ($) (Based on the number of shares August 2001–August 2005, i.e., ignoring the 2005 share split)	Operating earnings ($m)			
			Tax operations (includes international)	Mortgage operations	Business services	Financial adviser services
2004	704	3.98	638	678	19	-64
2005	636	3.84	664	496	30	-75
2006	490	2.98	590	322	53	-33

Source: H&R Block annual reports.

In 2005 and early 2006, H&R Block's managers were excited about both the tax business and the mortgage business:

> [W]e invested in the largest expansion of H&R Block tax office locations in the company's history, grew the scale of our Option One and H&R Block Mortgage origination staffs … each of these actions will allow us to be more successful in the future, despite the short-term earnings reductions they may create … Why did Option One increase its account executives in light of a more competitive market? Increasing the number of account executives was integral to achieving record loan volumes, as we did in the fourth quarter. Our new sales associates have allowed us to enter markets that are currently not served or underserved. They also enabled us to increase by more than 2,000 the number of active mortgage brokers who work with Option One.[158]

The directors really believed in the subprime model of originating mortgages and selling them to special purpose vehicles which then issued securitised bonds. They struggled to conceive that the merry-go-round might stop:

> Although we recognize there may be periodic market disruptions, we don't think it's realistic to think the secondary market would simply stop buying loans. In fact, the asset-backed securities market has experienced tremendous growth, with non-prime mortgage loans now making up $400 billion, or approximately 47 percent, of the total market.[159]

With hindsight, we know that much of this was pure hubris. As early as 2006, H&R Block's senior managers acknowledged problems with subprime, but they pointed at competitive threats rather than there being something fundamentally wrong with the business model: "In the case of our mortgage business, the competitive dynamics in the industry have created significant volatility in our results."[160]

But by then, there were signs of a slowing housing market and reduced demand for mortgages, leading to "compressed loan profitability"[161] – even though origination volume rose to $40.8 billion, making Option One the fifth-largest US non-prime lender.

Another $49 million charge was taken for legal settlements on the refund anticipation loans, causing a year-on-year lowering of profits in the tax division – the first decline for a very long time.

When sorrows come, they come not as single spies but in battalions, as written by Shakespeare.[162] The embarrassment levels were high as the directors admitted that the premier tax-calculating company had miscalculated its own taxes owing to states by $32 million. The company was also accused of fraudulently marketing individual retirement accounts (IRAs) by New York's attorney general – he sought $250 million in fines while stating that these accounts were "virtually guaranteed" to lose money for customers.[163]

Then, in January 2006, Chairman and CEO Mark Ernst had to explain on an investor conference call that software-related technology problems had left the company unprepared for a surge in January filings by taxpayers expecting refunds and "created a hole out of which we're working to climb". He revealed that the problem "cost us 250,000 clients" that were "unable to be recovered".[164]

At least they could console themselves with the thought that the business services division was on the up.

What happened after Buffett took his money off the table?

Meanwhile, of course, the subprime crisis was spreading like wildfire through the financial system, bankrupting many previously esteemed banks and financial institutions.

Table 4.5 H&R Block profits 2007–2009

Year end: April	Net earnings ($m)	Earnings per share ($) (Based on the number of shares August 2001–August 2005 – i.e., ignoring the 2005 share split)	Operating earnings ($m)			
			Tax operations (includes international)	Mortgage operations	Business services	Financial adviser services
2007	-434	-2.68	705	-1,183	58	20
2008	-309	-1.90	786	-1,166	89	10
2009	486	2.92	894	closed	96	sold

Source: H&R Block annual reports.

Managerial confidence seemed to be at a low ebb in April 2007, prompting an announcement of intention to sell Option One. The directors spoke of deteriorating conditions in the secondary market (those purchasing bonds secured on mortgages), "where reduced investor demand for loan purchases, higher investor yield requirements and increased estimates for future losses"[165] had lowered the value of non-prime loans. There were increasing problems with homeowners making late payments and defaulting. House prices fell all over the country.

The managers were all set to sell Option One to Cerberus Capital Management for about $300 million in 2007, but this failed. In the end, the directors simply closed down the mortgage origination business while selling off the loan servicing business. By the end of the year, H&R Block's shares had almost halved since 2005.

A boardroom battle in August–September 2007 led to a new group of directors taking over after 84% of shareowners voted in the new team at the September 2007 annual meeting. The new group was led by Richard C Breeden, a former chairman of the Securities and Exchange Commission from 1989 to 1993, whose investment fund held over ten million shares (1.8%).

The new broom boldly set out what had gone wrong in the 2008 Annual Report:

> Losses in discontinued operations, which were almost entirely a result of the Company's sub-prime mortgage lending subsidiary, were $1.6 billion ($4.81 per share) during these two years [2006 and 2007]. For almost a decade, internal focus on the tax business at H&R Block had been affected as the Company pursued a diversification strategy in financial services that failed to deliver on its expected benefits. For at least part of this time, the tax business seemed to drift, and overall corporate overhead costs spiraled upward.

So, they refocused on the core. Throughout the financial crisis, the original tax business just got stronger, with a pre-tax income in 2009 of $894 million. "Like many companies, we believe H&R Block will generate the most value by concentrating on what it does best," said the newly installed CEO.¹⁶⁶ In 2009, the financial services division was sold for $304 million.

Today, the stock price is more than treble its level at the start of 2010. The company's overriding focus has remained on tax preparations, with over 20 million Americans engaging its services today. Net income is in the $500–$600 million range, which is lower than it was a couple of decades before; but earnings per share are about double what they were back then following a series of large share buyback programmes.

Having lost his brother Richard in 2004 and then Leon in 2012, Henry Bloch died in April 2019, aged 96, surrounded by his family in his beloved Kansas City, Missouri, where it had all begun. Since stepping down from the board of directors in 2000, he had kept busy putting much of his fortune to good use in Kansas City, funding the arts, education and a business school, among many other things. The Marion and Henry Bloch Family Foundation is "committed to assisting the city's most vulnerable neighbors … Over the years, Marion and Henry Bloch learned that true success is not measured in what you get, but it is measured in what you give back".¹⁶⁷

Learning points

- **Share of mind is often crucial when valuing**. The extent to which a brand is permanently in people's heads when they think of a product area – for example, Coca-Cola in soft drinks, American Express in charge cards or H&R Block in tax preparation – can make a dramatic difference to pricing power, returns on capital employed and sustainability of earnings. This factor is not handed to analysts in an annual report or in any other written material. It is a fuzzy concept and must be estimated with a high degree of uncertainty. Yet it is often crucial. Businesses with a good share of mind can withstand managerial errors, as long as the core economic franchise is not damaged.

- **Buy into a good business when others are running away**. H&R Block's shares were down over 40% in late 2000 and early 2001 due to temporary operating problems and general pessimism following the dot-com bubble burst. Buffett saw that its longer-term prospects were good and so bought on PERs of around ten or 11.

- **The urge to diversify may lead to 'diworsification'**. Over the decades, H&R Block bought many other service businesses to provide alternative income sources. A high proportion of these failed to produce good returns on capital – many lost money. Having learned this lesson, these days H&R Block's managers stay within the tax calculation circle of competence, slightly extended to include a few minor complementary services.

- **Look out for danger**. Keep a close eye on the general business environment. In particular, scan for dangers building in the system. Buffett and Munger spent the largest portion of each day trying to, as they frequently said, "understand the way the world works". An important input here was the consumption of five or six newspapers daily. In the case of H&R Block, this allowed them to piece together crucial snippets of information – for example, large numbers of people with shaky credit histories taking out mortgages in 2006 combined with other data such as the prospect of rising interest rates, suspect banking models and the potential for herd-like behaviour in the securitised bond market. If you can mix them together, these ingredients – and some more – will help get you ahead of the crowd in recognising that trouble is coming.

Investment 5

SHAW INDUSTRIES

Summary of the deal

Deal	Shaw Industries
Time	January 2001
Price paid	$2.42bn
Quantity	87.3% in 2001 for approx $2.1bn Remaining 12.7% in 2002 for $324m
Sale price	Still held
Profit	$1.9bn returned in the first nine years. There were profits after that, but the numbers have not been made public.
Berkshire Hathaway in 2001	Share price: $62,500–$75,300 Book value: $57,950m Per share book value: $37,920

Shaw Industries is a carpet manufacturer. It was already the world's largest tufted carpet maker when Berkshire Hathaway acquired it in January 2001 and, in the years before and after acquisition, it added many other types of flooring, from wood to vinyl.

It is dangerous to pronounce on whether the Shaw Industries investment turned out to be a good use of Berkshire Hathaway's money. We are unable to gain access to data on Shaw's business profitability after 2009; but we do know that in many of those years, blighted by the Great Recession following the 2007–2008 financial crisis, it had lower profits than previously.

Profits (after tax and incremental capital expenditure) between 2001 and 2009 averaged $210 million, or 8.7% of the $2.42 billion paid for the company. In the years that followed, the business at first "continue[d] to struggle",[168] with profits in 2010 and 2011 at a fraction of what they were in 2006 (a high point when pre-tax profits stood at $594 million).

After 2011, there followed a gradual rise in earnings; but the decline in employee numbers from 25,492 in 2009 to 18,865 in 2024, despite the acquisition of substantial businesses, tells a story of a company that was not zooming away. I'll present the evidence as best I can – you can make up your own mind on whether Berkshire's money might have been better used elsewhere.

Where was Berkshire in 2001?

Berkshire's operating businesses were doing well at the turn of the millennium. Excluding insurance underwriting losses (2001 was a bad year for insurers, hurt by the 9/11 attack on the Twin Towers in New York), Berkshire Hathaway was making profits of $3–$4 billion per year (see Table 5.1).

Cash flow generated from operations was even better, at $6.6 billion in 2001, up from $2.9 billion in 2000. That meant Buffett had plenty of resources to hand to pay for the $4.7 billion of acquisitions in 2001, as bargains appeared in the malaise following the dot-com boom. Despite buying so much, Buffett had ample firepower left at the end of 2001, with Berkshire sitting on $5.3 billion in cash and over $24 billion in liquid bonds.

Table 5.1 Berkshire Hathaway's sources of reported earnings, 2000 and 2001

($m)	Pre-tax Earnings		Berkshire's Share of Net Earnings (after taxes and minority interests)	
	2001	2000	2001	2000
Operating Earnings:				
Insurance Group:				
Underwriting – Reinsurance	(4318)	(1416)	(2824)	(911)
Underwriting – GEICO	221	(224)	144	(146)
Underwriting – Other Primary	30	25	18	16
Net Investment Income	2,824	2,773	1,968	1,946
Building Products[1]	461	34	287	21
Finance and Financial Products Business	519	530	336	343
Flight Services	186	213	105	126
MidAmerican Energy (76% owned)	600	197	230	109
Retail Operations	175	175	101	104
Scott Fetzer (excluding finance operation)	129	122	83	80

($m)	Pre-tax Earnings	Berkshire's Share of Net Earnings (after taxes and minority interests)
Shaw Industries[2]	292	156
Other Businesses	179	103
Purchase-Accounting Adjustments	(726)	(699)
Corporate Interest Expense	(92)	(60)
Shareholder-Designated Contributions	(17)	(11)
Other	25	16
Operating Earnings	488	(47)
Capital Gains from Investments	1,320	842
Total Earnings – All Entities	**1,808**	**795**
	221	133
	(881)	(843)
	(92)	(61)
	(17)	(11)
	39	30
	1,699	936
	3,955	2,392
	5,654	**3,328**

(1) Includes Acme Brick from August 1, 2000; Benjamin Moore from December 18, 2000; Johns Manville from February 27, 2001; and MiTek from July 31, 2001.
(2) From date of acquisition, January 8, 2001.

Source: Berkshire Hathaway 2001 Annual Report.

The growth of Shaw Industries

Shaw traces its history back to the tiny Star Dye Company, which was bought by Clarence Shaw in 1946. It dyed rugs, bedspreads and robes in the floor-coverings capital of the US: the small town of Dalton, Georgia, home to over 150 carpet mills and 34,000 souls. The Star Dye Company established a good reputation and developed a respectably healthy clientele within Dalton.

Robert E ('Bob') Shaw – who was to sell to Berkshire in 2001 – was born to Clarence and Essie Evans Shaw in August 1931, 12 days before Buffett entered the world in Omaha. Bob attended Dalton High School, where his mother taught. Keen on football and basketball, he observed his own competitive nature as a young man in a reflective interview he gave at the age of 90:

> I played football and was a quarterback. I was also one of the worst students you can ever imagine. I always thought if you mathematically could get there quicker than your competitor, then you had a better chance to see just a little around the corner. I've always said if I'm in a poker game, if I can have one peek at their hole card I'm going to beat them. So it really is seeing a little more. Everybody sees a lot of things, but they're not willing to follow what they see.[169]

As a teenager, Bob drove a truck for his dad's company. After attending the University of the South in Sewanee, Tennessee, he took over as CEO following his father's death in 1958, knowing that he had to change the company. As the 1950s had unfolded, there was less demand for tufted bedspreads and robes, but more demand for carpets. Thus, Bob quickly retooled the company to start dyeing carpet. Sales rose to $300,000.

Elder brother JC Shaw[170] was also steeped in the textile and carpet industry that had kept Dalton thriving for decades. After Dalton High School, he earned a degree in textile engineering from Georgia Tech in 1950 and then took on various managerial roles at textile firms, including the challenge of creating a new carpet yarn division. Aged 29, he joined Marion Manufacturing Company in 1958 as general manager of Rocky Creek Mills' carpet yarn division. That year, he also inherited shares in his father's Star Dye Company.

In 1959, the brothers worked together when Rocky Creek Mills and Star Dye Company formed Star Finishing Company to dye and finish carpeting for other companies, with just ten employees. Despite being a director of tiny Star Finishing, JC was still primarily an employee of Rocky Creek Mills, and when it was bought he became general manager of the purchaser's automotive division for a while. But it wasn't long before JC left to establish his own carpet company in northwest Georgia.

The brothers reunited in 1967 when they created a holding company, Philadelphia Holding Company, to acquire the venerable Philadelphia Carpet Company (founded in 1846), a carpet manufacturing business. The holding company merged with Star Finishing the following year. Robert and JC were renowned for taking the risk of embracing innovations such as printed carpets and continuous dyeing ranges, and for implementing plans so efficiently that they significantly boosted profitability. The brothers recognised early that being a low-cost producer was vital to survival and profits. This meant, above all, gaining economies of scale. To this end, in 1971, the company was listed on the American Stock Exchange[171] after changing its name to Shaw Industries. By then, it had $43 million in sales and 900 employees.

Life on the stock market at the start was grand, with the share price rising significantly in the first year (see Figures 5.1 and 5.2). But the company had a terrible time of it in the recession of the early 1970s as the price of oil quadrupled, sucking money out of American pockets to pay more to members of the Organization of the Petroleum Exporting Countries (which provided over half the world's supply). Worse still for Shaw was the fact that the ultimate raw material for most carpet is crude oil; thus, carpet prices had to be raised just to break even.

There was some respite in the mid-1970s; but then in 1979, the Iranian revolution occurred, quickly followed by the Iran-Iraq war, which saw oil prices double. Operating in an industry that was particularly sensitive to both recession and oil prices meant that Shaw stock underperformed the S&P 500 for its first decade.

Figure 5.1 Shaw stock price (year end), 1971–1984 ($)

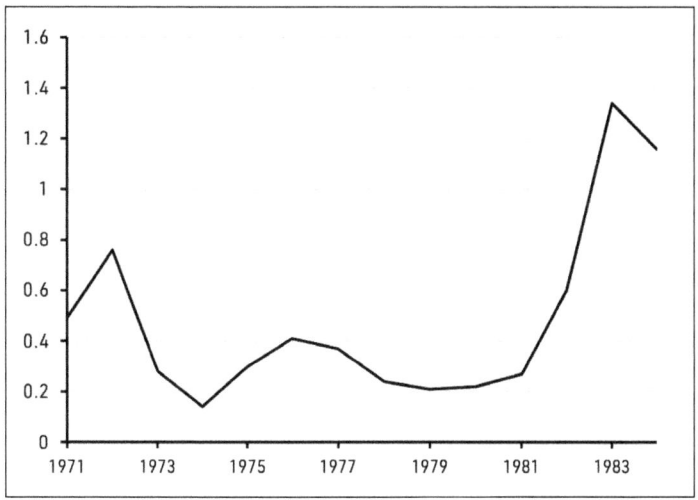

Source: Shaw Industries Securities and Exchange Commission 10-K filings.

Figure 5.2 Shaw stock price index relative to S&P 500 index (year-end), 1971–1984

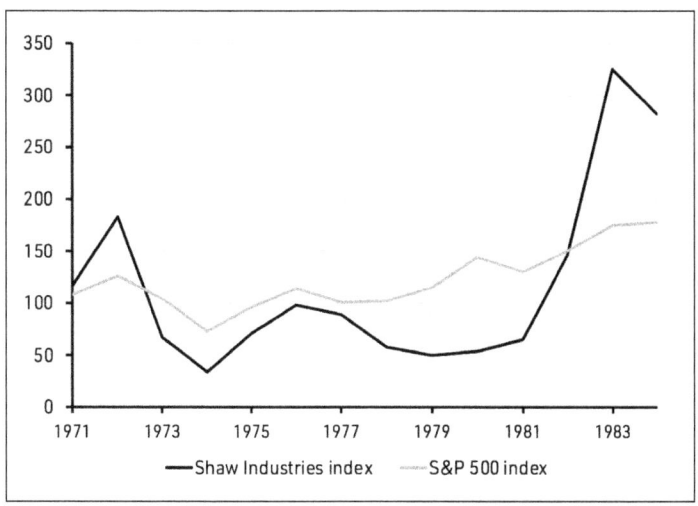

Source: Shaw Industries Securities and Exchange Commission 10-K filings.

It was a completely different story in the 1980s, when the company enjoyed terrific growth. By 1985, Shaw was included in the Fortune 500 list of the largest US corporations, with more than $500 million in sales and almost 5,000 employees. It got there by taking advantage of the recession of the early 1980s to buy other carpet manufacturers, making it the largest player in the US, as well as by maintaining high operational efficiency.

Another strategic move for Shaw was to become a wholesale distributor itself rather than selling through independent wholesalers, which tended to have good pricing power and therefore excellent profit margins. The Shaw family knew that this was a risky move because the industry doctrine was for various manufacturers to supply wholesalers, which then shipped out to retailers. Shaw was going into competition with its customers, which shocked many in the industry.

But they implemented it well and the gamble soon paid off, with retailers quite content to cut out the middleman too – as long as they got a better price. Besides, with Shaw being the biggest producer in the country, there would be a big hole in their retail offering if they excluded Shaw and bought only through the traditional wholesaler network.

As well as this 'forward integration', Shaw decided to 'backward integrate' – that is, buy up yarn-spinning mill companies to reduce costs, the benefits of which it could again share with retailers. As well as the biggest manufacturer, it became the most integrated, with the best economies of scale, making it *the* low-cost producer of nylon and polypropylene carpet.

Another pivotal move was the establishment of an in-house trucking operation, rather than relying on the dominant carrier used by other manufacturers. As volume throughput grew, Shaw's trucking network became increasingly efficient, with fewer empty routes, lower inventory levels in company warehouses and better service. With 1,000 trucks and 17 warehouses, it could offer fast delivery times. In addition, the fact that Shaw's volume was removed from the other logistics firms meant that they were less efficient, with more stop-offs at manufacturers, wholesalers and retailers over greater distances.

Bob and JC knew that they had to keep ahead of the game in so many ways. One of those was in new technology. So, when Du Pont in 1986 introduced stain-resistant fibres, Shaw was quick to move out its old inventory and refit its machinery, while competitors with less financial firepower remained hesitant.

Shaw's shares rose threefold over the late 1980s and then another fivefold in the early 1990s (see Figures 5.3 and 5.4) as it bought large carpet manufacturers and a fibre producer.

Figure 5.3 Shaw stock price (year-end), 1985–1999 ($)

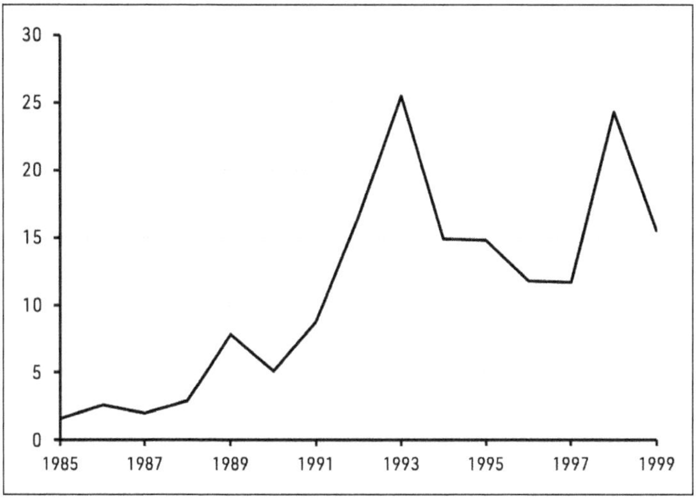

Source: Shaw Industries Securities and Exchange Commission 10-K filings.

Figure 5.4 Shaw stock price and S&P 500 index (year-end), 1985–1999 ($)

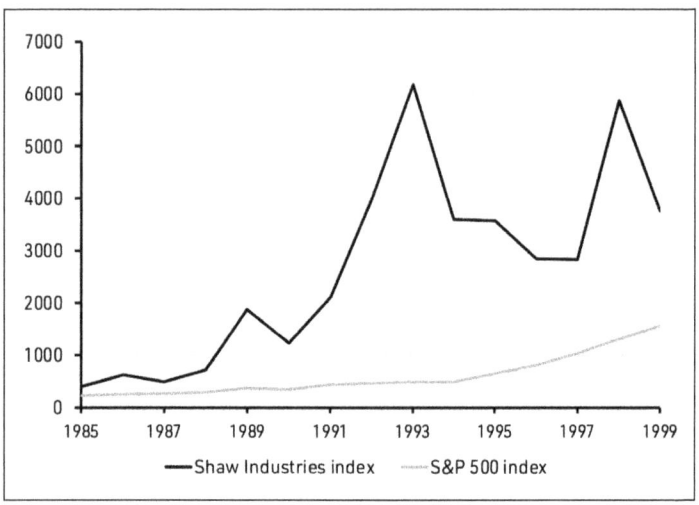

Source: Shaw Industries Securities and Exchange Commission 10-K filings.

The blunders of the mid-1990s

Business was booming for Shaw in the early 1990s. As Figure 5.5 shows, profits increased steadily to over $100 million and return on shareholders' investment was high: generally, the percentage return on equity capital was at least double that of the average company. Sales continued to rise for the rest of the decade (see Figure 5.6) as yet more companies were acquired. Despite booming sales, profits fell off a cliff after 1995 (see Figure 5.7). I suppose you could say that at least the company didn't make a loss. But the leaders knew they had messed up.

Figure 5.5 Shaw profit and return on shareholders' investment, 1985–1994

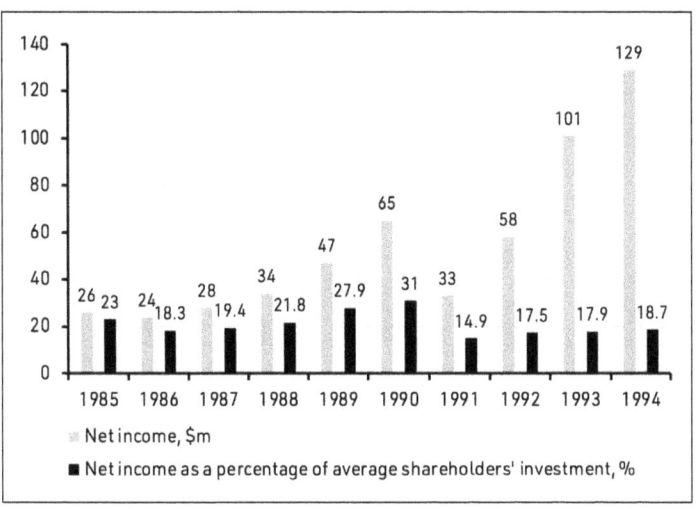

Source: Shaw Industries Securities and Exchange Commission 10-K filings.

Figure 5.6 Shaw sales 1985–1999 ($bn)

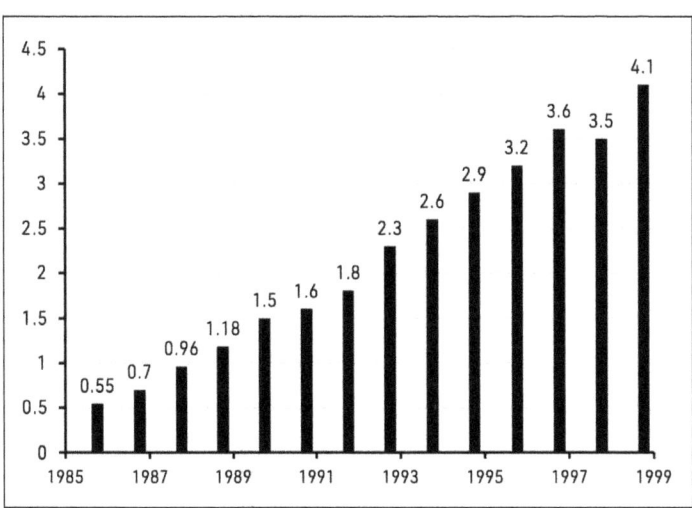

Source: Shaw Industries Securities and Exchange Commission 10-K filings.

Figure 5.7 Shaw Industries during the retail adventure

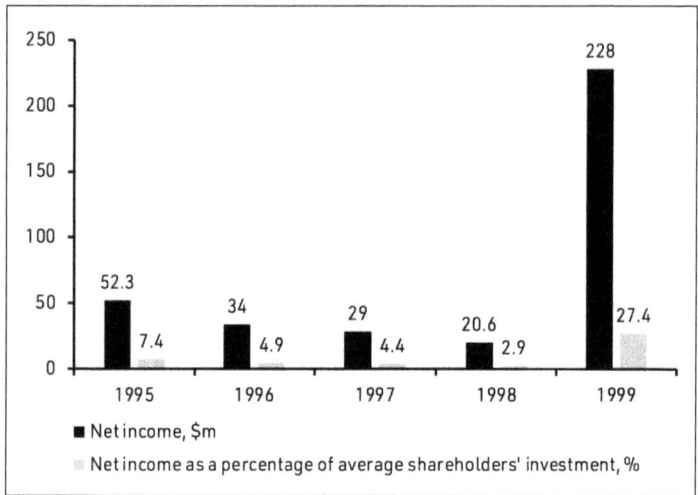

Source: Shaw Industries 10-K filings.

So, what went wrong? Following on from its successful vertical integration moves in yarn, logistics and wholesaling, in 1995 Shaw decided to go one step further and become a retailer. The company acquired large chains of floor covering retailers and bought individual stores at great cost (*Forbes* put this at $200 million).[172] It ended up with over 400 stores and was thus competing head-to-head with other retailers in town after town. I imagine you can already see the flaw in this strategy: Shaw wanted to continue supplying the vast number of independent retailers up and down the country while its own retail stores were undercutting those very same businesses.

Naturally, retail customers were furious. Why would they want to stock Shaw's carpets, they thought, when other suppliers were available? Shaw lost market share rapidly as both big players such as Home Depot and smaller stores dumped it. The costs of first building a retail business and then dismantling it almost wiped out profits.

In between marching up the retail hill and then marching back down it, Shaw's senior team had to try to motivate the managers of those 400 or so stores. These retailers had often been founder entrepreneurs, working all hours; but now they found themselves mere cogs in a larger enterprise, with fattened bank balances. In many cases they – how to put this politely? – shifted their work-life balance in favour of more leisure time.

Head office people were unable to step in or act as substitute managers because they didn't have a clue about retailing; they had spent their careers honing their low-cost manufacturing prowess. Shaw's US market share fell four percentage points during its retail excursion.

Another misstep was the purchase, for $100 million, of three UK carpet manufacturers in the belief that the UK market was fragmented and could do with both consolidation and the application of Shaw's advanced tufting technology. But it turned out that this was not enough to beat European competitors with their advantage of weakening currencies against the pound.

Chastened, Shaw threw in the towel in 1998, selling the UK business (for $100 million)[173] and the US retail stores (for $93 million),[174] and returning to its core competencies of efficiency in production and high-quality service for retailers.

Queen gets the red carpet treatment

This refocus was marked in October 1998 by a merger with another large Dalton manufacturer, Queen Carpets, for $470 million, mostly in the form of shares. The combined group commanded a 35% market share compared with the 28% of the previous leader, Mohawk.[175] It wasn't long before old retail customers returned to the fold. Sales rose and record profits were made in the year before Buffett decided to buy.

The Queen merger was astute. Bob wrote, in the 1999 Annual Report, that the move had already yielded in excess of $100 million in synergistic savings. He was very pleased with Queen's "expertise in styling, product development, and customer relationships … As we move forward, we expect to continue to benefit from the unique qualities that each company contributed in the merger".[176] Again, economies of scale through being both the largest and the most efficient manufacturer in the country led to lower costs.

Julian Saul had headed Queen alongside his father, Harry, since the 1960s, growing it to $800 million sales – making it the fourth-largest US carpet manufacturer. The Shaws and Saul had grown up in the same neighbourhood. Saul was nine years younger than Bob and, as mascot of the football team, would carry Bob's helmet. "We played softball and lots of sport together. We've been friends forever," Saul said in 2021.[177] They were such close friends that three years before the merger, when Bob told Saul that he was thinking of getting into the retail business, Saul responded in disbelief: "Bob, as a friend, I hope you don't do it. As a competitor, I hope you do it. It's not good. You shouldn't do it."[178]

When Bob finally saw sense and decided to get out of retail, Saul became more amenable to another of Bob's ideas: a merger between the two companies. Saul's experience and sound advice made him the perfect president of Shaw Industries.

The deal

In June 2000, Bob and Saul travelled to Omaha.[179] They were considering a merger with another firm and needed help from Berkshire's insurance division. The CEO of the target company travelled with them. Buffett was asked whether Berkshire would be willing to write an insurance policy to cover all future liabilities incurred by the company arising from asbestos exposure. According to Buffett,[180] the liabilities would have been "huge". If Shaw and Saul could not find insurance, the merger deal was off.

Berkshire was the go-to player in the insurance business for exceptionally large policies, but even it would never commit to an open-ended liability; it always put a cap on its exposure.

After some conversation, Bob and Saul concluded that if Berkshire was not willing to bet the ranch on the liability, then neither were they. As Bob was leaving, he asked Buffett about the possibility of an investment in Shaw Industries. Buffett was non-committal at that point, but his "interest in Shaw was sparked".[181]

A few days later, Bob sent Buffett a stack of information on Shaw Industries; and several days after that, he and Saul were back in Omaha to discuss a direct investment from Berkshire.

As they were leaving, Buffett asked the Dalton couple if they objected to Berkshire picking up some Shaw shares on the open market. Thus began Buffett's investment in Shaw. But a bigger deal was put on hold when, on 20 June, Shaw's largest customer, Flooring America, filed for Chapter 11. Flooring America's largest supplier was Shaw Industries and it was owed about $14 million, plus a promissory note of about $12 million.

Nonetheless, Bob continued the conversation with Buffett – and with Charlie Munger, who was then asked to cast his eye over the firm. By 20 October, they had a deal. Bob and Saul each wanted to retain 5%, and another 2.7% was set aside for directors and members of the managerial team. So initially, Berkshire bought 87.3% for $2.1 billion in cash at $19 per share – a good premium to the undisturbed price of $12.19, but significantly down on the $25 or so that the price had reached in both 1993 and 1998.

Shaw was then the largest business controlled by Berkshire, with 30,000 employees, sales of $4 billion and 100 manufacturing plants and distribution centres across the country. Corporate headquarters remained in Dalton, Georgia. In an interview with *The Wall Street Journal*,[182] Buffett emphasised his fondness for boring companies doing pretty ordinary things but doing them extraordinarily well: "The carpet business is a fundamental business. People will keep using carpet. It is a fairly easy business to learn."

The transaction completed on 8 January 2001. Bob was very pleased with the arrangement. Apart from walking away with plenty of cash, he was relieved of many of the pressures that listed companies are under:

> As a public company you can make the right long-term decisions and end up with some disappointing short-term results. That's when the stock price suffers ... [But within Berkshire] we think it will be easier to make long-term decisions without worrying about the short-term mentality of the stock market. That's

another benefit of being part of Berkshire. They are well known for their long-term views.[183]

A year later,[184] Shaw, Saul and their managers were sufficiently comfortable with Berkshire for them to swap their Shaw Industries shares for 4,505 shares of Berkshire Class A common stock and 7,063 shares of Class B common stock. Thus, Berkshire secured 100% ownership for an extra $324 million.

Buffett summed up the subsequent relationship with the team at Shaw at Berkshire Hathaway's shareholder gathering in May 2012:

> We want our businesses to run very autonomously, and we want the managers of those businesses to feel like they're their own business. That's enormously important at Berkshire. So we don't tell the people at Clayton Homes to buy their carpet from Shaw or to buy their paint from Benjamin Moore. We just don't do that.
>
> And you could say that's kind of silly, but any gains we would get from doing that, by selling incremental units, I think would be far offset by the change in the feeling of the manager as to whether they're really running their own business.
>
> We hand people billions of dollars and they hand us stock certificates and they have been running those businesses for decades in many cases. And we want them to feel the same way the next day, when they've got the money and we've got the stock certificates, as the day before when they had the stock certificates and we had the money.
>
> And the moment we start telling them how to change the way they operate, or to coordinate with this guy, or get this person's approval, or anything like that, you know, that just erodes that advantage, which we think is very substantial, that they have this proprietary feeling about their business.

What Buffett saw in Shaw

The top line of Table 5.2 shows reported net income over the five years leading up to Berkshire's purchase of Shaw. As discussed previously, there were some awful years. But when thinking of buying a company, Buffett always looked to the future. To help his thinking about likely futures, he separated out those past costs which were unlikely to be repeated from those which were normal costs of the daily running of the business. This is what I have tried to do in Table 5.2.

First, in 1997 and 1998, Shaw incurred exceptional expenses when it sold its retail businesses. It was reasonable to assume that this would not happen again – certainly not under Buffett and Munger's watchful eyes, and their control over capital allocation. So, to get to 'underlying earnings', we can start by adding back those exceptional costs.

Second, the sale of the UK business also incurred exceptional one-off costs, so we can also add those back.

Third, equities were sold at a loss. These were unrelated to the ongoing floor coverings business and were unlikely to be repeated, so we can add them back too.

Fourth, there were non-underlying 'non-recurring charges' that we can add back.

Finally, being intellectually generous to the directors, we might agree with them that the 'restructuring costs' they identified were genuine one-offs and unlikely to be repeated, so we can add them back also.

Table 5.2 Shaw Industries – an attempt to derive 'underlying earnings'

$m	1995	1996	1997	1998	1999
Reported net income	52.3	34.0	29.0	20.6	228.0
Add back loss on sale of residential retail business, net of tax benefit	0	0	23.3	92.7	2.4
Add back charge related to the disposal of UK assets, net of tax benefit			20.3		
Add back loss on sale of equity securities, net of tax benefit				13.4	
Add back 'non-recurring charges', net of tax benefit	4.1	26.5			
Add back restructuring costs, net of tax benefit	–	24.2	–	–	–
Underlying profit after tax	**56.4**	**84.7**	**72.6**	**126.7**	**230.4**
Shareholders' investment	710	672	638	797	869
Underlying profit after tax ÷ Shareholders' investment	7.9%	12.6%	11.4%	15.9%	26.5%
Shareholders' investment after deduction of goodwill	606	460	402	381	450
Underlying profit after tax ÷ Shareholders' investment after deduction of goodwill	9.3%	18.4%	18.1%	33.3%	51.2%

Source: Shaw Industries 10-K filings.

When all of those cost items are no longer regarded as relevant to underlying performance, we find that during those five years, profits after tax ranged from $56.4 million to $230.4 million. So, we are getting closer to a justification for paying $2.42 billion.

Now, I will throw in a consideration to which Buffett and Munger probably paid a great deal of attention: return on the amount of shareholders' money used by the business. Through these five years, shareholders' investment (net assets) was not as great as you might imagine for a manufacturing enterprise with over $4 billion in sales: it ranged from $638 to $869 million.

A large chunk of that shareholders' investment was not, in fact, assets available for the managers to use within the business, because it was the intangible asset labelled 'goodwill' arising from acquisitions. If we deduct the goodwill figures so that we come towards net tangible assets, the range for shareholders' investment being used in the business falls to $381–$606 million.

The return on that investment was 33.3% in 1998 and 51.2% in 1999. It might have flashed through Buffett's mind that this company would probably generate profits north of $200 million after tax on a net tangible asset base of, say, $500–$700 million. It simply didn't need to retain much of the profit made to expand production lines allowing growth. This meant that most of that profit could flow to Berkshire HQ in Omaha for deployment elsewhere.

This thought is reinforced by looking at the cash flow over those five years (see Table 5.3). In 1998 and 1999, cash flow – even after paying for necessary equipment – was nearer $300 million than $200 million.

Table 5.3 Shaw Industries – cash provided by operating activities

$m	1995	1996	1997	1998	1999
Cash provided by operating activities after net additions to working capital	161	166	139	378	394
Capital expenditure	−67	−107	−78	−65	−116
Cash flow after working capital and capex deduction	94	59	61	313	278

Source: Shaw Industries 10-K filings.

We can only imagine the smiles that must have appeared on Buffett's face as he read the numbers presented in Figure 5.8 in the years following the purchase. Profits more than doubled over the first six years. While we do not have access to all the net tangible asset figures for these years, we can deduce that, through acquisition and organic growth, this stood at over $1.1 billion in 2004 because Buffett wrote that: "Shaw, led by Bob Shaw and Julian Saul, earned an outstanding 25.6% on tangible equity in 2004. The company is a powerhouse and has a bright future".[185] Earnings after tax in 2004 were around $466 (1 - 0.35) = $303 million, assuming a 35% tax rate, which implies a tangible asset base of $1.183 billion – that is, tangible equity was about four times earnings after tax or, to be more precise, (1 ÷ 0.256) × $303 million = $1.183 billion.

Figure 5.8 Pre-tax earnings of Shaw Industries (Berkshire's share 87.3% in 2001, 100% thereafter)

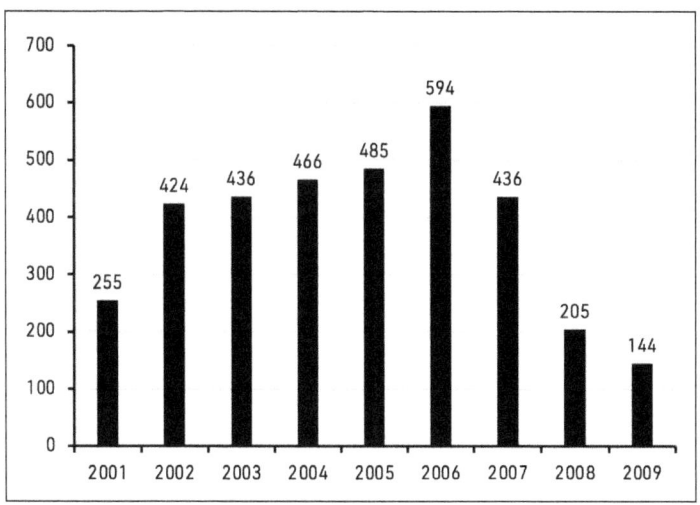

Source: Berkshire Hathaway annual reports.

Average profits before tax deduction over the first full nine years of Berkshire's ownership were $383 million. If we deduct 35% for tax,[186] the average return to Berkshire was $249 million. This is based on the assumption that Shaw did not need some of the cash it was generating to add to its fixed asset base.[187] So, let's take a look at the amount spent on capital items versus the amount deducted for depreciation and amortisation (deducted from profit), shown in Table 5.4.

If we deduct average incremental investment in capital items – that is, $39 million, shown at the bottom of the final column of Table 5.4 – then Berkshire Hathaway could take away approximately $210 million per year (i.e., $249–$39 million) in each of the first nine years to invest elsewhere. That is 8.7% of the amounted committed to buy Shaw: $2.42 billion.

Table 5.4 Shaw Industries – capital expenditures, depreciation and amortisation of tangible assets

Year	Capital expenditures (excluding those which were part of business acquisitions)	Depreciation and amortisation of tangible assets	Capital expenditures minus depreciation and amortisation
2001	71	88	–17
2002	196	91	105
2003	120	91	29
2004	125	99	26
2005	209	113	96
2006	189	134	55
2007	144	144	0
2008	173	150	23
2009	186	149	37
Average difference			39

Source: Berkshire Hathaway annual reports.

Clearly, this analysis lacks subtlety; it does not draw on the actual cash flows going to the Omaha office to be deployed into other investments. But as a rough estimate, I think it might give some insight into the returns from this deal over the first nine years.

After 2009, we have a problem, because in Berkshire's annual reports, Shaw's earnings are lumped in with those of Johns Manville, Acme Brick, Clayton Homes, MiTek and Benjamin Moore in the 'building products manufacturers' category. However, we are given some clues – first from what Buffett wrote in the annual reports and second from employee numbers (see Table 5.5). They do not indicate much volume growth.

Table 5.5 Information on Berkshire Hathaway building product manufacturers, 2009–2023

Year	Comment on Shaw in Berkshire annual report	Employees					
		Shaw	Johns Manville	MiTek	Benjamin Moore	Acme	Clayton Homes
2009		25,492	6,411	1,723	2,380	1,947	12,133
2010	"Our businesses related to home construction continue to struggle. Johns Manville, MiTek, Shaw and Acme Brick have maintained their competitive positions, but their profits are far below the levels of a few years ago. Combined, these operations earned $362m pre-tax in 2010 compared to $1.3 billion in 2006 … Shaw will spend $200m in 2011 on plant and equipment, all of it situated in America. These businesses entered the recession strong and will exit it stronger. At Berkshire, our time horizon is forever."	24,552	6,410	1,796	2,283	1,845	10,439
2011	"Last year, I told you that 'a housing recovery will probably begin within a year or so.' I was dead wrong … The four housing-related companies in this section (a group that excludes Clayton, which is carried under Finance and Financial Products) had aggregate pre-tax earnings of $227m in 2009, $362m in 2010 and $359m in 2011."	22,650	6,532	2,064	2,280	2,096	9,973

Year	Comment on Shaw in Berkshire annual report	Employees					
		Shaw	Johns Manville	MiTek	Benjamin Moore	Acme	Clayton Homes
2012	"Significant improvements in our carpet business, modest improvements in our other building products businesses in the U.S. ... In 2012 Shaw ... benefitted from the impact of price increases at the end of 2011 and beginning of 2012, as well as from relatively stable raw material costs in 2012, that resulted in higher margins."	22,312	6,841	2,037	2,240	2,117	10,575
2013	"Revenues in 2013 from our building products businesses increased 8% to about $9.6bn. These businesses benefitted from the generally improved residential and commercial construction markets ... Increased earnings were generated by building products businesses (13%)."	22,603	6,855	2,657	2,102	2,247	11,850
2014	"Revenues in 2014 from Shaw were relatively unchanged from 2013, reflecting the impact of the closure of its rugs division in early 2014 and lower carpet sales, offset by higher sales of hard flooring products. Pre-tax earnings in 2014 of the building products businesses increased 6% compared to 2013. Each of our building products businesses generated increased earnings in 2014 over 2013, with the exception of Shaw, whose earnings declined due to comparatively higher raw material costs."	22,074	6,852	3,006	1,908	2,257	11,988

Investment 5. Shaw Industries

Year	Comment on Shaw in Berkshire annual report	Employees					
		Shaw	Johns Manville	MiTek	Benjamin Moore	Acme	Clayton Homes
2015	"Revenues in 2015 of our building products manufacturers increased $192m (2%) over 2014. In 2015, the revenue increase reflected sales volume increases at Shaw, Johns Manville and MiTek, as well as the impact of bolt-on business acquisitions. The overall increase in earnings was primarily attributable to the aforementioned increases in revenues and lower average raw material and energy costs, partially offset by the negative impact of foreign currency translation and increased restructuring charges. Most of the comparative increases in earnings were generated by Shaw, Johns Manville and Benjamin Moore."	21,785	6,963	3,950	1,715	2,341	13,164
2016	"Building products revenues increased $456m (4.4%) in 2016 compared to 2015, reflecting volume-driven revenue increases by MiTek, Johns Manville, Acme and Shaw, as well as revenues from bolt-on acquisitions by Shaw and MiTek. The revenue increase reflected increased unit sales across several product categories ... Pre-tax earnings increased $11m (0.9%) in 2016 compared to 2015."	21,540	7,192	5,128	1,778	2,380	14,677

Year	Comment on Shaw in Berkshire annual report	Employees					
		Shaw	Johns Manville	MiTek	Benjamin Moore	Acme	Clayton Homes
2017	"Near the end of 2016, Shaw Industries, our floor coverings business, acquired U.S. Floors … USF … deliver[ed] a 40% increase in sales in 2017, during which their operation was integrated with Shaw's. This acquisition increased Shaw's sales to $5.7bn in 2017 and its employment to 22,000. With the purchase of USF, Shaw has substantially strengthened its position as an important and durable source of earnings for Berkshire."	21,867	7,309	5,738	1,772	2,408	16,362
2018	"Shaw acquired Sanquahar Tile Services in Scotland, which manufactures and distributes carpet tile throughout Europe … The pre-tax earnings increase [at] Shaw … sales increased 7.9%.... The comparative earnings increase reflected the effects of asset impairment, pension settlement and environmental claim charges of $107m recorded in 2016 by Shaw and Benjamin Moore. The comparative earnings increase also was a result of bolt-on acquisitions, partly offset by comparative declines in average gross sales margin rates due to higher raw material and other production costs."	22,660	7,801	5,670	1,764	2,353	17,144

Year	Comment on Shaw in Berkshire annual report	Employees					
		Shaw	Johns Manville	MiTek	Benjamin Moore	Acme	Clayton Homes
2019	"Aggregate revenues of our other building products businesses [other than Clayton] were $13.0bn in 2019, an increase of 2.8% versus 2018. Revenues increased for … hard surface flooring. Pre-tax earnings of the other building products businesses were $1.5bn in 2019, an increase of 8.2% over 2018."	21,094	7,769	6,159	1,848	2,117	18,533
2020	"Aggregate revenues of our other building products businesses [other than Clayton] were approximately $12.6bn in 2020, a decrease of 2.6% versus 2019. The revenue decrease reflected lower flooring volumes, partly attributable to the negative effects of the Covid-19 pandemic."	20,806	7,709	6,291	1,905	1,960	19,455
2021	"Aggregate revenues of our other building products businesses [other than Clayton] were approximately $14.5bn in 2021, an increase of 14.4% versus 2020 … Pre-tax earnings of the other building products businesses were approximately $1.7bn in 2021."	21,482	7,748	5,510	2,042	1,794	20,830

Year	Comment on Shaw in Berkshire annual report	Employees					
		Shaw	Johns Manville	MiTek	Benjamin Moore	Acme	Clayton Homes
2022	"Aggregate revenues of our other building products businesses [other than Clayton] were approximately $16.2bn in 2022. Significant cost inflation in 2021, that continued through 2022, largely drove the higher selling prices. Pre-tax earnings of the other building products businesses were approximately $2.4bn in 2022, an increase of 41.9% over 2021. Pre-tax earnings as a percentage of revenues was 15.0% in 2022, a 3.2 percentage point increase compared to 2021."	20,784	8,044	5,974	2,026	1,890	20,229
2023	"Aggregate revenues of our other building products businesses [other than Clayton] were approximately $14.5bn in 2023, a decrease of 10.0% versus 2022 … Pre-tax earnings of the other building products businesses were approximately $2.1bn in 2023, a decrease of 11.4% compared to 2022."	18,865	7,748	5,783	1,952	1,915	20,645
Change 2009–2023		-26%	+21%	+236%	-18%	-2%	+70%

Source: Berkshire Hathaway annual reports.

In August 2006, Bob turned 75 and expressed to Buffett a desire to retire as CEO. He stepped away from full-time work but remained on the board to advise on long-range initiatives. He promised not to overshadow the new leadership team headed by CEO Vance Bell – a 31-year veteran of Shaw Industries – and President Randy Merritt;[188] but "[I]f there's something they want to buy, they may ask me what I think,"[189] said Bob. Buffett was very happy with the succession, describing it as "the right call".[190] Two months before Bob stepped down, Saul retired as president. Shaw's sales are now above $7 billion a year.

Bob insisted throughout his career that he was not interested in building a business purely for the money, but that he wanted to create an institution that would last. Aged 90, he attested: "For me and people like Warren Buffett, it's not necessarily about the money. I drive a car that's 13 years old. It's about success and reputation."[191] In his tenth decade, he is still playing golf and helping out at Engineered Floors, a company he founded in 2009 when he "got bored" after four years of retirement. This private company with 7 million square feet of factory in Northwest Georgia produces soft surface flooring.

The Anna Sue and Bob Shaw Foundation also keeps him busy. It has given to dozens of organisations, particularly around Dalton. A major aspect of its giving has been directed towards helping children with autism spectrum disorder, attention-deficit/hyperactivity disorder and other learning and developmental disorders.

Learning points

- **Not all competitive advantages reside in brands and differentiation**. Being a low-cost producer can offer a competitive advantage to generate a decent return on shareholders' funds. Shaw – much like GEICO – operates in an industry where customers are very price sensitive: they are not willing to pay (much) extra for a brand-named product. So, the primary strategic focus of these businesses is to offer customers really good prices while maintaining satisfactory margins and return on equity; managers must continually strive to be the most cost-efficient. Bob and Saul had a long track record of this. Being the biggest in the industry also helps (if diseconomies of scale are handled well).

- **Don't upset your customers by directly competing with them.** Shaw infuriated its principal customers by running 400 retail stores across the US.

- **Companies with high returns on shareholders' equity are not necessarily good investments.** Much depends on the price paid for the profits and the cash flow likely to be generated. Shaw was in the ballpark of making around $200 million per year for shareholders while using $500–$600 million of their money. That is good business. But it's only a great investment if you can buy that earnings flow at a lowish price. Perhaps $2.42 billion was at the top end of a reasonable range?

A Note from the Author

Around this time, Warren Buffett brought six smaller companies into the Berkshire Hathaway family, most of which became stalwarts of the group. At first, I planned to omit them from this book series because Buffett does not provide profit numbers after buying. The companies have been absorbed within much larger reporting segments of Berkshire, such as "Retail" or "Building Products", and only group financial data is published in Berkshire's annual reports, rather than individual company figures. The sparseness of the numbers meant that I was unable to analyse the returns that Berkshire made on its outlay. In some cases, not even the amount paid was made public, let alone ensuing earnings.

On reflection, however, I figured that – even without numerical analysis – the stories of these companies are fascinating. If you go to the Berkshire annual meeting, you'll hear tributes being paid to these firms, all of which are still held today. If you venture into the hall next to the auditorium, you will also see their products on display. And they are open for business that first Saturday in May – for example, more than 1,000 pairs of Justin cowboy boots are sold during the annual meeting.

So, please forgive the lack of analytical detail in this part of the book; but I thought that you might find the origin stories, the deals and the subsequent lives of these companies within the Berkshire fold interesting nonetheless.

Investment 6

STAR FURNITURE CO.

Summary of the deal

Deal	Star Furniture Co.
Time	July 1997
Price paid	Undisclosed share payment
Proportion of equity	100%
Status	Still held

Warren Buffett likes furniture stores with strong franchises that dominate their geographies. It's an affection that developed following his 1983 purchase of the Nebraska Furniture Mart, with the brilliant Blumkin family forever deepening and widening the economic moat around their store in Omaha (see Volume 2, Investment 3). One of the first questions Buffett asked the Blumkin family was: "Are there any more at home like you?"[192] They told him about three "outstanding" furniture retailers in other parts of the country. At the time, however, none was for sale.

Over the years, Irv Blumkin maintained a friendship with Bill Child of R.C. Willey in Utah, one of the three retailers named. And, after 12 years of waiting, he eventually saw his chance to help both Berkshire and R.C. Willey. When chatting with Child at the 1995 San Francisco Furniture Mart Show, Blumkin began outlining his experience under the Berkshire umbrella. It wasn't long before Child was happy to sell to Berkshire too (see Volume 3, Investment 6).

Buffett now had two scouts in his search for the best furniture companies in the land. When Buffett asked Child the same question he had asked the Blumkins, the same two names were mentioned – a reassuring confirmation. The first was Star Furniture of Houston, which was duly acquired in 1997.

The final company on the list was Jordan's Furniture, which dominated Massachusetts and New Hampshire. It was acquired 16 years after Buffett first took an (intellectual) interest in it. He had watched it go from strength to strength, but it wasn't until the Tatelman brothers were ready to be partners in the Berkshire's team that he approached them. That is a story for the next chapter.

The beginning of Star Furniture

Star started life as a grocer in downtown Houston in 1912, but it wasn't long before it was accepting furniture in exchange for groceries. It operated on the lower floor of a three-storey building. The other two floors were occupied by a "hotel of some questionable repute", according to owner and leader Melvyn Wolff, who was later to sell to Buffett. "My father told me that the people upstairs used to say that the downstairs of their brothel was occupied by a furniture store of questionable repute," he quipped.[193]

Wolff's father, Boris, was a penniless Russian *émigré* with no command of English, who had escaped a work camp in 1918. But by 1924, he had saved enough (Wolff estimated this at between $1,200 and $1,500) to buy an interest in the furniture store, becoming the fourth partner with a one-quarter share. The injection of cash from Boris and another partner allowed Star Furniture to put a downpayment on the building, moving out the hotel and exhibiting furniture on all three floors. They targeted blue-collar workers, offering them all their furniture for a dollar down and a dollar a week to pay off the debt.

Hit hard by the Depression, they nevertheless promised staff that none would be laid off and duly kept that vow – a triumph in itself. When the Second World War further dented sales, the partners concluded that the business could not support the owners and their families. One partner left to start his own furniture business after selling his stake to Boris and Mrs Louis Getz. The fourth partner had died a few years before.

By 1950, the company had six stores. At the time, Wolff was 19 and was planning a career in law. He had already started studying at the University of Texas in Austin when his father had a heart attack. Wolff asked his father whether he would like him to come home and help look after the business until he was back on his feet. Boris didn't want to interrupt his son's education, so Wolff came up with the solution of living in Houston for a year, working at Star and attending night school at the University of Houston: "My dad would spend an hour or two in the store every day, but he never recovered to the point that he could assume a workload."[194]

Wolff duly "got the furniture business in [his] blood"[195] and never went back to the University of Texas. However, he continued at the University of Houston, graduating in 1953, and then did a two-year stint in the US Army as an officer in Korea. He joined Star properly in 1956. At the time, annual revenue was less than $2 million.

In 1962, within a fortnight, both Boris and Mrs Getz died, leaving the five second-generation partners to decide what to do. "I was the youngest of that bunch, but I somehow conned the rest of the group into making me president,"[196] said Wolff. The business was not healthy, experiencing periods of either tiny profits or losses, with a large debt load and negative net worth. Furthermore, a competitor 20 times its size spent a lot more on advertising and blocked Star from carrying all the furniture lines it wanted by securing exclusive rights.

Then came the announcement they had been dreading: the bank wanted its loan repaid. After a lengthy search, Melvyn secured the backing of another bank and then presented a radical plan to the partners: sell two stores, including the main downtown one, and use the money raised plus the issue of long-term notes at junk-bond interest rates to rent a large warehouse/showroom which had been abandoned by a competitor. The partners didn't like the risk, so instead, they accepted Wolff's offer to buy them out in 1964.

Wolff persuaded his sister, Shirley Toomim, to give up her interior design business so that she could head up store design and display.

They made a great team and by 1997, Star had ten stores in Houston, one in Austin and one in Bryan, and was generating $110 million in sales. The pair had concluded in the 1960s that continuing to directly challenge a competitor 20 times their size was a silly approach because it was attacking a "superior force along a broad front".[197] Far better was to carve out a niche. So, they concentrated on selling to upper-income customers, offering affordable style and superior service. "Different by Design" was their USP and slogan. They were also clever in choosing locations on major freeways and more upscale areas.

Selling the business

Wolff and Toomim had the vast majority of their family's net wealth tied up in the one business, so naturally they wanted to diversify. Also, they were concerned that any estate taxes due would be covered through the forced sale of stores, displacing their employees, whom they cared deeply about. An initial public offering (IPO) and a trade merger to another furniture store chain were considered. But these solutions proved unsatisfactory because they failed to afford any reassurance about the preservation of Star's unique business culture: the team could lose the autonomy on which the company's competitive advantages had been developed. "We had spent our lifetimes building an organisation of people who really depended on the firm for their income, and we wanted it to last,"[198] said Wolff.

Blumkin of Nebraska Furniture Mart and Child of R.C. Willey had long extolled the virtues of Buffett to Wolff, particularly when it came to maintaining the autonomy of businesses and supporting the long-term futures of staff. A mutual friend, Bob Denham of Salomon, told Buffett two days before the 1997 Berkshire shareholders' meeting that Wolff would like to talk. At Buffett's invitation, Wolff travelled to Omaha to attend the meeting. Buffett reported that Wolff "spent his time in Omaha confirming his positive feelings about Berkshire. I, meanwhile, looked at Star's financials, and liked what I saw."[199]

A few days later, they met in New York and a deal was quickly agreed. "We've made most of our deals in one meeting. This one took two hours and 20 minutes in a hotel room in New York. That's par for the course," said Buffett.[200] According to Wolff, Buffett "asked the most piercing questions", including why one footnote in a 1996 report was worded slightly differently from the same footnote in a 1994 report. Wolff said that blew him away: "How can someone read three years of 30-page financial statements and note different wording of a footnote?"[201]

Even more astonishing was the absence of any formal due diligence, employment contracts or non-compete agreements. No one went to Houston to look at the company before the deal. "There was a handshake," recalled Wolff. Buffett wrote in his 1997 letter to shareholders that: "I had no need to check leases, work out employment contracts, etc. I knew I was dealing with a man of integrity and that's what counted."

The all-share deal was completed on 1 July 1997. Wolff really wanted uninterrupted continuity and "selling the company for stock meant that there would no longer be any tax consequence to our death, at least not for the company".[202] Also, the stock deal allowed Wolff and Toomim to "join up with a group of people that we couldn't be happier to be a part of. We believe it's the finest family of companies ever assembled under one corporate name".[203] In June 1997, Wolff told the *Omaha World-Herald* why he appreciated holding stock in Buffett's Berkshire: "We like what he has done with his company and how he makes his stock values grow."[204]

The amount paid has been kept confidential, but it's interesting to note that Berkshire had an entry in its 1997 accounts for "Common stock issued in connection with acquisition of business" of $72.7 million. (That said, caution is required in interpreting this – for example, there might have been deferred consideration paid in later years. Unlike in the 1995 accounts, the last word in that entry was "business" in the singular.)

On the sale of the company, Wolff and Toomim gave $1,000 to every Star employee for each year of service. This act of generosity cost them $1.6 million. Buffett was most impressed with the way the siblings shared their good fortune with the people in the business who had helped them succeed: "Charlie and I love it when we become partners with people who behave like that."[205]

What happened afterwards?

When Buffett eventually travelled to Houston to talk with the staff, he was asked how many of his people he would be sending down from Berkshire headquarters to become part of the company. He responded: "I've only got 11 employees, and that includes the receptionist and secretary. So I don't have anyone to send!"[206]

Executive responsibilities remained exactly the same after the transaction as they had been before. Wolff thinks this is a great strength of the Berkshire method, as the teams within each subsidiary feel a sense of ownership of their small part of the overall empire:

> Because Warren hasn't interfered in any way in our business our management team doesn't feel like they're working for Berkshire. They think they're working for Star Furniture Company. That's where their focus is. And they're not worried about how General Re is doing, or how Dairy Queen is doing, or anything else. They are devoted, day-to-day, about making this a better company.[207]

And the non-integration formula works. For example, within three years, Star's revenue had doubled to nearly $200 million.

There hasn't been much interaction with the other furniture companies within Berkshire. There is a kind of mutual-help group, allowing staff from the four companies to consult each other to solve particular problems, but this is purely informal and based on friendships and respect for knowledgeable fellow retailers.

Wolff describes Buffett's attitude as follows:

> I bought four freestanding, well-managed furniture companies; don't screw it up. Just keep running your companies like you do. I've got no objection to your meeting together and loving each other and so forth. But don't look for synergy for my sake.[208]

When asked what's the best thing about being part of Berkshire, Wolff replied that it's Buffett himself: "When you ask him a question, you won't get a snap answer, you'll get sound advice."[209] And Buffett's ability to motivate his managers goes beyond sage counsel and money. Many of his managers are multi-millionaires or billionaires themselves, and yet they carry on working. Wolff said:

> I have to remind myself that this isn't just my company anymore, that I am not working to make money for myself and my family anymore. Because I'm really not ... I took on a responsibility to Berkshire's shareholders ... you become self-motivated ... [to create] the best furniture company, although not necessarily the biggest ... I'm always saying 'What's the next goal?'[210]

It's worth noting that Star has not grown much beyond the base it had in 1997. Today, it has merely ten stores, all in Texas – seven in Houston and one each in Austin, Bryan and San Antonio. This is typical Berkshire Hathaway: managers are told to go for expansion where an additional dollar of investment will generate value for shareholders (i.e., a suitably high rate of return), but to remember that will only be where there is real competitive advantage. This awareness will likely cause you to limit expansion, because the franchise – resting on your reputation, market dominance in a certain geography or some other factor – is unlikely to stretch very far. If you've reached the limit, send any earnings not needed for franchise maintenance to Buffett to allocate to other businesses that can generate value with the marginal dollar. Capital allocation is what he does.

Wolff and his wife set up a family foundation, the Cyvia and Melvyn Wolff Charitable Trust, which works in six areas: education, religion, health, the arts, the underprivileged and "other". They also endowed the Wolff Center for Entrepreneurship at the University of Houston, which regularly takes the top half of the class to Omaha to learn from Buffett.

Wolff stepped down as CEO in 2004 but kept working as chairman of the board until he passed away in 2017, aged 86. On hearing the news of his death, Buffett – who had attended every store opening – said of Wolff:

> The first day I met Melvyn, I knew he would be a wonderful partner and friend. More than 20 years later, his every action had confirmed that initial appraisal. I would see him regularly with students from the University of Houston that he brought to Omaha. They loved him as I did.[211]

Toomim – born three years before Melvyn, in 1928 – remains vice president of Star Furniture.

Wolff said to an audience of graduating students in Houston in 2008:

> In each challenge, there will be a hidden opportunity for those clever enough to find it. When the world looks easy and everything is on an upswing, it is much harder to unseat the protectors of the status quo. Fresh, innovative ideas carefully implemented will carry the day.

He added:

> You must know that to whom so much is given, so much is expected. Make a commitment to yourself to experience the joy of sharing your good fortune. There is no better feeling than the satisfaction of making a difference in the lives of others.[212]

Learning points

- **Patiently observing good companies from a distance for many years, waiting for the right moment to buy, is wise.** But it takes remarkable fortitude and a long attention span. Star Furniture was on Buffett's buy list for 14 years before the opportunity to fulfil his ambition arose.
- **Buyers of a business who offer continuity of teams, culture, uniqueness and HQ will have the edge.** Owners who really care about their people, customers and business are attracted to Buffett's promises of autonomy and permanence.
- **Giving acquired teams the freedom to manage promotes a sense of ownership, pride and gratitude in reciprocation of such generous trust.** Wolff said that after the acquisition by Berkshire, his managers still felt like they were working for Star day to day as they nurtured their creation.
- **Only expand business operations if an additional dollar of investment will generate value for shareholders (i.e., a suitably high rate of return).** Like many Berkshire companies, Star has barely grown in terms of number of outlets or sales. It sticks to those areas generating high returns, where it has a competitive advantage.

Investment 7

JORDAN'S FURNITURE STORES

Summary of the deal

Deal	Jordan's Furniture Stores
Time	November 1999
Price paid	Undisclosed cash payment
Proportion of equity	100%
Status	Still held

Following his successful 1983 investment in Nebraska Furniture Mart, Warren Buffett put another three furniture retailers on his list. These were the best in the business, according to Nebraska Furniture Mart's Irv Blumkin. Buffett persuaded R.C. Willey's Bill Child to sell in 1995, followed by Star Furniture's Melvyn Wolff and his sister, Shirley Toomim, in 1998. Finally, in 1999, he completed the set by buying Jordan's, a New England chain with the highest sales per square foot of any US furniture store and a legendary reputation for its in-store advertising and entertainment. Buffett thus achieved his goal of gathering together America's four most outstanding furniture retailers.

The establishment of Jordan's Furniture Stores

Samuel Tatelman – the grandfather of brothers Eliot and Barry, who would eventually sell Jordan's to Berkshire – was born in Russia in 1889. After coming to America, his family settled in the Boston,

Massachusetts area. A shoemaker by trade, Samuel decided to start a business selling furniture from a truck to supplement the family's income. Eight years later, in 1926, Samuel teamed up with his brother-in-law to open a store in the Boston suburb of Waltham. The business lasted two years; by 1928, Samuel felt the need to open his own store, again in Waltham. When asked why the name Jordan's was chosen, Barry said that his grandfather told him it was simply pulled out of a hat.[213]

Samuel's son, Edward, joined the business in 1940 at the age of 27, after studying at Boston University. Although by then the store had moved to larger premises in Waltham, Jordan's remained small, with a total of ten people working in the business.

Third-generation Eliot (born in 1946) and Barry (born in 1950) recall their father coming home and telling them stories about the store around the dinner table.[214] They were keen to get involved and started working part-time in the store at elementary school. "When we were kids, there were three generations working at the Waltham store. We used to all go out to lunch together, which was fun,"[215] recalled Eliot. He was paid ten cents an hour to dust, while his younger brother got five cents to clean ashtrays. Ever since, Barry has maintained that Eliot was overpaid!

The boys admired the principles by which their father and grandfather ran the business. "It was about being good to your people, being honest to customers and treating people fairly," said Eliot.[216]

Eliot went on to study at Boston University with an eye on joining the business, which he duly did in the early 1970s. Barry was keen on the arts and studied drama in New York State. His original ambition was to be an actor. But after a year, he decided that route was not right for him, so he transferred to Boston University, majoring in advertising and public relations. The move was inspired by elder brother Milton, who had forged a career producing ads for motion pictures and consumer products in New York City. "After listening to Milton's stories and having him share his experiences with me, the subject interested me, so I decided to pursue advertising,"[217] explained Barry.

He found college itself less interesting than the associated internships: while working at a TV station, he helped brainstorm ideas for commercials, and later he worked as a movie and theatre critic for a local magazine. On graduating, he was all set to work as a copywriter at an advertising agency.

But then he sat down with his father, Edward, who was thinking about following Samuel into retirement in 1973. His dad asked him: "Why go to work for someone else when you can work for yourself? You want to do advertising? It's yours. I'm here if you need me."[218] Thus persuaded, Barry joined his brother Eliot in the family business.

Barry's enthusiasm for promotion and Eliot's love of business practicalities (merchandising, systems, accounts) made a great combination. The brothers had remarkable respect for each other, as Barry explained:

> There were of course times when Eliot and I had different opinions, but knowing that every idea or inspiration could turn into an opportunity, I was not too concerned whose idea was used. He could try his first, and then I could always try mine next. The fact is that no business issue is worth fighting over. Family should always come first![219]

Barry said his greatest joy came not from the success of the business but from the way he and his brother stood by each other over the years.

Eliot and Barry sprinkle some magic

Jordan's wasn't much of a business back then, with a mere eight employees. But at least it was run as these 20-somethings wished. Their father told them that he would "always be there for us if we needed him, but that the business was ours to run and that we were in charge".[220] The brothers appreciated this approach: "Because my father really stepped back, he allowed us to try things differently, and that's why Eliot and I became creative in our own sense," acknowledged Barry.[221]

For a time, much continued in the same way – such as old Samuel sitting in a rocking chair in the ground-floor window to greet customers as they came in through the door and then get them to a salesperson.

But there were also new innovations: clowns to entertain customers, handing out balloons and colouring books for children, and free snacks. "Making customers feel at home, feel relaxed, is important, because these are big-ticket items here, and making that type of purchase can be stressful," said Ron Sickels, a sales assistant in the early 1970s. "So the Sweet Station, where we have cookies baking, coffee, soda and popcorn available, is the fun factor."[222]

Bob Mackenzie, Waltham sales manager, added: "You're not just selling a piece of furniture – you're establishing a relationship."[223] Steve Casavant worked at Jordan's for 16 years and commented on the attitude that helped the company excel: "Customer service, the way you handle and treat a customer, is crucial. No pressure sales. Be helpful."[224]

Barry and Eliot were determined to develop a unique culture at Jordan's. An important element was to make both work fun for employees and shopping fun for customers. Boring newspaper ads were dropped in favour of lively, jokey radio and TV slots, with the brothers playing starring roles, mostly spoofing movies. They quickly became known throughout New England as pioneers of 'shoppertainment'. Shopping for furniture is normally about as enjoyable as going to the dentist, admitted Hershel Alpert, a furniture retailer in Seekonk, Massachusetts, adding: "To appreciate what Barry and Eliot Tatelman have accomplished at Jordan's in metropolitan Boston, you have to remember that they are selling *furniture*. How can they be making so much money – and having so much fun?"[225]

It was Milton who came up with the idea of switching all advertising to radio (and later to TV). In New York, he had heard some compelling ads featuring two guys talking and thought that Barry and Eliot could try something similar. Barry was certainly up for it, drawing on his drama school experience. He was less sure that Eliot would be convinced, "but he was game".[226] The three brothers spent a lot of time coming up with funny scripts, variously described as "goofy", "tongue-in-cheek", "silly" and "self-deprecating". The brothers were happy with being "hammy impresarios" who pitched products – without ever mentioning price – often parodying national ads by companies such as The Gap and Volkswagen, or spoofing movie scenes.

Milton had worked on commercials for major movies such as *Rocky* and *The Godfather*, so he had plenty of ideas for pastiches.

The brothers made hundreds of ads. Through humour, they sold an image of their stores and themselves as honest, reliable and fun. Across metro Boston, they became known as simply "Barry and Eliot". So talented were they that they gained this fame from spending just 1% to 2% of their gross revenues on advertising – far below the industry norm of 6%. Britt Beemer, an industry analyst with America's Research Group, surmised:

> The number one reason for their success is that people believe in the company. The more you get people to believe in the company, the less you have to keep lowering and lowering and lowering your prices to get people to buy from you.[227]

The typical furniture retailer goes heavy on "one-day only" sales, "limited offers" and "big discounts". In the early 1970s, Jordan's followed suit, but the brothers soon got fed up with that. "We realised we were spending more time changing tags and more money paying for tags. And it wasn't legit. Your staff couldn't feel good about it, not if they were honest. How could it be $899 this week and $799 the next week? It didn't make sense."[228] They didn't want to wheedle money out of people's wallets that way. Instead, they wanted to build long-term, quality relationships, so they decided on a single-price policy and never held sales, all while making shopping fun.

Just as things were starting to take off, Eliot, Barry and their three siblings lost both their grandfather and their father within 13 months of each other: Samuel in August 1979, aged 89, and Edward in September 1980, aged 67.

Spreading the fun around New England

Barry in particular was keen to do business differently:

> We wanted our place to be a little out of the boundary, or out of the paradigm. The problem is many corporations have regulations and hierarchy that make people counterproductive. They knock down everyone's creativity, excitement and thrills

from what they enjoy doing. I think everyone has a great amount of creativity. As long as they don't get pushed away by corporate rules, they can flourish.[229]

So, when a colleague suggested that all sales assistants dress up in tuxedos for a day, the brothers were all for it; as they were with the idea of giving a rose to every customer collecting furniture, or offering free hotdogs, or washing windscreens, or dimming the lights when someone was trying out a bed.

In 1983, the brothers opened a second store 38 miles north of Waltham, in Nashua, New Hampshire. Their original store – a mere 32,400 square feet, with its early 20th-century downtown storefront – harked back to the pre-mall shopping era; whereas the Nashua store was double that size and freshly built in 1983. It was very modern in style: geometric, with clean lines. It soon got around that in Nashua, customers would be greeted with chocolate-chip cookies or doughnuts.

Four years later, the brothers opened a third store in Avon, Massachusetts, 26 miles south of Waltham. This was even bigger, at 85,000 square feet, with a glorious modern curved glass façade. Opening day caused the largest traffic jam ever seen in Avon. The brothers had to put out messages on the radio to ask people not to come. Of course, that just encouraged more shoppers:

> Our promotion went too well. Everybody came to our store, and there was a two-and-a-half-hour wait in line. It was a cold February day, and as the customer flow got out of control, we went to the radio to beg people not to come. We even promised to keep our discount prices for weeks.[230]

It wasn't long before the Avon store had pink markings in the parking lots and a laser light show to liven things up. Looking to ramp up the fun volume further, the brothers came up with the idea of erecting a Ferris wheel in the store. But installing such an enormous structure simply proved impossible, so they settled on Motion Odyssey Movie (MOM). MOM's 48 cinema seats acted like a flight simulator, moving in eight directions, while people watched a thrilling movie on a screen four storeys high. This was such a large undertaking that there were five years of planning before it was opened in 1992, at a cost of $2 million.

The original MOM included a 15-minute journey produced by George Lucas. All profits were donated to charity (there was a charge for a seat). An instant hit, it generated $250,000 in profits after paying salaries, operating costs and debt service in the first year alone. The ride was later revised and rebranded as *The Polar Express 4-D Experience*. It was a great way to get kids enthusiastic about going anywhere near a furniture store, taking the pressure off their parents while they shopped. Barry described his goal as follows: "We want people to stop, take a look, go over to MOM and – who knows? – maybe they'll buy a sofa, too."[231]

Soon, retailers from all across America were turning up to see MOM. One of the biggest names asked Eliot how he might get something similar for his own stores. Eliot responded: "Don't waste your money. It's not going to work … There's more to it than just a 'MOM thing.'"[232] He was referring to whole package of 'shoppertainment' and the culture that he and his brother had created. He also believed that:

> Everybody's idea of entertainment is different. That's one of the problems that a lot of people who try to do this don't get. It has to be the right kind of thing in the right environment and the right personality to the company.[233]

Later, Jordan's bought an "Enchanted Village" Christmas scene, created in the 1940s by a Bavarian toy maker. It had up to 60 animated figures, each dressed in traditional costumes, performing motorised movements in an elaborate old-style village. Eliot remembers being entranced by it in a famous Boston store when he was five or six. Jordan's staff spent a lot of time lovingly restoring it to bring some Christmas cheer to the Avon store each winter.

In 1997, Barry and Eliot won an award for their socially responsible entrepreneurship. They donated about 50 pieces of furniture each week to the New England Coalition for the Homeless and helped to support local children's charities.

In 1998, the last of the four Jordan's stores to open before Berkshire's purchase was in Natick, Massachusetts, 12 miles southwest of Waltham. This one was a whopping 120,000 square feet, with a striking glass frontage, and featured a recreation of New Orleans' Bourbon Street inside, complete with a nine-minute Mardi Gras parade and a riverboat with a Dixieland band playing on deck. There were also life-sized robots modelled on jazz greats like Louis Armstrong, as well as the Tatelman brothers themselves. The Louis Armstrong figure emerged from a wall and played "When the Saints Go Marching In" every 45 minutes.

"While Eliot and I conceived and set into motion the culture that is Jordan's Furniture, it is up to our employees to take it from there," said Barry. "And they do. I'm amazed at how often I hear comments such as, 'What do you put into the water? Why are your people always smiling?'"[234] It helped that the average employee stayed with the company for over ten years – a sign of a well-managed firm.

The deal

With annual sales of around $250 million and 1,200 employees, Jordan's was thriving and Barry and Eliot had no intention of selling. In fact, they had already turned down several unsolicited offers because they didn't want to lose control of their creation. Then Barry met his old friend Irv Blumkin of Nebraska Furniture Mart at an Anti-Defamation League[235] dinner in New York. Blumkin asked if he would be interested in meeting Buffett. They weren't meeting him with the idea of selling. They just wanted to meet him.

Thus, an arrangement was made for Barry and Eliot to show Buffett around the Natick store in August 1999, while he was in Boston for the Gillette board meeting. The brothers picked him up from the Prudential Shopping Mall in central Boston. They went to the carpark but couldn't find their car, "so all of a sudden we were walking with the richest man in the world and searching for our car. The scene certainly made an impression," recalled Barry.[236]

But Buffett was impressed even before he had even met the brothers, as his other furniture chiefs had been singing their praises. The buzz he saw at Natick confirmed his view that Jordan's Furniture was "truly one of the most phenomenal and unique companies that I have ever seen. The reputation that Eliot and Barry have earned from their employees, their customers, and the community is unparalleled. This company is a gem."²³⁷ At the end of the meeting, Buffett told the pair that if they ever wanted to sell, he would be interested in buying.

This set the brothers thinking. They already knew that Buffett wanted the founders/leaders of his businesses to stay on board and carry on, with very little input from Omaha. He would need them to continue developing the business in the way they thought best. This was ideally suited to Barry and Eliot, who were still brimming with ideas and determination to preserve the unique culture of the firm.

Another factor was succession planning. Only one member of the next generation had shown an interest in the business at that point and the brothers wanted to be even-handed:

> You want to be fair, but what is fair? What if one of the kids wants to go into the business but the other doesn't? What happens when they get married and their wives have opinions about what's fair? We started to think that if we did sell the company, we wouldn't have family problems.²³⁸

Barry later added: "[B]eing fair is important because money can really break up a lot of good family ties."²³⁹ Each brother had two children who either were in college or had recently graduated. By selling, they would give their children the freedom to choose any career they wished. "A lot of people have family businesses and force their kids to go into it. Mine and Eliot's goal is to have happy kids who can do exactly what they want to do when they want to do it," Barry told the *Boston Globe*.²⁴⁰

They mulled over things for a month or so and then told Buffett they would like to discuss the idea with him further. Buffett asked for some financial figures. Two days later, he put in a written offer, the first page of which involved Buffett waxing lyrical about the qualities of the business the brothers had built. Buffett also wanted confirmation that they would continue working for the business for the rest of their days. While they couldn't make such an open-ended commitment, they did tell Buffett that they had nothing else planned for the near future and would never leave him high and dry.

The sale price has never been disclosed, but that hasn't stopped people from guessing. For example, Arthur Lubow in *Inc Magazine* suggested a figure of $225 million, quoting "an inside source".[241] Andrew Kilpatrick observed that "top furniture stores often sell for the same amount as their annual revenues – in this case $250m".[242] Ronald Chan put the offer at $225 million to $250 million.[243] In 1999, the *Boston Business Journal* wrote: "The deal is estimated by analysts to be worth $200m to $300m."[244] Joshua Myerov in the *Boston Globe* mentioned "a reported $225m".[245]

The brothers knew that, had they kept hold of the business and continued to build it, they probably would have sold it for a lot more. But they believed it was best not to be too greedy:

> Barry and I realise we can have pretty much anything we want. But it reaches a point where you ask yourself, 'How much more do I need, and for what?' We like doing what we are doing; we like the challenge and the excitement of it, but it's not about the money anymore … What the deal does is provide tremendous security for our families, and that's really important to us.[246]

In typical style, Buffett didn't even ask for an audit. As Barry said: "It's a new concept in business. It's called trust."[247]

Berkshire announced a definitive agreement on 11 October 1999, in which Barry said: "We are very excited about this venture. Berkshire Hathaway and Jordan's are a perfect fit. Nothing in the company will change … except for the fact that our growth potential is huge with the financial support of Berkshire Hathaway." Buffett added:

> Future plans for other Jordan's Furniture locations all over New England will continue to move forward. Community outreach with organizations such as MA Adoption Resource Exchange and other various charities will continue to be a strong part of the Jordan's business philosophy.

The deal closed on 13 November 1999. Afterwards, Buffett was incredibly impressed by the brothers' generosity to those who had helped build the business. In his 1999 letter to Berkshire shareholders, he wrote:

> Barry and Eliot are classy people – just like their counterparts at Berkshire's three other furniture operations. When they sold to us, they elected to give each of their employees at least 50 cents for every hour that he or she had worked for Jordan's.

This payment added up to $9 million, which came from the Tatelmans' own pockets, not from Berkshire's. And Barry and Eliot were thrilled to write the checks.

Other beneficiaries of Barry and Eliot's generosity at that time were children affected by HIV. For example, the brothers paid for a camp where these children could have some fun in the outdoors. It was a cause close to their hearts because their brother Milton had died of AIDS in 1993, aged 50. Eliot, his wife June,[248] their sons Josh and Michael and various cousins and friends helped out at the annual camp. The brothers also continued the habit of visiting a different high school every week to give a talk to encourage children to think outside the box and do things differently.

Berkshire Hathaway now owned four furniture retail businesses, each of which was still run by the original family and each of which dominated its territory, selling more furniture than anyone else in Massachusetts and New Hampshire (Jordan's), Texas (Star), Nebraska (Nebraska Furniture Mart), and Utah and Idaho (R.C. Willey). In his 1999 letter to shareholders, Buffett enthused:

> There's no operation in the furniture retailing business remotely like the one assembled by Berkshire. It's fun for me and profitable for you. W. C. Fields once said, 'It was a woman who drove me to drink, but unfortunately I never had the chance to thank her.' I don't want to make that mistake. My thanks go to Louie, Ron and Irv Blumkin for getting me started in the furniture business and for unerringly guiding me as we have assembled the group we now have.[249]

Buffett's style post-acquisition

Barry and Eliot envisaged continued steady growth after the deal, even mentioning a potential quadrupling of sales to top $1 billion one day. Soon after selling, they convened a meeting with the other Berkshire Hathaway furniture retailers in one of their stores to discuss how the four might work together. About 75 people turned up. Afterwards, Barry spoke of the remarkable similarities he discovered: all had started as family businesses, each with a long-term focus; all had earned respect in their communities, leading to carefully managed profitable growth; and all had held on to good staff for decades. Barry acknowledged that, while the brothers had been in their own cocoon for years, "there's more than one way to skin a cat. You always think the way you do something is the best … we found out that even though other people might do things differently it can still be very successful".[250]

While they continue to discuss ideas for improvement today, the four Berkshire furniture businesses are still very much independent of each other and there is no pressure from Omaha to merge or even to collaborate – that's entirely up to them. Eliot observed:

> The beautiful part about Warren is that when we joined forces with him, absolutely nothing changed. We called him the day after we got the check – we both got on the phone – and we said 'Okay, Warren, you're up. What do you want from us? Do you want us to call every day? … What do you want us to do?' And his answer was 'What do you want? You want to call me every day, call me every day. If you don't want to call me, don't call me. It's, like, just keep doing what you've been doing.'[251]

Barry described Buffett's greatest asset as his ability to analyse people, what they are like at their core – he's a great judge of character. And when he finds people whom he likes and trusts, he demonstrates his admiration and faith by handing over control (except for higher-level capital allocation). Furthermore, said Barry:

> He's a great motivator, and a very down-to-earth guy. He has the ability to put everyone at ease and make you feel special … no one is afraid of him. We really love the guy. He's become a friend, almost like a father figure … he always says something funny, you always get a laugh, you always have a good time … you can call him as often or as little as you want and he's always got an answer for you … He knows about everything.[252]

Barry also observed that Buffett is not driven by money *per se*, but just enjoys the game, the work and the people he is with. And he has kept everything simple – for example, driving a six-year-old car and living in the same modest house for decades – adhering to values that ensure a happy and fulfilled life.

Some growth over the next quarter of a century

In 2002, Jordan's took the fun to the next level with the addition of an IMAX 3D theatre inside the Natick store. It's not a small one either, with 262 seats. Munching popcorn, Buffett said at the opening: "These fellows are the kings of excitement. I was at this store about three years ago, and it knocked me out. Now, they've added this. No one is going to catch them."[253]

Another store was opened in Reading, 17 miles from Waltham, in October 2004. It too had an IMAX theatre (500 seats), as well as "the largest ropes course in the world", 32 feet high and including a 69-foot zipline. From the ropes, you can view whimsical sculptures of famous Boston landmarks, many made out of millions of jellybeans. And there's a gigantic fountain to boot.

Two other notable events occurred in 2004. First, the original Waltham store closed down – not because it lacked customers, explained Barry, but because "it doesn't represent Jordan's the way we are today".[254] Second, a 750,000-square-foot warehouse and office complex was opened in East Taunton, 42 miles south of the old Waltham store.

In 2005, the warehouse underneath the Avon store was converted into the 50,000-square-foot Colossal Clearance Center, selling discontinued stock, excess orders and scratched or dented items.

Barry left the company in December 2006 to pursue his dreams in the entertainment industry, but continued to help out with ideas, particularly on promotions. He went on to become a Broadway producer of shows such as *Dirty Rotten Scoundrels* and *The Book of Mormon*. He also dabbled in Hollywood as the principal of a new film company called Filmshop and worked on a TV series. Today, he divides his time between homes in Martha's Vineyard and Florida. Away from stage and screen, he plays golf and works on charitable endeavours. He says that, while he misses the wonderful people at Jordan's, he has moved "on to new things; I'm excited. I love being creative. I am now working with creative and wonderful people."[255]

Eliot took the helm and now runs Jordan's with his two sons, Josh and Michael (both co-CEOs) – the fourth generation of Tatelmans.

Over the years, Jordan's garnered much attention through its "monster deals". For example, in 2007, it offered to refund the cost of furniture purchases during a five-week period between 7 March and 16 April if the Boston Red Sox won the World Series. Over 30,000 customers participated in the promotion. The odds were not all that great when the offer was made, because the Sox had won only once in the previous 88 years.

But they ended up taking home the trophy in the October final, so Jordan's refunded over $30 million on sofas, beds, dining-room tables and more. Joe and Jennifer McEachern of Danvers, Massachusetts received about $12,000 back. In all, 25,000 families obtained refunds. This may seem like a crazy gamble by Jordan's, but it was in fact an astute move: first, because of the widespread publicity it garnered the company; and second, because Eliot knew of a certain large insurance company in Omaha willing to insure against the possibility of a win for the Red Sox. Thus, the family could still root for the Sox throughout the season.

Jordan's has run many similar promotions since. For example, in 2008 and 2014, it agreed to pay out if the Red Sox won the Series again (they didn't, in either year). In 2021, the company pledged that if the Red Sox pitched a no-hitter between 3 August and 3 October, all furniture and mattresses bought between 14 April and 16 May would be free. In 2023, if any Red Sox player hit for the cycle (i.e., hitting a single, double, triple and home run in one game), all furniture purchases at Jordan's Furniture would be free.

In 2011, the J-Team – as the Tatelmans call their people – opened a fifth store in Warwick, Rhode Island. The 100,000-square-foot store is home to the Splash Experience, a 15-minute Las Vegas-like spectacle of dancing fountains, synchronised laser lights and video.

Four years later, in December 2015, Jordan's opened the doors of a sixth store in New Haven, Connecticut, over 160,000 square feet in size. Buffett was on hand to cut the ribbon at the grand opening. The store features "the largest indoor adventure ropes course in the world", with two 60-foot-high ropes and a 48-foot-high freefall jump, as well as a less adventurous course for kids under 48 inches. The zipline spans a

1,000-nozzle water show with state-of-the-art lights, sound and music. Ice cream and pizza are also on offer.

In 2020, South Portland, Maine got its own Jordan's outlet. This seventh store has 120,000 square feet of display space, some of which is taken up with yet another giant ropes course. And in 2023, an eighth opened in Farmington, Connecticut. The 120,000-square-foot store features an 80-foot-long LED screen that displays scenes from around the world, sporting events, beautiful landscapes and historical landmarks. Customers also pass through an 8-foot LED tunnel to enter the store.

A long way travelled, feet firmly on the ground

The Tatelman family have come a long way from their eight-employee business of 1973 to one with square footage of more than 1 million and over 1,000 employees. Eliot summed up the culture that drove this growth:

> We want to be the best, not the largest … the challenge for us is to do things in a different way than other people, and see smiling faces on our employees and smiling faces on our customers … [If smiles are] your motivation rather than just the bottom line, then the bottom line comes anyway. It really does.[256]

On how to measure of success, Barry commented:

> [N]ot how much money … but success to me is really about how to achieve a balanced life. For example, spending time with my family, doing well in business, contributing to charity, having good friends, staying creative, and also getting respect from the community. When my father, Edward, passed away in 1980, everybody in town came to his funeral to pay tribute. He died without an enemy. Money can't buy that. Perhaps the number of people who attend one's funeral is a measurement of success.[257]

Learning points

- **Differentiation can take many forms**. Selling furniture is boring. Most stores present a selection of products for you to walk around, but it's hardly an exciting prospect. Jordan's has differentiated itself in the market by making its stores fun places to be – even children like visiting them.

- **Investing is about the intangibles**. Many people think investing is about numbers. But numbers only get you so far. For most companies, the numbers are easy to understand and therefore thousands of investors can analyse at that level. The great investors know that the most important aspects of a business to investigate are the intangibles, such as the extent to which the firm is respected in the community, has name recognition, is run by trustworthy people or has a fun reputation.

- **Relationships are vital**. Barry and Eliot had no intention of selling their business, but the opportunity to work alongside Buffett first intrigued them and later charmed them. The relationship is built on a high degree of trust, freedom, respect and good humour. So many rapid-fire takeover merchants just don't get that.

- **Be decent, honest and fair**. Businesses run on the principles of being decent to their staff, being honest to customers and treating people fairly are often worth scrutinising to see whether they would make good investments.

Investment 8

BEN BRIDGE JEWELER

Summary of the deal

Deal	Ben Bridge Jeweler
Time	July 2000
Price paid	Undisclosed
Proportion of equity	100%
Status	Still held

The family that created Ben Bridge Jeweler took a conservative approach to expansion, to say the least. For their first 56 years of operation, spanning three generations, they had only one store. There was quite an acceleration after that; but they remained cautious, so that by its 88th year, when Berkshire Hathaway acquired the company, there were still just 65 Ben Bridge Jeweler stores.

The story begins in Poland, at a time when Jews were oppressed under the Russian czars, who restricted where they could live, whether their children could go to school and even the professions they could enter. Families often depended on the kindness of strangers to survive. The Jewish people have a tradition of *tzedakah*: a blend of justice and charity, a sense of fairness and a duty to take care of your neighbour.

Over the next 120 years, from generation to generation, the Bridge family have upheld the *tzedakah* principles of their Polish ancestors – to the point where, five generations down the line from their arrival in America, the family decided to give away $9 million of the funds they received after selling to Berkshire Hathaway. They sat down and thought carefully about how to share this windfall fairly among their employees. They are also well known in the Seattle area as generous benefactors and contributors to the community.

The first 56 years

In the early 1900s, Joseph Bryczkowski – who would later change his name to Joseph Bridge – left Poland to join his brother Alex in America. Alex had moved to the country back in 1886 and had set up a store in Seattle to outfit gold seekers headed to Alaska. By the time Joseph arrived, Alex already owned several stores and was a wealthy man.

In 1906, Joseph's wife, Fannie – a well-educated woman who spoke six languages – joined him from Poland with their three children, including ten-year-old Ben. Fannie insisted that, once they arrived in America, they would all speak English.

At 18, after graduating high school, Ben worked at a wholesale grocers and department group called Schwabachers in Seattle. He was soon appointed manager of the candy and tobacco department; but when America joined the First World War in 1917, he was one of the first to sign up due to his love for his adopted country. As a radio operator in the Navy, his job was to listen for enemy engine sounds; and he handled communications on a submarine chaser, fighting the Austro-Hungarians in the Adriatic. On his return to America in 1919, he joined the Naval Reserve and began working in Schwabachers again.

Then he met Sally Silverman, whom he married in 1922 – which is where the jewellery shop comes in.

Sally's parents, Sam and Fannie Silverman, owned S. Silverman Jeweller, a watchmaker and jewellers in downtown Seattle. The Silvermans had arrived in America from Ukraine around 1905. At the time, the Russians were 'drafting' Jewish boys into their army from as young as 12, sending them to military school and then forcing them to spend 25 years as a soldier. To save their boys from ending up as cannon fodder, many families fled the country. Within seven years of their arrival in America, Sam had opened S. Silverman Jeweller.

Sally quickly persuaded her new husband to join her parents' business. Ben became a partner and the name of the business was changed to Silverman & Bridge. Then, in 1927, the Silvermans moved to California for health reasons and Ben bought out their share of the Seattle business by borrowing against some insurance policies. The store was once again rebranded, to Ben Bridge Jeweler.[258] Meanwhile, in Los Angeles, the Silvermans opened a new store – on Broadway, no less.

Ben and Sally's two sons, Herb and Bob, both worked in the store as children. Herb, who was later to become an admiral as well as a very successful retailer, recalled:

> I started working at Ben Bridge Jeweler as soon as I could see over the counters. Early on my jobs were simple, like sweeping floors or polishing silver, of which there was plenty. Eventually I ran errands and helped customers with simple things, like buying a clock or taking a watch for repair. I even had a small workbench where I did simple repairs.[259]

Ben was strict but loving with his boys. And he passed on his proclivity for hard work. Herb was only nine when he decided to get a 'real' job away from the store. He sold newspapers to commuters on the Kirkland Ferry, rising at 5:00 am to do so. He later did a paper route, which required him to get up at 3:00 am to deliver 100 newspapers. This was all before school; and after school, his father expected him to help out in the store unpaid. Herb worked there on Saturdays too: "I looked forward to going … I was energised by the store, by what was happening, and the people on both sides of the counter … that's our name on the front door."[260]

Ben was a man of honour. During the Depression, he struggled, but it was imperative to him that he pay his bills in full and on time, despite nearly being forced to declare bankruptcy. He would race down the street to hand a customer change they had left behind in the store. He considered it vital to meet his obligations and do things properly. This was another trait passed on through the generations. "He'd lend money to someone down on their luck, with little or no hope of getting it back. He'd bail one person out of jail and help another with their rent"[261] – *tzedakah* in action.

Born in 1931, Bob was six years younger than Herb and the pair were firm friends for life. Bob was "likeable, lovable, and charming",[262] according to his older brother. Their mother, Sally – like Warren Buffett over in Nebraska at that time – would regularly wander over to a stockbroker. She loved to play the stock market and "she was good at it",[263] said Herb. Her husband tolerated her buying and selling, but avoided it himself, being much more comfortable with things that he could control and anticipate.

The family were not avid synagogue attendees. Herb later said: "[T]he dogma of religion falls flat for me. To me the keys to life are deeds, high moral character, and charity. That's my religion."[264]

When Herb was 16, Japan bombed Pearl Harbor. He was very keen to join in the fight as a Navy pilot but had to wait six months to turn 17 and graduate from high school before signing up as an aviation cadet. The Navy was swamped with volunteers in their 20s, so young Herb was told to go off to university for a while until he was called up. After two quarters at the University of Washington, still impatient to fight, he called the recruiter and said: "Sign me up and send me to boot camp. I don't care where you put me, but I want to put that uniform on."[265] So he ended up being a very lowly yeoman despite obvious officer potential – and he loved it.

While Herb was serving in the Pacific aboard the destroyer *Doherty*, he received a present in the mail from his father on his 18th birthday – a simple letter, which read: "Dear Herb: Happy birthday. You are now one-fourth owner of Ben Bridge Jeweler. Sign the enclosed and return."[266] It was a note for $6,000.

Fed up with swabbing decks and scraping paint, Herb heard about the possibility to train as an officer. After passing a test, he was sent to the University of Washington in the autumn of 1943, and then to Columbia University to train as a fighter director officer on an aircraft carrier guiding pilots to intercept incoming enemy aircraft. He served near Okinawa in the four months before the war ended.

Discharged in 1946, Herb walked into the family jewellery store, proud in his officer's uniform. Ben looked up from serving a couple of sailors and said: "Herb, that uniform sure looks good on you. Now why don't you go in the back and hang up that pretty jacket and get this place swept out?"[267] One of the sailors exclaimed: "You can't talk to an officer like that!" Ben replied: "I can talk to *that* officer like that – even if *that* officer becomes an admiral some day!" It was said in jest, but Herb did eventually become an admiral by rising through the ranks of the Naval Reserve – a commitment he took on despite working full time at the jewellers.

After spending a year finishing his degree and marrying top pharmacy graduate Shirley, Herb returned to the store. But then the Korean War broke out and he left to serve in Asia for a couple of years, returning in June 1952 for his brother Bob's commissioning as an officer in the Navy after graduating from the University of Washington. Herb was best man at Bob's wedding the day after the commissioning.

Bob had been running the store alongside Ben while Herb was in Korea. Bob had also received a one-quarter share in the business on his 18th birthday. Herb wanted to be satisfied that Bob had been treated fairly, so he said to his father and mother:

> Look, you made me a quarter owner in the company and now you've done the same for Bob. But I've had six years of equity building up, and that would give me an upper hand in ownership forevermore. I want you to arrange things so that Bob's share of the store is the same as mine ... I care about my brother and I want a mutually beneficial partnership with him.[268]

Once an officer, Bob went to serve his country and it was Herb's turn to work in the store. When the Korean War was over, Bob was also discharged and also joined the Navy Reserve, again rising through the ranks for the next 20 years.

In 1954, when Herb was 29 and Bob 23, a predicament arose in the business. "That problem was my father,"[269] said Herb:

> The quintessential micro-manager, he was unable to accept any input, big or small, in running the store. I'd have an idea and Dad would smile at me and say he'd tried that in 1928 and it didn't work, or that the time wasn't right, or that it cost too much, or some other sorry explanation. I'd plead my case and he'd calmly say that I just didn't understand. Dad had his way of

doing things and he never gave an inch … Bob was content … With Dad and me it was a collision between two bulls because we were too much alike. Not that it was highly contentious or volatile, because it wasn't. Dad was patient with me, we loved each other very much, and we had a good relationship. It's just that my frustration was building up.[270]

Herb resolved to find work elsewhere so that he could learn about how to expand a business and then return to the family business once his father had retired. He found such a job in Denver, managing three stores for a national retailer. When, in the autumn of 1954, he told his father that he intended to leave for Denver in the new year, Ben – appreciating Herb's initiative and need for independence and personal growth – said: "If you've made up your mind, go do it." Thus, Herb and Shirley put up their house for sale and made preparations to leave – until Ben called a family meeting and announced: "Herb, you are not leaving. It's me who's leaving."[271]

Everyone was thunderstruck, not least Sally – Ben was only 58 and had boundless energy, and Sally wasn't sure she wanted her husband around all day, interfering with how she spent her time. They all tried to talk him out of it "for Mother's sake" (Ben was a man known to number his books and date canned food). But Ben was adamant he "didn't want to be the one to drive the family apart", explained his grandson Ed Bridge. "He wanted the family business to be a unity venture."[272]

When it came to the valuation of his half of the business, Ben simply suggested: "You two get together with the accountant. I know you'll do the right thing."[273] And so it was that two 20-somethings came to own Ben Bridge Jeweler, after paying for the shares in instalments. Meanwhile, to everyone's surprise, Ben took to retirement like a duck to water. He became head of the Jewish Community Center and the Jewish Federation, and pursued a host of other charitable activities. It would be another ten years before he darkened the door of the store. Herb and Bob had complete control and received no criticisms or comments from their dad.

Herb believed that, in his heart of hearts, his father was unable to delegate – and delegation was what the business needed. The two naval officers were very good at that. "The problem was, early on we'd look around to delegate and only see each other,"[274] said Herb with a wry smile.

Herb and Bob expand

It was pretty easy to split roles between the two: Herb was the salesman, while Bob had more business savvy thanks to his degree in business studies, experience as a naval supply officer and attention to detail.

At first, they were ultra-cautious – after all, their parents' pensions and their young families depended on the flow of payments from the business, and perhaps their father's conservativism made sense. Increasingly, though, they felt the urge to grow. This meant they would need good people to delegate to – and good people would be attracted to a business that offered opportunities for promotion. This prompted them to consider expansion.

Their first step was somewhat anonymous and limited. At the time, manufacturers wanted to control the prices at which retailers sold their goods. They would threaten stores that did not abide by the price floor with a refusal to supply. But Herb and Bob knew their customers and thought they could attract a lot more business if they lowered prices in certain settings.

A discount store, PriceMart in Seattle, offered other retailers space under one roof with a no-frills ambience. Ben Bridge Jeweler took some of that space in the late 1950s, but did not use the company name, so no one knew there were Ben Bridge people behind the counter. Jewellery and other goods were sold at a reduced margin of, say, 10% or 12%. Thus, a watch with a recommended retail price of $95 could be sold for $70; and because of the greater throughput, profits were good. And the brothers learned a lot: Bob developed his ability to manage high volumes of purchases and manage cash flow, while Herb broadened and deepened his knowledge of sales and marketing through alternative channels.

Their next step was a response to a threat. America's first suburban shopping mall was built in Seattle in 1950. The downtown retailers saw this as a danger and banded together in a bid to save the traditional shopping heart of Seattle. They went to the big retailers – Nordstrom,

JC Penney, Bon Marche and Frederick & Nelson – to ask for their support in making downtown more vibrant. Thus, an organisation was formed. Herb and Bob became well known as the organisers; so when, in the mid-1960s, JC Penney asked around for the best and most entrepreneurial people in the jewellery business, the brothers' names kept coming up.

JC Penney wanted Herb and Bob to operate several in-store JC Penney-branded jewellery departments. It so happened that their number one store in America was in Seattle and Herb and Bob got to run that one and six others. In all, JC Penney eventually had 300 outsourced in-store jewellery departments across the country. The brothers were able to observe first-hand how JC Penney implemented its policies and practices across the chain. And they learned how to operate in a shopping mall setting, where much of their subsequent expansion took place.

JC Penney organised an annual contest between the different jewellery vendors in its department stores and every year Herb and Bob's stores would come first, second and third, with all seven stores featuring in the top ten. "We'd been brought up in the business, we were gemologists [gaining such a qualification is prestigious], we had all the contacts, and we knew how to do things right," wrote Herb.[275]

Delegation to good employees was also key: "To us, it was all about the people. We wanted employees who cared, who would act as the Ben Bridge or Sally Bridge of [their] store."[276] But still the brothers could not offer much in the way of career progression.

So, they decided to open a second Ben Bridge Jeweler store in 1968. It was located in the Southcenter Mall in south Seattle and was managed by Bob. They had to choose distinctive merchandise carefully, because they also ran a JC Penney's jewellery department in the same mall. The Ben Bridge store carried a higher class of merchandise.

The new store was a great success and it wasn't long before they planned a third – this time at the Northgate Mall, Seattle. The owner of the mall was willing to throw out Zales, a national chain of jewellers, and put Ben Bridge Jeweler in the same spot, mostly because the Bridge brothers were 'good citizens'. This notion of being a good citizen, in contrast to the way much other business is conducted, stayed with the brothers over the years: reputation really counts. Three other stores quickly followed – one in Seattle and the other two a few miles down the road in Tacoma and Olympia, Washington.

Now that they were operating on a broader scale, with seven outlets in JC Penney and six standalone stores, they could afford buyers that travelled to Asia to get the best merchandise at better prices, bypassing wholesalers.

But the relationship with JC Penney was deteriorating due to a switch in the department store's policy on discounted jewellery. At first, it was offering 10% off, but the Bridge brothers recognised they had been forced onto a slippery slope – next year, the discount would have to be 15% to maintain sales momentum and so on. All of this undermined customer perceptions of value.

It was then that JC Penney offered the brothers all 300 of its in-store jewellery departments:

> Bob and I asked ourselves, did we want to be at the whim of their executives, where one might wake up in a bad mood and we're out on the street? Plus we wanted to chart our own course. It was an easy decision for us both.[277]

The brothers travelled to visit the New Yorkers, not only turning down the offer but terminating the relationship completely.

Their staff were offered a choice: stay with JC Penney or go with them. Employees in all seven chose Ben Bridge Jeweler even though no managerial positions were vacant at the time. They all stayed for many years thereafter, with three rising to the position of vice-president. Herb and Bob were also becoming more adept at staying out of their managers' way, recognising that:

> They often knew better than we what was best for their store. It took a few years, but we came to realise that our jobs were to keep people on course while cheering them on, which is what every good leader should do.[278]

It was 1980 when they first stepped outside of Washington state, opening a store in Oregon, followed by one in California in 1982. This expansion was not driven by self-interest – as they put it, "we could make as good living with ten stores as we could with 70".[279] Rather, they expanded so that they could say to their people: "[L]ook, you do things right and you can move up in the company, there's room here for you to advance. Come grow with us."

Herb and Shirley had two children, while Bob and his wife, Bobbi, had three. Two of the five showed interest and aptitude for the business from a young age: Jonathan (Jon), born in 1950, son of Herb and Shirley; and Edward (Ed), son of Bob and Bobbi, born in 1956.

Jon and Ed go bigger

Jon and Ed had both worked in the business as boys, sweeping the floor and polishing silver. Like his father, Jonathan joined the Navy and graduated from the University of Washington (magna cum laude with an honours degree in economics in 1972). After serving during the Vietnam War, in 1973 he returned to the university to attend law school, while still in the Navy. He then worked as a staff judge advocate for a few years until he left active duty and joined the Navy Reserve – a family tradition – rising to four-stripe captain. In 1981, as a 31-year-old officer and a lawyer, he joined Ben Bridge Jeweler full time. He started on the sales floor, but later did a stint as chief financial officer (CFO).

Ed had joined the business three years earlier, in 1978, after obtaining a degree in business from the University of Washington (he graduated phi beta kappa). At first, he worked on the sales floor; but following the retirement of the company's CFO shortly after his arrival, Ed stepped into the role. Subsequently, he became head merchandiser.

His uncle Herb said of him:

> Ed came in as a businessman and he was instrumental in not only expanding the business, but also in keeping us profitable by pinpointing when a store should be closed. There were locations that no matter what you did – change managers, tweak inventory – nothing worked. Ed was our watch dog and did a fantastic in making those calls.[280]

By 1980, there were Ben Bridge Jeweler stores in 11 states and new outlets were opening at a rate of two or three a year. Herb recalled:

> When people ask how we did it we answer: Very simply, hire the best of the best and then we gave them the tools to succeed. We provide good merchandise, attractive displays, ongoing training, sincere customer support, and a culture of professionalism and trust. We don't keep secrets from our managers. We hire people who love jewellery and the emotions that are evoked when a person receives a loving, symbolic gift from someone they love.[281]

By 1990, when Herb and Bob handed over the title and responsibilities of co-CEO to Jon and Ed, there were 39 stores: 20 in California, one in Alaska, one in Hawaii and the rest in Washington State and Oregon.

The deal

While the family felt a real sense of achievement from growing the business and creating new opportunities for their people, Herb and Bob were thinking about what might happen should they die and how best to manage the transition to the next generation, with an eye towards fairness, managerial continuity and estate taxes. Jon's wife, Bobbe, was a partner in a law firm and her colleague suggested that Herb and Bob each be issued so many shares at $750 per share, and for that $750 be frozen, never to increase. That way, all future gains could be passed on to the other shareholders, their heirs.

The idea was implemented and each year the five children were gifted a set amount, regardless of whether they worked in the business. Herb and Bob's sense of fairness and commitment to prioritising family harmony above all else meant that every member of the next generation was treated equally.

By the 1990s, the children each held a substantial amount of stock. But the company wasn't paying any dividends, so there was no income generated for them. By then, this generation had children of their own – along with the expenses that come with parenthood – while Bob and Herb were in their 60s. "It seemed time to take stock and consider how to tap the company's assets,"[282] said Herb.

Investment 8. Ben Bridge Jeweler

Jon and Ed commissioned an appraisal of the business. They were all shocked at the high valuation that came back (the figure is undisclosed, but revenue in 1998 was $137 million). The next move was to let potential buyers know that the Bridge family might be willing to sell or do some other deal. Two national companies expressed an interest, "but neither was a good fit",[283] as they would have wanted to move the headquarters from Seattle. The family's view was that Ben Bridge Jeweler was a Seattle company through and through. Even worse was the lack of any reassurances of security for their loyal staff. "We had people who'd been with us 35, 40 years, these people were family to us, and we weren't about to sell them out to the highest bidder. We could never betray our people like that,"[284] insisted Herb.

They also considered an IPO or a leveraged buyout, but fate intervened. Bob and Barnett Helzberg Jr had been friends for many years, often taking skiing trips together. Helzberg had sold his jewellery chain, Helzberg Diamonds, to Berkshire Hathaway back in 1995 (see Volume 3, Investment 5). Bob learned from Barnett that Buffett was a quality guy to do business with and surmised that Ben Bridge Jeweler would be a great fit with Berkshire Hathaway. Its culture of prudent growth and spending, reputation for integrity and highly competent managers were right up Buffett's street. And Berkshire had proven to be a wonderful home for dozens of other family-owned businesses with similar dilemmas to those faced by the Bridge family. Bob asked Helzberg to forward the appraisal on to Buffett.

Buffett was interested and spoke on the phone with Ed. They got along fine, so Ed forwarded some figures. Buffett liked the annual same-store sales growth numbers: 9%, 11%, 13%, 10% 12%, 21% and 7% over the previous seven years – "a truly remarkable record".[285] Ben Bridge Jeweler now had 62 stores in 18 states, with a 63rd about to open. Buffett was also impressed by the "extraordinary reputations"[286] of the family and the business. He enthusiastically said to Ed: "You guys are great, great, great."[287] Buffett consulted Jeff Comment, who had taken over the operation of Helzberg Diamonds when it was sold to Berkshire in 1995, who confirmed Helzberg's view that "Ben Bridge was a business full of people with great character. They had a nice niche in the marketplace".[288]

However, just when it looked as though things were moving towards a deal, a strategic buyer (i.e., one in the same or a related industry) increased its offer. "I think," said Ed "that we probably could have received 20% more from this buyer than we got from Berkshire. But I also think we would have destroyed the business if we had gone down that way."[289]

Buffett had named his price, half in cash and half in stock. Both sides also agreed not to make the price public. Within days, in December 1999, they had a deal – "just like that".[290] They still hadn't met; "I buy companies all the time over the phone,"[291] Buffett told Bridge.

The deal was inked on 18 May 2000 and took effect on 3 July. Jon wrote to employees:

> Our success has and always will be our people. By entering into this alliance, we will continue the tradition of our grandfather and fathers in overseeing the management as well as the long-range planning of the company. This arrangement will provide for the smooth transition from this generation to the next – a concern that has been at the center of this action.[292]

They looked forward to being part of Berkshire, which Ed called:

> … the finest family of companies ever assembled under one corporate name. Warren Buffett, Chairman of Berkshire Hathaway has demonstrated a legendary record of protecting the unique characteristics of individual businesses in a diverse portfolio of companies. We're excited to be a part of it.[293]

For his part, Buffett added: "I can't tell you how pleased we are to enter into this association with Ben Bridge Jeweler. Run by an outstanding management team, Ben Bridge will be a great addition to the Berkshire family."[294]

A condition of the sale was that Bob and Herb would stay on in salaried positions for as long as they lived, and "Warren was fine with that".[295] Buffett also said that he would only buy the business if Jon and Ed continued to run it. He told them: "We don't need a non-compete, because I know you would never do anything to hurt the business."[296] Ed was very impressed by this level of trust: "[W]hen someone tells you something like that, you have to listen."[297] Buffett also insisted: "I don't want to do a contract, because I don't want you to stay if you're not happy."²⁹⁸

When Warren did finally meet the family, Ed recalls that as he and Buffett drove past a See's Candies store, Buffett mentioned the store's exact sales figures. Ed was amazed. Buffett responded, "[W]ell, I love numbers."²⁹⁹ That just confirmed the wisdom of a warning Ed had been given by the head of another Berkshire business: never show Buffett a figure that you don't want him to see, because he'll remember it.

Herb and Bob's payout had been frozen at $750 per share two decades previously, so they did not get a very big cheque; but their children "did pretty well".³⁰⁰

It was Ed and Jon who decided to share the windfall with the people who had helped the family succeed. They set aside $9 million and devised a formula that included everyone, with those who had worked the longest and those in more senior positions getting more. The bonuses were paid in three instalments: one-third on completion of the deal; one-third one year after that; and one-third on the two-year anniversary of the sale. Thus, they incentivised people to stay during the period of uncertainty following the takeover, giving Jon and Ed time to prove that Ben Bridge Jeweler was still a great place to work.

Clearly, Ed and Jon had absorbed the family tradition of *tzedakah*. As proud father and uncle Herb wrote:

> [N]o one ever gets anyplace by himself or herself; and if you do, you've done something in a hollow way. I get teary-eyed even now, a decade later, talking about how Ed and Jon knew that those who create the wealth should share the wealth.³⁰¹

Buffett was likewise impressed:

> In their typically classy way, the Bridges allocated a substantial portion of the proceeds from their sale to the hundreds of co-workers who had helped the company achieve its success. We're proud to be associated with both the family and the company.³⁰²

What happened afterwards?

After the sale, Herb and Bob asked Buffett when he would like to do his due diligence, check the inventory and audit the books. Buffett's response was: "I don't do due diligence. I don't need that. I wouldn't have bought you if I didn't trust you."[303] The brothers were both astonished and greatly heartened by this message.

Buffett also set the tone in his 2000 letter to Berkshire shareholders:

> No one wanted another jewelry chain to come in and decimate the organization with ideas about synergy and cost saving (which, though they would never work, were certain to be tried). I told Ed and Jon that they would be in charge, and they knew I could be believed: After all, it's obvious that your Chairman would be a disaster at actually running a store or selling jewelry (though there are members of his family who have earned black belts as purchasers).

The relationship has since deepened and whenever Buffett flies to Seattle to play bridge with Bill Gates, he also spends a day at Ben Bridge Jeweler – all the managers there know him. Jon and Ed have even invited suppliers to meet the legendary investor.

Ed reflected on 18 years of experience working in Berkshire Hathaway:

> There was very little change, and that is unique to Warren and Berkshire's culture. It's one of leaving the operating units alone as long as they are doing a good job. When I talked to Warren in 2000, he said, 'We don't delegate, we abdicate. We don't have time to meddle.'[304]

However, Buffett did encourage delegation *within* the firm, to enable it to grow. There was also money available, as Ed Bridge acknowledged: "We have had great financial strength behind us. We were strong financially before [Berkshire], but knowing [there are] billions in backing helps me sleep better at night."[305]

But still, the growth rate was prudent. Thus, it took 18 years to go from 63 stores to 95. By then, almost half (46 stores) were operating as Pandora Stores, the world's largest jewellery brand. These were run as franchises. Starting in 2010, Ben Bridge Jeweler later became the largest Pandora franchisee in North America.

In the 21st century, another generation entered the business. As is the family tradition, Lisa (daughter of Ed and Pam) started cleaning store counters as soon as she was tall enough to reach them. After graduating with honours from Washington University in St Louis and attending the Gemological Institute of America, she started her career at Ben Bridge Jeweler in the buying department.

By 2010, she was vice-president of education and in 2015 she launched her namesake range of jewellery, the Lisa Bridge Collection, which became one of the company's best-selling lines. In 2017, she assumed the role of president and chief operating officer (COO) on Jon's retirement. Buffett welcomed the passing of the baton to the younger generation: "With the challenges facing retailing, I am excited to have someone passionate for the jewelry business with creative ideas and an understanding of today's consumer at the helm. Lisa has retailing in her blood."[306] Buffett was earning a reputation for appointing women to leadership positions: Beryl Raff was chairwoman and CEO at Helzberg, while Karen Goracke succeeded Susan Jacques at Borsheims.

Ed continued as CEO until 2019, when he handed over the post to 33-year-old Lisa. "It brings me great joy to know the company will be in such capable hands," he said. "Lisa will surely propel the business into its next phase and a bright future."[307]

Lisa's brother Marc also worked in the store as a youngster, being paid 25 cents per hour to search through old envelopes to make sure there weren't bits of scrap metal or stones left behind: "If we found something (and it only happened once or twice) we got a 25 cent bonus."[308] After studying at Washington University in St Louis, the London School of Economics and then law school at the University of Washington, he joined Ben Bridge Jeweler as associate general counsel and helped to prepare the company for the "internet thing".[309]

But his real passion was helping customers to find a wonderful piece of jewellery. He had risen to the position of vice president of marketing when, in 2017, he announced his intention to leave the family business and set up his own jewellery store. He explained:

> When you work in a family business it's hard to evaluate your own capacity. You get opportunities you wouldn't have anywhere else. You are … shielded from the reality of ordinary jobs … Once you're in, it's hard to imagine doing anything else. After our son Asa was born, I began thinking about the example I wanted to set for him. Whatever his dreams might be, I hoped he would have the courage and confidence to pursue them. And then I had to look in the mirror. Did I have the confidence to follow my own dreams? Was I too afraid of hard things? Was I willing to bet on myself?[310]

He duly established a jewellery store business far from the family's outlets, in Arlington, Texas.

Following Ben Bridge Jeweler's "most successful year yet",[311] in 2022, Pandora Group decided to stop franchising its brand and product in the USA, so it bought back all the Pandora franchise stores run by Ben Bridge. This reduced the company's store count dramatically, down to 37 (in nine states) and a mere 425 employees – significantly fewer than the 700 or so the company had in 2000 and a fraction of the 1,159 it had in 2016. Lisa said:

> The cornerstone of our business is building customers for life and that is why we first fell in love with Pandora. This has been an important and successful chapter in our history and we know our team will be in excellent hands as a part of the broader Pandora organization … We are excited to fuel our Ben Bridge growth.[312]

What happened to our leaders …

Jon retired in 2017 and has been active in many non-profits, from the Alliance for Education and the Jewelers of America Political Action Committee to the King County Mental Health Board and the Center for Children and Youth Justice. He also teaches at the University of Washington. He said:

> I think education in general has been the thing that has been most important to me, and caring for younger people. As I said in our business, the most important word in the English

language is the word empathy. That has not changed in my outlook over the years, make the world a better place; leave it better than when you got on the planet.[313]

Ed continued as CEO until 2018. Now officially retired, he remains a vital source of sage advice when daughter Lisa calls. He has also been actively involved in many non-profits, including Jewelers for Children, the Jewelers Vigilance Committee, the Jewish Federation of Greater Seattle and the Seattle Victims Fund.

Now in his 90s, Bob is still happy to give Lisa a helping hand when needed. Steeped in *tzedakah*, he has also thrown himself into community projects since his retirement. He championed countless causes, including helping the homeless of Seattle by building low-income housing. The organisation he founded has provided thousands of homes. When he co-chaired the King County United Way Campaign with son Jon in 2000, they raised $93 million for education, the arts and hunger projects. Buffett and Gates helped by giving a presentation to those who donated more than $25,000. "Warren and Bill engaged in a spontaneous, interesting repartee that everyone enjoyed,"[314] said Herb.

In subsequent years, over $100 million was raised in total. Bob pulled in Buffett again to help raise money for the City Club, a female alternative to the Rotary Club, which at the time refused to admit women.[315] There were dozens of charitable ventures after that.

Meanwhile, Herb was still going into the office every day in his 80s:

> [T]he business is Jon and Ed's to run … I'm the connecting fiber. I knew grandpa Silverman, who opened the first store; I grew up under the watchful eye of Ben Bridge, a micro-manager; Bob and I raised our sons with our father's mindset; and now I see that same character in my grandkids and Bob's grandkids … I'm an important piece of the furniture.[316]

A few years before his death in 2018, aged 93, Herb said that his kids and grandkids were his and Shirley's[317] "ultimate success story": "It doesn't matter how grand your achievements, it doesn't matter the awards, accolades, or tributes; what ultimately matters is your kids and family. To have kids who develop into better people than you."[318]

Herb also shared his views on the topic of morality in business with students at the University of Washington:

> I believe morality should be the foundation of any business education. I believe with all my soul that business is a medium to improving the community and improving the world … I believe that our future business leaders should be given a moral compass indicating that success is not making millions for yourself while creating misery for others. Success is when you help create an environment that brings a decent living through rewarding work to many, not just a few at the top … I learned from my Grandpa Bridge to be of service, to live according to the *tzedakah* blend of charity, justice and fairness. *Tzedakeh* has been my lifelong moral compass that's never steered me wrong.[319]

Learning points

- **Kindness in business is not a weakness.** The Bridge family were raised on the principle of *tzedakah* – a blend of justice, charity, a sense of fairness and a duty to take care of your neighbour. The people around them – employees, suppliers, customers, Warren Buffett – bore witness to their acts of decency and compassion. Because they exhibited a firm moral base, integrity and generosity, they attracted good people.

- **Slow and steady is often the best way forward.** It was decades before a second Ben Bridge Jeweler store was opened. Even at the company's fastest expansion rate, it was opening a mere two or three per year. It's important to get this right and avoid too much risk. But some growth was pursued as a way to enable the company's loyal and competent employees to progress in their careers.

- **Family unity is more important than money.** Each generation considered it vital that all family members benefit from the businesses, whether or not they worked in it. Ben Bridge sacrificed his leadership of the company to prevent tension in the family.

- **A good reputation can open many doors.** The Ben Bridge Jeweler team were often treated favourably, especially around Washington

State, because they were regarded as good citizens. Buffett would not have bought the company if it lacked an excellent reputation.

- **Maximising wealth is often less important than doing right by your people**. The Bridge family could have received 20% more money by selling to someone other than Berkshire. However, the other potential new owner was likely to damage the company culture, the lives of its staff and its unique team spirit.

- **Being a 'good home' for a family business enables excellent businesses to be bought at merely fair prices**. Buffett's no-interference policy, commitment to maintaining the company culture and genuine admiration for his leaders elicit reciprocal respect and warm relations, often permitting Berkshire to offer a lower amount of money compared with less-attuned buyers.

Investments 9 and 10

JUSTIN BOOT AND ACME BRICK

Summary of the deal

Deal	Justin Brands and Acme Building Brands
Time	July 2000
Price paid	$567.6 million in cash for Justin and Acme together
Proportion of equity	100%
Status	Still held

It may seem strange that Buffett bought a company which manufactured both cowboy boots and bricks; the two products hardly go together. But they were made by the same company in 2000 when Berkshire bought it – and they had a lot more in common than one might imagine. Both had their origins in frontier days in Texas, close to Fort Worth.

In 1879, the founder of Justin Boots turned up in a dusty town of 200 people, four saloons and four doctors to fix up the fighting cowboys moving up the Chisholm Trail. When he arrived, he had just 25 cents in his pocket; but his new friend the barber lent him all his savings – a grand total of $35 – to help him start making boots. It was such a rough place that Justin felt a strange sense of pride when he saw that two hanged outlaws were both wearing boots he had made.

A few miles away and 11 years later, a man was searching for the perfect piece of land on which to dig out clay/shale to be used to make bricks. There had to be a supply of coal too, and easy transport to the main towns along railway lines. Paying just over $4 an acre and then building a kiln, he created the Acme Brick Company.

Eight decades later, these two players were the biggest names in their respective fields across America. They came together in 1968 with a plan to open up the holding company to outside shareholders on a stock exchange, under the leadership of the grandson of the founder of the boot company, John Justin Jr. Thirty-two years after that, when John Jr was looking to settle his estate, aged 83, Berkshire bought all the company's shares for $567.6 million.

Buffett could see that Acme Brick had strong market positions in the 250-mile radiuses around each manufacturing plant, because the cost of bringing bricks from further away was prohibitive. Thus, the brick business was highly profitable. The cowboy boot business was more variable, with some periods of high demand and good profits and others when high fixed costs and reduced interest in boots resulted in losses. Nevertheless, buoyed by their Old West heritage, Justin Boots and its other brands, such as Nocona and Tony Lama, led the market and could command a premium.

Justin Brands

In the years following the American Civil War, cowboys would drive their cattle from southern Texas, across the Red River, through Indian territory and up to the Kansas rail stops along the famous 1,000-mile Chisholm Trail. It was tough work – and it was tough on their footwear. At a bend in the Red River stood the tiny town of Spanish Fort (population 200; 20 buildings), the last stop before Indian lands. In 1879, a 20-year-old Herman Joseph (HJ) Justin arrived in town with just a rucksack holding all his worldly possessions, including his precious hammer and awl – he had been apprenticed to a cobbler in Gainesville, Texas, and these were the tools he needed to work leather. Spanish Fort lacked a bootmaker and HJ spotted an opportunity.

But when he stepped down from the spine-rattling wagon, he only had 25 cents in his pocket. He needed a job, so he went to see the barber-cum-bathhouse owner and was put to work sweeping the floor. After a few weeks of heating water for the longhorn drivers for their longed-for soaks, he noticed a cowboy in the barber's chair wearing boots that were falling apart and offered to fix them up as good as new. Thus, the boot business began in a rickety wooden lean-to at the back of the barber's shop on a couple of pieces of scrounged lumber.

The next day, another customer appeared needing his boots mended. Word was travelling fast in the local saloons. While HJ was earning some money from repairs and was thus surviving, he was not getting to design and make boots, his ultimate goal. He was on the verge of giving up on Spanish Fort when he spoke with his new friend the barber, Frank See:

> Frank, I am going to have to leave. I can't get by at this unless I can get hold of some money. Have you any money? If I can get enough to buy a little stock, just two or three hides, I'll make the world sit up and take notice that H.J. Justin can make the best boots in the world.[320]

See handed over all his savings – $35 in total – to HJ. The first pair of boots made were sold for $9 to See, who wore them riding around his ranch until 1905. Other orders quickly followed. At first, HJ often had to wait until the weather was good enough to work outdoors because the lean-to was so small. Then he moved up in the world – into an eight foot by eight foot shack, on which he painted the words "H.J. Justin, Boot Maker".

HJ's boots were made to last, tight fitting to provide a sure footing, but comfortable. The high leather top protected against rattlesnakes, brush and bad weather. The high heel kept feet firmly in stirrups and dug in when roping on foot. Most were plain black, made for robustness and selling at $8.50 a pair (about a week's wages for a cowboy); but HJ then started to experiment with decorative stitching (which also strengthened the boots) and later with colourful inlays. Justin's reputation for quality boots travelled the length of the Chisholm Trail; in its first year, turnover reached $1,000.

By the time he married Annie Allen in 1887, HJ was struggling to keep up with the orders, even with Annie working long hours to help. Then a Montana rancher reported that many cowboys in his state wanted made-to-measure boots, but couldn't travel to Texas to be measured. So Annie and HJ devised a mail order system, sending out a tape measure and foot chart so that customers could measure various parts of their feet and legs. So many mail orders poured in that HJ enlisted the help of his brother William – and later his two sons, Vane and Bill, would also work for the company.

By 1889, the cattle drives were slowing as railways were built out across Texas. Spanish Fort residents had hoped that the Missouri, Kansas & Texas Railway would come to their town, but it was routed further south. HJ was dependent on the railroad to ship his mail order boots, which made it inevitable that the business would have to move to a railroad town. The family chose Nocona, 19 miles away. In fact, most of Spanish Fort chose to move to Nocona (named after a Comanche chief who had died in a battle with Texas rangers in 1860).

HJ, Annie and their one-year-old son, John Sullivan (later to be John Justin Sr), moved into two rooms at the rear of a boot shop. They had seven children and subsequently moved to a big house built by HJ on land behind the shop. After a few years of school, from age 13 onwards, the children were expected to work in the shop from 6:00 am to 6:00 pm, six days a week, although on Saturdays they could sometimes stop at four – all for 25 cents a day. It wasn't all work, however: there was a backyard laid out with swings, slides and other play equipment. Children came from all over town to play on them; as subsequently did older townsfolk for dances and parties hosted by HJ, who loved to dance.

HJ and Annie's self-measuring system became increasingly popular, and HJ decided to approach merchants and department stores in cities throughout the West to offer them a dollar for each order he received using his measuring blanks. They sold a lot of boots. Events such as cattlemen's conventions also provided canny marketing opportunities. By 1908, annual production was over 1,000 pairs made by a dozen workers, generating revenues of $12,000.

John Sr, then aged 20, and his 18-year-old brother Earl began running the business at home while HJ was on the road talking to merchants. HJ decided to make his two eldest boys equal partners in the business and changed the name to H.J. Justin & Sons. Twenty-five pieces of machinery, including Singer sewing machines, were added, as well as more staff.

By 1909, the company was selling in 26 states, Canada, Mexico and Cuba; and by 1915, its 25 boot makers could turn out 25 pairs a day and ship to 36 states and a collection of countries around the world. By then, its reputation was so strong that buyers would pay the $12 for a pair upfront.

In 1915, HJ fell ill with a mysterious ailment. He searched the country for a treatment, but to no avail, and he died in 1918 – a year after his grandson, John Sullivan Justin Jr (who later sold the business to Buffett) was born to John Sr and his wife Ruby. The founder left behind a magnificent mission statement, an inspiration to future generations:

> No boot shall ever bear the Justin brand unless it is the very best that can be produced from the standpoint of material, style and workmanship … It is my wish that I leave behind me an institution which will uphold the standards and spirit of the true West.[321]

At age six, John Jr began helping out at the company's recently built new factory as an unpaid assistant to cousin Bill, putting laces in calf-length boots mostly destined for oilfield workers (who had to deal with a lot of mud), then a booming industry in Texas.

By 1922, the company's 36 employees were making up to 9,000 pairs a year, which generally sold for between $16 and $22. The next year, a 50-page catalogue was produced which included HJ's statement about the standards and spirit of the West on the inside front cover, as well as his photo. A cadre of travelling salesmen were also recruited, selling to stores in small country towns.

In 1925, the business moved 90 miles south to Fort Worth – a fast-growing meat-packing and oil-drilling metropolis with a population of over 125,000. This gave it access to better banking facilities, freight connections (the town was a rail hub) and a larger pool of workers. The exodus was handsomely subsidised by the Manufacturers and Wholesalers Association of Fort Worth, which didn't want Dallas, Abilene or Waco to attract the Justin business. Six hundred people moved, including 70 employees.

When his sister Enid announced that she was staying to make boots in Nocona, John Sr said that she would lose every cent; while brother Earl added sadly, "Hon, don't you know, it won't be much longer when there won't be any cowboy boots worn at all?"[322] Enid shot back, "Why, Earl, we'll always eat meat and the cowboys will always have to ride the range."[323] She started the Nocona Boot Company and was a tough and determined competitor of H.J. Justin & Sons for many years – a rivalry that didn't end until the companies merged in 1981; and the Nocona brand remains strong even today.

John Justin Jr

John Jr liked to work. So, after each day at junior high school, from 5:30 pm to 11:00 pm, he put in a stint as a delivery boy for a pharmacy. He also worked as a morning paperboy, getting up at 4:15 am to make his rounds. Frustrated because his father wouldn't take him into the business – John Sr wanted his son to go to college – at 16, he went to look for a job in Washington DC. After working there for about two years, he transferred to Dallas and then finally went to Oklahoma Agricultural and Mechanical College. After one year, he transferred to Texas Christian University in Fort Worth.

In the evenings, he and fellow student Charles D Tandy – later to found the giant Tandy Corporation – would head for a garage to make leather belts from scrap, often until dawn. They made good money selling the belts to Fort Worth stores.

According to John Jr, his father was pessimistic about the future for cowboy boots:

> My dad ... felt that with automobiles and sidewalks, people wouldn't need boots any more. He just sort of felt that boots were a lost cause. So they began playing down the cowboy boot

side of the business and they began concentrating on work boots and on making shoes.[324]

They also added military boots, a line of fancy English riding boots and even golf shoes. Many of these diversifications failed to make money, but the cowboy boots ploughed on, generating good returns and keeping the payroll steady throughout the Depression. The company received a boost from the new trend for women to wear cowboy boots. It also sold to truck drivers, railroad workers and pilots all over the country.

John Jr quit college in 1937 but was given a menial job at the family's factory, earning just one-quarter of the minimum wage. After a year of that, he decided to go back into the belt-making business. The move was a great success – not least because his dad and uncles agreed that their salesmen could sell the belts alongside footwear. When war broke out, John Jr joined the US Merchant Marines and persuaded his mother to manage the Justin Belt Company while he was away. He served three years in the extremely dangerous North Atlantic on liberty ships dodging German U-boats to bring food and soldiers to Britain.

The Justin Belt Company thrived and by 1950, sales had reached $500,000. H.J. Justin & Sons was also doing well, making work shoes and boots for workers in essential industries as well as military boots. In 1943, sales topped $1 million. The square dance craze that swept the nation in the late 1940s also helped to boost cowboy boot sales. The back cover of a booklet explaining the dance moves read: "You can dance all night and dance a little longer in easy-feeling Justin Boots."[325] At first, 10,000 copies were printed and sent to the company's 2,000 retail dealers across the country. But demand was so strong that more than 100,000 ended up being printed.

The 33-year-old John Jr celebrated the twelfth anniversary of his profitable belt company in 1950 with its 30 or so staff. His longtime secretary, Dorothy Morell, recalled that after crediting the wrong customer with a cheque bearing a similar name, John Jr said: "As long as you're breathing, you're going to make mistakes. But we learn from them".[326] She recalled:

He was an easy person to work for. His office was always open to people. He was never sarcastic and he never spoke harshly to any of the employees. If he criticised you, it was only with good reason. If he felt you were doing the best that you could, that was good enough for him.[327]

While John Jr was happy with the belt business he had created, he still had a hankering to run the family boot business: "Going back as far as I can remember, running this company was what I wanted to do."[328]

By 1950, the boot company had reached crisis point. HJ had never set out a line of succession and there had been years of internecine conflict between three of his sons. Thus, there was no strong sense of direction or leadership, to the point of occasional chaos, with orders countermanded, resulting in lost market share.

Uncle Earl had watched John Jr grow his belt business from scratch. Impressed, he concluded that John Jr should lead the management of the boot business. He said: "John, we really have to have some new blood. We really need somebody like you to take over and run the company."[329]

John Jr thought he might face serious opposition from Uncle Avis; while his father's negative view of the future for cowboy boots meant that John Sr wouldn't be too keen either. So he explained to Earl that he didn't want to get "into the middle of a family squabble ... I'm used to running my own business and would only be interested in the job if I was assured of having complete control".[330]

"That's what I'm asking you to do," came the response.

John Jr wrote a letter to the board explaining that he would need absolute authority if he were to take the reins at the boot company. The only exception was if the board members were unanimously against a particular decision. In a side room at Youngblood's Fried Chicken, after a good meal, his letter was read out and circulated. Uncle Avis objected: "I don't know why we need this ... I don't know why we need anybody else in here."[331] This led to a major argument between the brothers.

John Jr watched this play out and then said to Earl: "I appreciate your asking me, but this is what I told you I didn't want to get into. Thank you and goodnight."[332]

With that, he walked out of the room.

John Jr thought that was the end of the matter, but a few days later he received a phone call from Earl to say that Avis was extremely upset and wanted to sell his stock. "Are you interested?"[333] John Jr rushed to speak with his Uncle Avis: "I understand you want to sell your stock."[334]

"I sure do. Do you know anybody that wants to buy it? This business is killing me. Everything is wrong."

"How much do you want for it?"

"$150 per share."

That was $50,925 for his 339.5 shares. Avis was the company's largest shareholder. Earl had 320 shares, John Sr had 183 and John Jr already owned 104. Put all these votes together and they had a majority (more than 50%).

Avis went down to the vault and returned with handfuls of stock certificates. He signed the back of them and John Jr wrote a cheque (he had a prearranged loan available). John Jr then walked over to his father's office to break the news. John Sr nearly fell out of his chair. Then he embraced his son and said, "We need you."[335]

John Jr skipped town for a few days while Aunt Enid vented her fury. She was annoyed that with the departure of Avis, she no longer had a conduit for information at the company.

When Earl died two years later, John Jr bought his 320 shares, plus a few more from Earl's family.

John Jr rapidly expanded the business, particularly the cowboy boots side: "People just didn't think of us as shoe people. You build your reputation on what you do best."[336] This was in direct contrast to the brothers' strategy – they had been losing $1.25 on every pair of shoes.

When, at 5:00 am one morning in 1951, he sent a bunch of his men armed with crowbars to destroy the shoe-making machines, his father – on hearing the racket – came rushing in and ordered them to stop. He was still convinced that shoes were the future and boots were in decline. John Jr was scared that his dad would have a heart attack, he was so wound up. He eventually managed to persuade his father to go with him to the office where they could talk quietly and calmly. In the end, John Sr accepted the inevitable, especially in light of the authority the board had granted John Jr; but he still disagreed. Also done away with were English riding boots, cavalry boots and all boots except cowboy boots.

Another shift in the business saw the introduction of boots with pointed toes for "cowboys who drove pick-up trucks around their properties",[337] alongside the round-toed traditional boot for line riders and fence riders (something else John Sr opposed). And John Jr thought it wise to move on from all-black boots; competitors were stealing a march on them by offering boots in many colours.

In addition, the factory needed modernising. The workers suffered in the heat in the summer and froze in the winter, and the lighting was really bad. All this was improved for the company's 100 workers and new machines were installed, from boot turners to boot dryers.

Meanwhile, John Jr – now 36 – was a very eligible, handsome bachelor. One tabloid wrote the headline: "You'll get a boot out of this, girls – here's a Texas millionaire neither old, married nor smelling of cattle or oil."[338] But the same month that article appeared, November 1952, John Jr met widowed Jane Chilton Scott, the mother of two small children, at a ball. They were married in January 1953.

Jane was shocked that her new husband didn't wear cowboy boots; he didn't want to "out-cowboy" the real cowboys. "John, here you're the president of the world's leading cowboy boot company and you don't wear boots."[339] Henceforth, he became a walking advertisement for Justin Boots.

In 1954, rodeo riders started wearing tennis shoes so that they could jump off a horse, run and catch a calf to throw it and tie it up. The Rodeo Cowboys Association thought tennis shoes did not fit the image, so they ruled that all competitors should wear cowboy attire, including hat and boots. Calf-ropers knocked on John Jr's door to say they didn't want the traditional high heel because it prevented a rapid dismount. He and his team designed a flat-heel boot called the Roper. It became popular with the general buyers, not just rodeo riders.

Another innovation came about due to John Jr's allegiance to Texas Christian University. He designed a special pair of boots to wear when he went to watch the games – in purple and white, with a horned frog inlay on the front. He was soon deluged with requests from other fans. Then the media caught on and fans from other colleges wanted their own mascots inlaid in their boots.

John Jr's two companies came together in 1955 when H.J. Justin bought a controlling interest in the Justin Leather Goods Company for $100,000.

John Sr remained active in the business until his death in November 1959, aged 71. During his lifetime, boot production had increased from 15 pairs a week to 1,000 pairs a day.

The company was already nationwide by 1960, but three-quarters of its trade still came from Texas, Oklahoma, California, New Mexico, Arizona, Colorado, Wyoming and Oregon. Then there was a cowboy craze and people started demanding boots in all sorts of fancy hides, from ostrich to alligator and snakeskin – which commanded high prices.

By the time John Jr celebrated his 50th birthday in 1967, he had bought out all the other shareholders. He loved his job and had a happy family life: "I figured I really had it made."[340] But then, in the autumn of 1968, he had a major scare after being rushed to hospital with appendicitis: "I began thinking about what would happen to the company if something happened to me. Everything I had was tied up in the company. I didn't want Jane saddled with having to try to run it."[341]

John Jr discussed the matter with his lawyer, Sproesser Wynn, who also happened to serve as legal counsel to First Worth Corporation. This had been formed in August 1968 to hold the Acme Brick Company. Wynn suggested a merger as a solution. First Worth Corporation was shortly to have an IPO, which would give Justin's stock a market value and a place to sell should he wish. And if he did die, his widow would be able to cover the estate taxes through a few stock sales.

Acme Brick Company

The Acme Brick Company grew to be America's largest brick manufacturer, producing over one billion bricks in the year before Warren Buffett bought it. By then, the company was 109 years old – and those 109 years were a rough ride. It was established in late 19th-century Texas, when the state was developing at a rapid rate. As urbanisation increased, so too did the demand for more durable and grander buildings than log cabins. There was an obvious need for robust building materials.

Dallas merchant George Bennett wanted to satisfy this demand by building a pressed brick factory. To do so, he would need to find a source of clay or shale, fuel, plenty of labourers and transportation to a reasonably adjacent market – it is expensive to move bricks relative to their value, so brick makers tend to be local.

After two years searching for a location offering all these factors, Bennett came across land on a tributary of the Brazos River five miles from Millsap (slightly north and east of the centre of Texas). It was an old relay station on a stagecoach route with a population of 100. Crucially, the land was on the railway route, with Fort Worth a mere 46 miles away and Dallas 78 miles. The Mineral Wells and Northwestern Railroad could carry bricks to retail points in Southwest Texas.

Bennett had shale samples tested by a brick machinery company in Chicago – it was of good quality and colour. Coal was also found in the area. He purchased three 160-acre tracts of land for just over $4 an acre in 1890. Buildings were needed for machinery, horses, mules, tools, a blacksmith and a repair shop.

Production started in 1891 at the plant (around which a settlement grew, to be called Bennett, after George). In return for the considerable expenses incurred to that point, Bennett was entitled to most of the $100 shares issued in 1891; in all, $52,000 was called for.

Despite bringing in experienced brickmakers, the plant had more orders than it could fill. At first, more kilns were added; then a new plant was built to take production to 75,000 bricks a week made by 300 workers.

By the turn of the century, as well as hundreds of homes, landmark buildings in Dallas had been constructed using Acme bricks ('acme' means 'the highest point'). And in 1901, the company received a large order for a huge meatpacking plant in Fort Worth, for which it needed to step up production to two million a month. The small settlement of Bennett still has a brick plant in operation today.

Throughout these formative years, Walter Bennett, George's teenage son, would go to the plant, putting his hand to every task. During a world tour at the age of 15, he collected such a variety of brick from Europe, Asia and South America that he would later establish a small museum.

During the 1907 recession, triggered by panic over the San Francisco earthquake and Wall Street's excessive speculation and excess borrowing, George died, aged 54, on a trip to Galveston, having fallen ill with stomach issues. His 21-year-old son, Walter, was passed over for the role of company president. Instead, he became vice-president and general manager, under the 'leadership' of a man who seemed to spend little time at the plant. As the recession deepened, wage cuts were imposed and strikes ensued, resulting in the closure of the plant. From 1908 to 1909, there were periods when the plant was opened by hiring local farmers; but there were many idle times. The ongoing effects of the recession prompted the decision, in 1910, to shutter the plant entirely.

Things were looking bleak. But then a friend of Walter's – a Texas Pacific Railroad train conductor – made his train stop, unscheduled, in Bennett. He had news: the town of Midland in West Texas had been almost completely razed to the ground by fire and was in sore need of bricks to rebuild.

They needed to act fast. James Fender, an old school friend of Walter and now a general manager of Acme (covering timekeeping, bookkeeping, sales and shipping), rushed to a banker in Millsap to borrow enough money to cover expenses for a trip to Midland. He returned with a very large order. The company rehired and fired up the kilns – it was back in business.

Two years later, Acme bought Denton Pressed Brick Company, 38 miles north of Fort Worth. In 1916, the name of the company was changed to Acme Brick Company and 29-year-old Walter was appointed as president.

The First World War was a boom time for brick makers, as all kinds of manufacturing firms across America ramped up production. Acme opened branch sales offices in San Antonio, Houston and West Texas.

The period after 1918 was even better. As automotive transport took off, there was a need to replace muddy streets with paving brick; the oil industry was expanding and building fancy brick offices; sewerage pipes (made in Denton) were being laid; and families wanted brick homes. Expansion continued through the 1920s, including into states beyond Texas, with sales offices opening all over the southwest.

The following plants were built or acquired:

- 1920–1921: Plant built in Perla, Arkansas.
- 1923: Fort Smith Brick Company, Arkansas, agreed to merge with Acme Brick.
- 1924: American Brick and Tile Company, Oklahoma City was bought. It had an Oklahoma City plant and one in Cleveland, Oklahoma.
- 1925: Plant built in Tulsa, Oklahoma.
- 1926: Arkansas Brick and Tile Company bought with plants in Malvern, Pine Bluff and Little Rock.
- 1927: Wichita Falls Brick and Tile Company, Texas bought.

By 1928, Acme had approximately 900 employees producing 165 million bricks a year – a peak that would not be exceeded for another two decades. With the start of the Great Depression in 1930, sales fell to just 98 million bricks and the company closed several plants and 16 of its 28 sales offices.

By 1934, sales had fallen to 20 million bricks and the company was on the brink of collapse. But the management team, under the inspiring leadership of Walter, managed to pull it through. However, the strain of this period had a deleterious effect on Walter's health and he died in 1935.

William Bryce – a prominent Fort Worth businessman and adviser to Acme – assumed the role of president of Acme following the death of his friend Walter. In 1941, Bryce switched position to chairman, appointing James Ernest Fender as president with day-to-day executive responsibilities. An "extrovert salesman",[342] Fender had worked for the company since 1907 and was its longest-serving employee. He managed to increase brick sales to over 100 million in 1942, helped by wartime reflationary spending.

Surviving the Great Depression as a brick maker was a remarkable achievement in itself. Because so few made it through in a healthy state, Acme found itself at an advantage as America went on a spending splurge during and after the Second World War. In 1944, Acme bought a Clinton, Oklahoma plant to help meet the anticipated boom in housing and construction materials after the war. Several more acquisitions followed:

- 1945: Bishop Brick in Garrison, Texas. It came with a plant in Houston.
- 1945: Garrison Vitrified in Garrison, Texas.
- 1950: Monroe, Louisiana.
- 1950: Baton Rouge, Louisiana.
- 1954: Buffalo Brick and Tile in Buffalo, Kansas.
- 1954: Alexandria, Louisiana.
- 1954: Waskom, Texas.
- 1958: Kanopolis, Kansas.
- 1958: Great Bend, Kansas.

Between 1945 and 1950, sales tripled from $3 million to $9 million. When Fender retired in 1959, at the age of 76, Acme had 19 manufacturing plants and 32 sales offices in five states and was manufacturing 300 million bricks a year. The 1960s marked another great decade of growth and prosperity for the company: in 1965, shipments topped 433 million.

By the late 1960s, competition for brick from concrete, asbestos cement, aluminium, steel plastic and adobe brick had intensified. Acme decided to embrace the trend rather than fight it. Thus, it acquired businesses in fields such as lightweight aggregate block, cinderblock and precast and prestressed concrete. One acquisition came with patents for 'Featherlite' blocks, still a very successful product today.

The Justin Companies and Acme combine

The 22 November 1968 edition of the *Fort Worth Star-Telegram* carried the following story: "Two of Fort Worth's oldest manufacturing companies – perhaps the two very oldest – joined Thursday under the aegis of a three-month-old corporation that bids fair to become a conglomerate."

DO Tomlin, then president and general manager of Acme, had long dreamed of forming the First Worth Corporation, incorporating both Acme and Justin Industries. In late 1968, John Jr and Tomlin reached a deal:

- First Worth would exchange 72,225 shares for all outstanding stock in H.J. Justin & Sons;

- 37,775 shares of First Worth stock would be exchanged for all stock of the Justin Belt Company; and

- If the price of First Worth stock was less than $23 per share three years afterwards, John Jr would receive additional First Worth stock to make up the difference.

John Jr became the company's largest shareholder. The structure was created in a way that allowed the two entities to stay essentially autonomous, with John Jr remaining actively in charge of all boot and belt operations. John Jr was also a director and member of the executive committee of First Worth.

But not long after the completion of the merger, John Jr became increasingly annoyed and started to think that he had made a dreadful mistake. Only two days after the deal closed, three men carrying clipboards and stopwatches appeared in his office at the boot plant. When he asked them what they wanted, they said, "We're from First Worth. We're here to do some time studies in your factory."[343] He was incensed because he had agreed with Tomlin: "You're in the brick business. I'll run the boot business. I don't want anyone messing with me at all. If you want to know anything, call me and I'll come over."[344] The three men were politely shown the door. Tomlin did apologise, but John Jr started to worry "what I had gotten myself into".[345]

Then came another mistake: a board meeting was held in New Orleans in 1969 with no expense spared – a private jet, a fleet of stretch limousines, plush rooms, lavish gifts for the directors' wives who were in attendance, fancy dinners. "I found myself wondering what it all was costing the company," mused John Jr.[346]

And then another: Tomlin and Wynn shocked John Jr by deciding behind his back to withdraw the IPO. Not only did John Jr and his family lose the easy ability to sell his shares, but the company also lost access to the finance needed to fund its ambitious expansion plans, such as expanding boot production. Even worse was the reason for the withdrawal: the auditor had discovered problems in the financial statements. And the other directors had already spent $139,000 on consulting and other fees on the IPO.

John Jr was:

> really worried. There were so many mystifying things happening, things coming to light, that I hadn't known about … I was really frightened that I had made a serious mistake that could cost me everything I'd worked for … It finally got so bad that I was having trouble functioning.[347]

Head lowered in despair, he was walking through downtown when he was so overcome with emotion that he had to lean against a 'No Parking' sign for fear of passing out. An oilman friend saw him and asked what it was that was so serious. On hearing John Jr's tale, he suggested going to see a certain aggressive young attorney. They marched over to his office there and then.

The attorney immediately saw that the level of misrepresentation John Jr had suffered called for suing to nullify the merger. As they started down that path, the other directors made an extraordinary offer: if John Jr dropped the lawsuit, the management of the entire corporation was his – he would become president and CEO of First Worth Corporation.

John Jr's attorney pointed out that Acme Brick was not making any money, whereas Justin Boot Company was, and had a great future. Why not take the chance to walk away from bricks through annulment of the deal?

But John Jr accepted the offer. After all, such litigation can go on for years, with appeals and countersuits; and meanwhile, the company would be rudderless. That was no good, as all his net worth was tied up in First Worth stock. "I gave it a lot of thought," he said, "and I finally decided my best course was to take over management of the company and try to pull it out."[348] At a fraught board meeting, Tomlin was replaced by John Jr and, as the largest stockholder, Justin quickly elected a new slate of directors.

The situation was bad. "John's timing couldn't have been worse," recalls Ed Stout, Acme's vice president in Little Rock at the time and later president of Acme Brick:

> Acme Brick had always been subject to the cycles in housing starts, and in 1969 housing starts dropped rather dramatically … Also, a number of acquisitions … we didn't seem to run them very well … we were strapped for cash … we purchased all those companies for cash … So here's John, the third generation of a family business that's been going for nearly a century. He's traded for stock that's going down the tube. I could understand how he felt.[349]

By the early 1970s, John Jr had a comprehensive grasp of the brick business. He had to learn fast because the chief of bricks had resigned in 1969 along with Tomlin, so John Jr took on leadership there as well. Often wearing old jeans and scuffed boots, he would drive out to the local Fort Worth brick plant to work alongside the clay extruders and kiln loaders. "You'd be surprised by how much information you can get that way," he said. "It was a constant learning process."[350]

Towards the end of 1970, hardly any brick orders were being received as the housing slump continued. Nevertheless, John Jr decided to be bold and began building up inventory in anticipation of an economic rebound – it turned out to cost much the same to keep operating at a low level as to shut down altogether because the fixed costs were still there. His bravery paid off in 1971 as house building picked up to over two million starts. In 1972, sales rose to $63 million; that same year, the company changed its name to Justin Industries Inc and First Worth became nothing but a bad memory.

On being appointed Acme president in 1973, Stout faced a massive problem: natural gas prices had jumped after the Middle Eastern oil embargo. Acme had long ago shifted from coal to natural gas to fire its bricks and heating bill was its largest cost after labour. Undaunted, the team set about entering the oil and gas exploration business. They duly struck gas, in substantial quantities. Combined with efficiency improvements, this lowered the cost of brick production (at some plants, gas consumption was cut by two-thirds). By 1978, market-set gas prices were ten times the level of 1972, so competitors were struggling; whereas Acme sold nearly 550 million bricks that year and the business was nicely profitable.

The holding company reported net sales of $184.5 million in 1979 – quadruple the $46.5 million recorded in 1971. John Jr had seen the potential for risk reduction in combining the bricks and the boot businesses right from the start:

> Acme's sales fluctuate with the homebuilding market. But the boot business is different. It's a lot more stable. The boot company does reasonably well even in periods of economic downturn. In good times it makes a lot of money. So Justin and Acme made a good combination.[351]

On the 100th anniversary of the founding of H.J. Justin, Bootmaker, 60 salesmen descended on Spanish Fort for a three-day conference on the very spot where the first shop was located. John Jr was presented with a deed for the land on which they stood. That same year, an article in the *Washington Post* enthused about the latest rage: "[N]ationwide the fastest-moving fashion in western chic is the cowboy boot – with $200 million in business this year alone. And Washington is no exception to the trend … sales are really booming in New York."[352] The company was struggling to keep up with demand, even though it was turning out 2,600 pairs a day. The 1980 release of the movie *Urban Cowboy*, starring John Travolta and Debra Winger, further boosted the rage for western gear.

By 1980, Aunt Enid – now 86 – was still very much in charge of the Nocona Boot Company, making more than 1,250 pairs of boots per day and $1 million profit a year. One day she called John Jr and asked if he wanted to buy her out. A deal was agreed, but the ever-capricious Aunt Enid soon wanted to back out. After a court case, the deal went through in 1981 for just shy of $9 million.

Despite the success of the boot business, it was the brick business that turned out to be the real cash cow – in the good years. Even in 1979, bricks accounted for 82% of the company's profits. When recession hit in 1982, the popularity of cowboy boots faded and the division fell into losses, with excessive inventory and staff. Housing starts also collapsed, so large group losses were recorded. But Acme kept pumping out the bricks (at a lower rate than normal, but much more than the market then demanded), waiting for the upturn – after all, bricks have a long shelf life. The gamble paid off again as housing starts jumped in 1983 to 1.7 million and the company shipped a record number of bricks – close to 600 million.

The year 1990 was a great one, with bumper sales of nearly $315 million and net income of $7.3 million. The company's success was noticed in the financial markets (Justin Industries was quoted on Nasdaq) and an offer came in to purchase all its shares for £157 million. The bidders had built up an 11.6% stake, but to buy the rest they were reliant on loans. The resulting company would have a lot of debt.

John Jr had been courting the company's main rival bootmaker, Tony Lama, based in El Paso, for 20 years. This finally paid off just as Justin Industries came under offer. It was announced that Tony Lama would be bought for cash and Justin Industries would assume its pile of debt. However, the bidder's bankers baulked at the level of debt that the combination of Justin, Tony Lama and the acquirer would have, forcing the bidders to lower their offer – which was, of course, rejected by Justin Industries' shareholders.

When the bidders walked away, a relieved John Justin said: "When you have a company as old as we are and as close as we are, you hate the thought of someone new coming in and tearing everything up."[353] He was full of confidence about the future: "[W]e own the Justin, Nocona and Tony Lama boot lines – the best names in the business. Combine that with the market strength and brand recognition of Acme Brick and we're in a very good position."[354] Wall Street agreed and pushed up the shares.

In 1994, John Jr, then aged 77, was diagnosed with leukaemia and given six months to live if he didn't receive treatment. With his tough, pragmatic mindset, he put himself through punishing chemotherapy, losing his hair and 20 pounds in the process. Although he recovered from that illness, other health issues meant that by the late 1990s, he had to resort to a wheelchair and a walker to get around the office; but he was determined to continue working notwithstanding.

Then disaster struck: in 1998, a new computer system was planned, designed to integrate all of the footwear divisions, creating efficiencies and lowering costs. However, it did not work out that way. The goal was to synchronise accounting and purchasing, production and personnel – but the outcome was chaos. The new system was launched just before the busy Christmas season; it failed and the company lost many sales. It took almost two years to sort out the mess, all while competitors eroded market share. In June 1999, John Jr decided to restructure the company into two operating divisions: footwear and building materials.

Randy Watson – often described as the quintessential Texan in his humble yet larger-than-life way – was appointed president and CEO of the boot business, Justin Brands, at the age of 41. In the previous seven years, as sales manager and then vice president of marketing, he had grown accustomed to John Jr walking up to him and asking deceptively simple questions that required a nuanced and intellectually challenging answer, such as "Are all our customers happy?" or "Are all the boots being made right?" He had to think deeply before responding to his mentor.

Both John Jr and Watson were committed to upholding the integrity and reputation of the Western brands they were proud to sell. Paraphrasing Buffett, Watson said: "Brands take more than a century to build, but they can be lost in a moment."[355] He also reflected Buffett's managerial style by first making sure the right people were in the right place and then "stay[ing] out of their way".[356]

But in 1999, Watson was forced to intervene in a big way. Over the previous five years, revenue from footwear had declined by 26% and a $9.2 million operating profit had turned into a $16 million annual loss. Watson decided to close two of the company's five factories. To stay motivated during these hard times, Watson referred to Theodore Roosevelt's speech on "The Man in the Arena", delivered at the Sorbonne, Paris, on 23 April 1910:

> It is not the critic who counts: not the man who points out how the strong man stumbles or where the doer of deeds could have done better.
>
> The credit belongs to the man who is actually in the arena, whose face is marred by dust and sweat and blood, who strives valiantly, who errs and comes up short again and again, because there is no effort without error or shortcoming, but who knows the great enthusiasms, the great devotions, who spends himself in a worthy cause; who, at the best, knows, in the end, the triumph of high achievement, and who, at the worst, if he fails, at least he fails while daring greatly, so that his place shall never be with those cold and timid souls who knew neither victory nor defeat.

Watson would never forget the scenes at the two factories he shut down on one day in 1999 – about 500 jobs were lost. Gut wrenching though this was, he knew it was necessary to strengthen the organisation for the long run.

Acme Building Brands was now headed by Harrold Melton, a 40-plus-year veteran of the company. He was delighted to be president and CEO of the division when, on the last business day of 1999, the company's one-billionth brick for the year was made (the company had 22 plants at the time). He was also proud that when Texans were asked to name a brick brand, 75% named Acme, compared to just 16% for the runner-up.

John Jr became chairman emeritus of the Justin Industries board and was succeeded as president and CEO of Justin Industries by JT Dickenson, a 25-year stalwart of the holding company. John V. Roach, the CEO of Tandy Corporation for much of the 1980s and 1990s, succeeded John Jr as chairman of the board of Justin Industries.

The deal

Given his failing health, John Jr thought it prudent to settle his estate and concluded that it would be best to sell the entire company, so the directors began preparing for sale in 1999. Roach hired New York investment firm Donaldson, Lufkin and Jenrette to deal with potential acquirers. Word quickly spread and the directors started to receive enquiries, including from the three big brick companies in North America. There was a lot of interest in buying either the boots or the brick business, but no one was interested in both.

Acme's in-house attorney, Jeff Bodley, contacted a friend in New York who reached out to Buffett to bring Justin Industries to his attention.[357] Buffett recalled:

> On May 4th, I received a fax from Mark Jones, a stranger to me, proposing that Berkshire join a group to acquire an unnamed company. I faxed him back, explaining that with rare exceptions we don't invest with others, but would happily pay him a commission if he sent details and we later made a purchase. He replied that the 'mystery company' was Justin.[358]

Buffett was interested and so quickly scheduled a visit to Fort Worth. He also spoke with Melinda Gates, a Dallas native, who told him that everybody in Dallas knew Justin boots and Acme bricks.

He then contacted Roach, who asked: "Warren, how do we want to go forward? Do you want to send in some accountants to review the books? Do you want to have factory tours and review the operations?"[359] He responded:

> John, you know Berkshire Hathaway's headquarters operates with only 12.8 employees and I don't have anybody to send to do a review of the books, or to visit the plants either. If anybody's going to come, I'm going to have to come myself.[360]

Thus, in June 2000, Buffett visited Fort Worth to meet with John Jr and Roach. Buffett asked John Jr to tell him the real history of the business and afterwards Buffett described Berkshire Hathaway for three-quarters of an hour. The pair clearly impressed each other. Buffett spent the rest of the morning with Watson and the afternoon with Melton. Buffett was very interested in what both had to say about the people at Justin Brands and Acme, such as who did what, as well as their operations and prospects. What were their competitive advantages, positioning and market share? Who were their main competitors?

When Melton handed Buffett an information pack on Acme, the first thing he looked at was the average tenure of employees: 27.2 years in finance, 21.8 years in production and 14.8 years in the field. "He wanted people who demonstrated they could perform successfully over a long period of time," explained Melton.[361]

Buffett added:

> [W]hen Harrold [Melton] and I first met, he talked about how a home is the largest single investment made by most families. I must say, that like most people, I took the beauty and permanence of my brick home, purchased in 1958, for granted. Then I realized that my total expenditure in maintaining the brick exterior of my home for forty-two years was zero! How many thousands of dollars would I have spent maintaining another type of exterior during the ensuing four decades? Early in my business career, that money spent on maintenance would have been unavailable to invest in quality stocks and companies.[362]

Acme's marketing team later latched on to this statement and, together with Buffett's picture, promoted the idea of brick being a great investment.

Melton became an instant admirer:

> I've been around a lot of bright people in my life, but I have never seen anyone who grasps the essence of a business the way Warren Buffett does. It doesn't take long for him to make a decision. He is really, really quick.[363]

As Buffett was leaving, he told Roach that had seen everything he needed and that he never bought a business that had to be fixed. Dennis Knautz, vice president of finance, accompanied Buffett to the airport.

"It was essentially a handshake deal," said Knautz. "He decides what a business [is] worth. And he liked the look of the management team."[364]

However, there were still other parties interested. So, Roach set a date for a board meeting a few weeks later, at which all proposals would be considered. Within hours of meeting the team, Buffett faxed in his offer: $22 per share – a 23% premium to the $17.88 closing price the day before. Buffett phoned to see whether the fax had arrived and added: "I haven't shown it to my attorney yet, but this is what the deal is."[365] Roach was pleased with this sequence of events, as "sometimes attorneys have a way of prolonging and complicating deals".[366] The $22 per share was quite high compared with the trading ranges over the previous three years (see Figure 9.1).

Figure 9.1 Justin Industries, stock trading range, 1997–1999 ($)

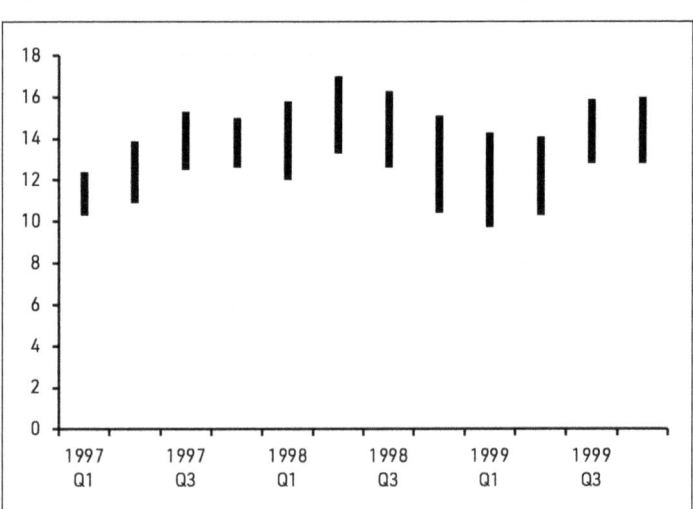

Source: Justin Industries 1999 Annual Report.

Buffett went on to state:

> [The] incredible value that brick delivers has made Acme a household name in their primary market. We place a high value on investing in companies like these with strong brand positions in their markets like Coke, Gillette, GEICO, and American Express. We know that these companies achieve strong brand preference by consistently delivering superior products, service, and value.[367]

Roach said that Buffett drove the pace of the deal:

> We almost had to slow him down he moved so fast ... Anytime I called and asked him a question, I usually had a response in writing in a minute. He's the only person from Berkshire Hathaway who I talked to in the whole process.[368]

When Buffett first made his offer, Roach told his staff to arrange for a due diligence process from Omaha. It was quite a shock to find that this consisted of just a few questions about tax liabilities and insurance reserves.

Buffett was invited to make a short presentation at the Justin Industries board meeting along with other bidders, but he was unable to make the date. Bob Denham, from Berkshire's law firm (Munger, Tolles & Olson), made a short presentation instead. At 5:00 pm, Denham was told by the Justin directors that they would like to work with him on a definitive contract for the purchase. This took a couple of days and was announced a week later, on 20 June. The tender offer of $22 per share to acquire all of the stock, including John Jr's 20% holding, closed on 1 August 2000.

Roach stated in the announcement that:

> John Justin and I are extremely pleased that one of America's most admired companies is acquiring Justin Industries. Warren Buffett's and Berkshire's business philosophy will provide current management the opportunity to build on our strong market presence and on our corporate traditions. We believe this acquisition is great for our shareholders, our customers, our employees, and our communities.[369]

Buffett responded:

> We not only encourage extraordinary autonomy in our operating businesses, we depend on it. Justin will fit this pattern perfectly. It is an absolutely first-class business run by first-class people. The managers who have produced Justin's outstanding results will continue to run operations from Fort Worth just as they have in the past.[370]

In celebration, John Jr gave Buffett a pair of ostrich-skin cowboy boots.

One of the few changes agreed was that the holding company would disappear and the footwear company would henceforth report to Berkshire separately from the brick company. Harrold Melton said that move "took a lot of overhead out of our business".[371]

What did Warren Buffett buy?

Earnings per share in 1999 were $1.43, so Berkshire paid a price-earnings ratio (PER) of $22 ÷ $1.43 = 15.4. The multiple is much higher if the denominator used is the average earnings over the previous few years – profits were lower from 1995 to 1998 (see Figure 9.2).

Figure 9.2 Justin Industries Group net income, 1995–1999 ($ million)

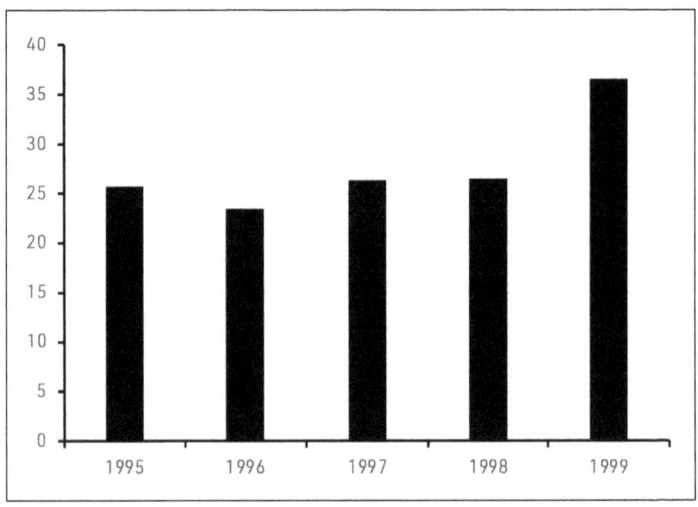

Source: Justin Industries 1999 Annual Report.

The natural delivery radius for bricks is about 250 miles around a plant, meaning that local manufacturers often have a cost advantage, giving them a competitive edge within their geographies. You might say that Acme Brick had a series of economic franchises in these radiuses around its plants. The large sums needed to establish a factory and distribution network presented another barrier to entry.

A month after the merger, Roach was asked whether he thought Buffett had bought Justin Industries for the boots or the bricks. The logic of his reply is aligned with the evidence in Figures 9.3 and 9.4:

> [T]he value of the company is really in the brick and building materials business. It's not very glamorous, but it's the big cash producer overall ... out of [the $22 per share] probably $18 should be attributed to the building materials and the other $4 to the footwear business ... the real reason Warren was interested in Justin was that we had a strong competitive position, strong market share in each of our businesses, old and well-established trademarks that were highly recognised, and management teams that he was comfortable with ... a high level of integrity.[372]

Figure 9.3 Justin Boots and Acme Building Products Revenue, 1995–1999 ($ million)

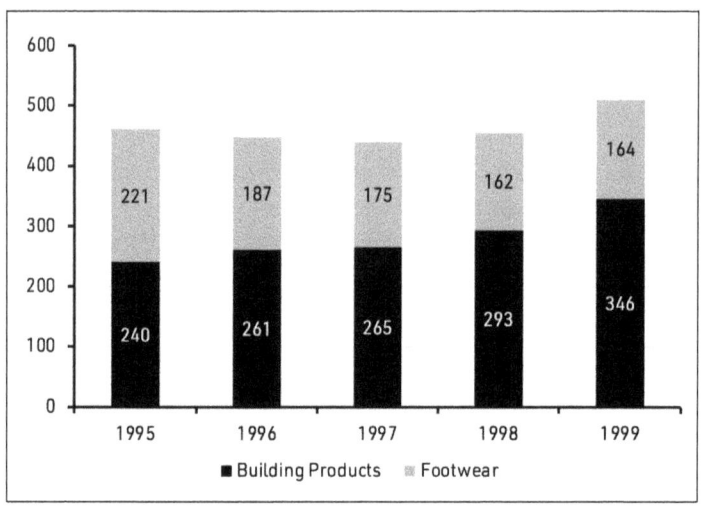

Source: Justin Industries 1999 Annual Report.

Figure 9.4 Operating profit of the footwear and building materials divisions and central overheads, 1995–1999 ($ million)

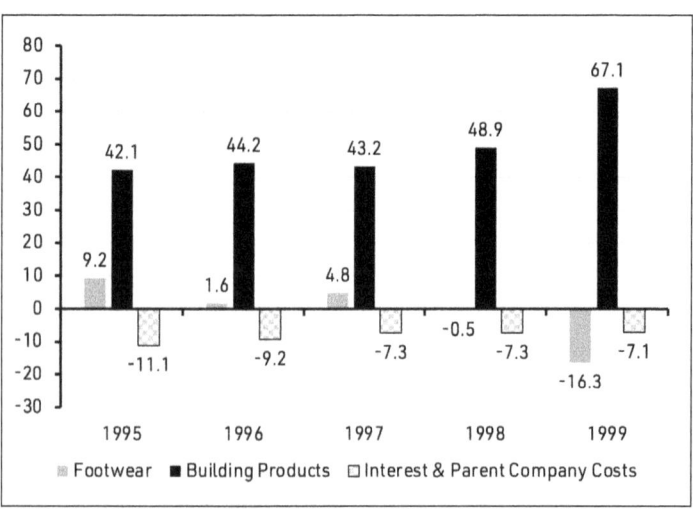

Note: Totalling the three components equals income before taxes.

Source: Justin Industries 1999 Annual Report.

Return on shareholders' equity in recent years was okay, at around 10%; but given the fixable problems at Justin Boots, there was some potential for it to rise to the levels seen in 1992–1994 (see Figure 9.5).

Figure 9.5 Justin Industries return on shareholders' equity, 1990–1999 (%)

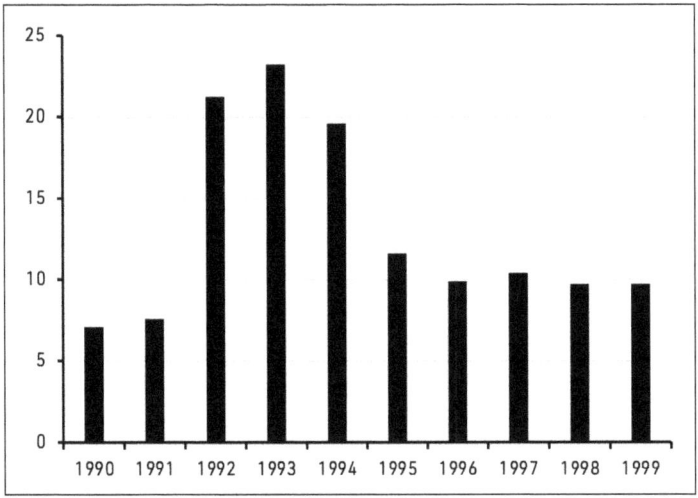

Source: Justin Industries 1999 Annual Report.

What happened afterwards?

At Justin Brands, Watson was grateful that Buffett was different from most acquirers in that he left managers who were passionate about what they did to just get on with it. He said:

> Unlike Berkshire, many corporate raiders never seem to leave good businesses alone. They feel the need to make changes even when a business has worked perfectly well for generations. It is funny how these raiders want to see results in a short period when they should notice that tested and true businesses take years to build![373]

Watson suggested that one of Buffett's great talents is the ability to make managers and owners perceive the benefits that come with being part of Berkshire. The testimonies of current Berkshire managers attract likeminded business owners to the Berkshire family.

Melton, the boss of Acme, was keen to reassure employees that joining Berkshire was a major positive:

> The acquisition will be a very beneficial thing for Acme's homebuilder customers. All the things that Mr. Buffett and Berkshire Hathaway believe in – continuity, sound conservative business practices, and growth with stability – are excellent fits with Acme Brick Company's century-old philosophy. Our new ownership will enable Acme Building Brands to continue making the necessary investments in manufacturing and distribution to stay abreast of our customers' growing needs.[374]

Melton considered Buffett to be:

> a terrific boss. He grasped the essence of our business immediately, and he never interfered with my operation of Acme. He was normally available by phone when I had a reason to contact him, and he was always gracious and helpful.[375]

Buffett enthusiastically supported Melton's expansion of the brick business. Thus, it continued to acquire brick makers in Arkansas, consolidating its dominance in that state; and then added plants in Mississippi, Tennessee and Colorado.

As promised, headquarters remained in Fort Worth. Knautz described Buffett's approach as:

> pretty much a hands-off management style. At first, we didn't know what the rules were, especially for financial reporting. But we quickly learned to send the reports to Omaha instead of downstairs to Mr. Justin. It was pretty autonomous. Mr. Buffett told us we could call him every day.[376]

Buffett likes to see monthly figures and discuss the general business climate half a dozen times a year but otherwise leaves his managers to get on with things. Knautz later added that "within the Berkshire family is the ability to keep managing a wonderful business without worrying too much about producing short-term results at the expense of long-term value".[377]

Sadly, John Jr passed away not long after he had arranged the sale of the company, on 26 February 2001; but at least he died knowing it was in good hands.

After 40 years with the business, Melton retired in 2005, to be succeeded by Knautz. He took up the mantle during a boom: record brick sales had been set for 15 years in a row. In early 2006, over 100 million bricks were being made each month. However, this was to come to a grinding halt in 2008 as the Great Recession took hold – just when Acme was crowned the largest brick manufacturer in the United States. Whereas in 2006 American producers were churning out 9.5 billion bricks, by 2010 this figure had fallen to 2.5 billion. And these are businesses with high fixed costs, given the capital that must be committed. Production was curtailed and employee count dropped from 2,892 at the end of 2006 to 1,845 in December 2011. Ultimately, half of the company's brick plants were closed. But still, operating losses were made every year from 2009 to 2013.

By contrast, all the company's sales offices remained open during the Great Recession. "If you close a sales office, you're leaving that market. It's like pulling your hand out of a bucket of sand. It's harder to get back in," explained Knautz.[378] They had long ago learned that bricks are cyclical and you've got to be ready for the inevitable upturn, even if that means building up stock and incurring temporary losses. The company could bear the losses not only because it had built-in resilience and a can-do culture, but also because it had solid financial backing from Berkshire.

In 2012, demand for bricks began to increase again and a backlog of orders started to build, encouraging the company to ramp up production. But it wasn't until 2014 that volumes sufficed to break even. Having weathered the recession as America's largest, most respected brick producer, with strong resources, Acme was in a position to further dominate the industry, as so many competitors had been weakened. Plants were bought in Alabama, adding to the 2008 expansion in Minnesota.

By 2014, Justin Brands was selling into 40 countries, with major distribution centres in Canada and Belgium. Watson stepped down in 2019 but soon decided retirement was "overrated". Instead, he got back into the boot business with his family – thus, R. Watson Boots was born.

After delivering 32 billion bricks over a 40-year career with the company, Knautz retired in 2023, with operations chief Watson taking over as president and CEO. Acme appreciates loyal and experienced people: Watson had also put in over 40 years with the firm, mostly on the production side.

Judging by the number of employees (see Figure 9.6), brick production has not increased significantly under Berkshire ownership – although more automation may have reduced staff numbers while maintaining high output.

Figure 9.6 Number of employees working for Justin and Acme, 2003–2023

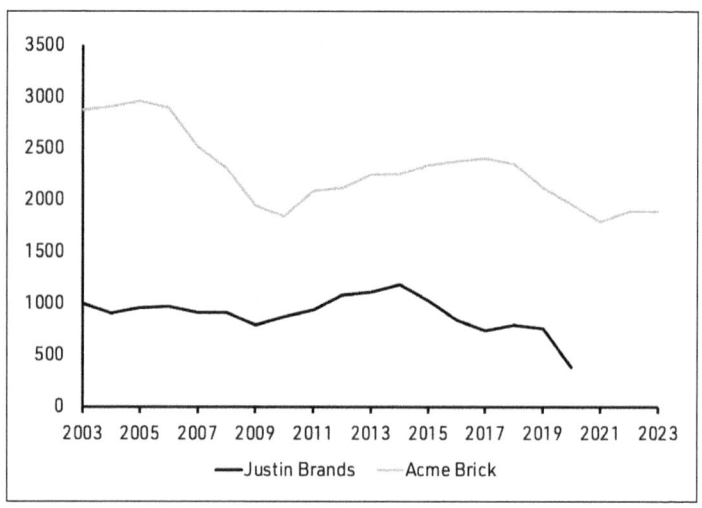

Source: Berkshire Hathaway Annual Reports.

The number of employees making boots for Justin Brands has dwindled in recent years. Today, most production is outsourced to China and other Asian countries. Whether this has damaged quality and image is much debated by buyers of cowboy boots. These days, only select styles are made in the United States, and then with 'global parts'.

Learning points

- **Good businesses come in many forms, including those that enjoy pricing power due to their geographical position**. The cost of transporting bricks means that local producers can often price significantly above cost. Other types of pricing power include:
    - strong brand loyalty (share of mind) (e.g., Coca-Cola, See's Candies);
    - low-cost production (e.g., GEICO, Shaw Carpets); and
    - duopoly/oligopoly (e.g., Moody's).
- **Search for businesses that are very good at holding on to the best people**. John Jr was hardworking, rational and driven; but he was also kind, understanding and open. He had many loyal friends inside and outside the company.
- **Sticking to an area of business in which you are well known, where you can differentiate and apply your experience, is better than venturing into seemingly attractive growth areas**. John Sr pushed into shoes because he doubted the future of boots. His son saw that the company had no competitive advantage in shoes, failing to draw on its heritage, customer recognition and skill set. Also, the shoe market is fiercely competitive.
- **Mergers can be fraught with problems**. After the merger with Acme, John Jr discovered that he had been misled. There was also an extravagant senior management team and a culture of management by numbers rather than getting to know the people and secure buy-in.
- **Company founders and longstanding managers hate the idea of a corporate raider taking their creation and tearing it apart**. This fear often leaves an opening for Buffett, whose promise to preserve the team, culture and HQ location can be trusted.
- **Deals are made by able businesspeople, not by lawyers**. Both Buffett and Roach agreed the fundamentals of the deal for Justin Industries. Lawyers are prone to "prolonging and complicating deals", according to Roach.

- **Leave a good business alone**. If you are running a conglomerate, it is usually best to ensure that the businesses you are buying are well managed (otherwise, don't buy), and to leave those managers to get on with it. That way, you'll get greater commitment and expertise. Be helpful but don't interfere.

- **Tell managers to focus on long-term value.** Too many company managers are instructed to sacrifice long-term shareholder wealth creation to meet short-term targets. This frustrates them enormously because it is so irrationally shortsighted.

Investment 11

BENJAMIN MOORE

Summary of the deal

Deal	Benjamin Moore
Time	December 2000
Price paid	$1.01 billion in cash
Proportion of equity	100%
Status	Still held

The most interesting aspect of the Benjamin Moore story is that it describes a rare case of Warren Buffett becoming so annoyed with the direction of a company that he sacked the CEO. At the time of buying, Buffett made a promise that the paints, stains and varnishes manufactured by the firm would continue to be sold through its network of independent distributors – something that took decades to build. While the other major makers sold most of their paint through big-box stores such as Lowe's and Home Depot, Benjamin Moore had stuck strictly to thousands of small stores all over the United States and Canada. Each dealer was certified by the company and there was a special culture – an intimately connected eco-system, built on trust.

Benjamin Moore offered a premium product and charged a premium price through knowledgeable retailers who were thoroughly trained in the Benjamin Moore way. These people had committed large amounts of money and time to become partners with the company, so it was important for Buffett to reassure them that the relationship would continue. They were loyal to Benjamin Moore and Buffett reciprocated that loyalty with a solemn promise.

But in 2008, a new leader, Denis Abrams, was attracted by the siren voices of the big-box stores to sell paints, stains and varnishes to them. Volumes would soar and so would profits, so they claimed. And that was true in the short term.

But the move was wrong in Buffett's eyes – not just because it shattered the wall of integrity that both Buffett and Benjamin Moore had spent decades building, but because it was bad strategy on two counts. First, as soon as the certified distributors caught wind of the plan and saw their loyalty thrown back in their faces, they started to rebel, looking to other sources of income and badmouthing Benjamin Moore. Second, while the biggest retailers may offer boosts to profits in the short run, they are renowned for putting the squeeze on supplier margins over the long run. Far better, thought Buffett, to stick to selling a premium product – used by architects, industrial coating users and house owners alike – in a superior way and at a consistent premium price, even if at lower volumes.

Further exasperating retailers, Abrams told his sales team to convince these distributors that they should deal only in Benjamin Moore paints and remove other brands; the salesforce was even empowered to threaten refusenik retailers with the promise that company-owned stores would open nearby to compete with them. And there were other irritants, including increased inventory financing costs and being billed for advertising that never appeared.

These moves caused a lot of pain; but eventually, Buffett righted the ship.

The origins of Benjamin Moore

Benjamin Moore, born in County Monaghan, Ireland, arrived in New York in 1872. The 17-year-old found work in a paint factory and then as a paint salesman. Eleven years later, he managed to put together $2,000 to start his own business with an older brother (who left the business shortly afterwards).

The powdered form of paint they made contained everything that house painters needed apart from the water to be stirred in. This (almost) ready-made paint was a boon to those not willing to collect together the various ingredients, as they had previously been forced to do. The product was called Moore's Prepared Calsom Finish and was sold exclusively through independent retailers in nine colours. From the start, they were determined to build a reputation for manufacturing excellence and quality, even if they had to charge more for their product.

They didn't have to wait long to turn a profit: that came in 1884, an impressive $2,000. Unfortunately, that year their little factory in the loft of a three-storey building was destroyed when a fire broke out on a lower floor. Everyone escaped and Moore was the last person to leave as he rescued what he could. Within three days, he had found new premises in another Brooklyn loft and was back in business.

In 1892, Moore introduced a superior white paint, called Muresco, which quickly became a bestseller. This variant maintained its position as the number one calcimine paint in the United States for a large part of the early 20th century. Curiously for a white paint, it contained Irish moss, as well as Pennsylvania clay. Eventually, it was made in 32 different colours. Other bestsellers in the company's fields of specialised paint included one for coating cement and Moore's House Paint.

From the start, Moore was willing to sacrifice market share by charging a premium price for a higher-quality product in terms of durability, colour spectrum and pigment. Also, from the beginning, the company established a distribution method – trading through Benjamin Moore-certified independent paint dealers – that reinforced its niche appeal to people wanting both quality products and quality service from retailers, who made great efforts to inform customers about paint differences.

In 1911, Moore gave a talk at the Brooklyn YMCA entitled "The Basic Principles of the Successful Man", in which he said:

> The chief characteristics of a truly successful business man, in my opinion, are:
>
> 1. **Intelligence**, which is the basis of what is known as good horse sense,

2. **Industry**, without which intelligence is as futile as is intelligence without industry,

3. **Integrity**, for if the results of a man's intelligence and industry are not achieved through sincere motives, honest methods and service to his fellows – his employers, or employees, his trade, his community, and the world at large – they do not constitute genuine success.[379]

These principles are incorporated in the company logo – still used today – consisting of three pyramids, two of which form a stylised 'M'. The three sides symbolise these basic values of intelligence, industry and integrity.

On the issue of integrity, Moore expounded:

> First … a fair deal for everyone. Second … the giving of value received without any graft or chicanery. Third … a recognition of the value of truth in the representation of our products and an effort at all times to keep the standard of our goods up to the highest mark. And last … the practice of strict economy without parsimony.[380]

By 1897, the business was increasing sales at such a rate that it had to establish factories in Chicago and Cleveland. Then in 1906, it pushed into Canada. In 1907, the first chemist was hired and the research department was established. A major advance that year was the launch of a non-lead matte oil paint that could be washed over and over, called Sani-Flat.

In 1917, Moore stepped down at the age of 62 and named his nephew, Livingstone P Moore, as his successor. He died in 1925.

As part of its programme to inform customers about paint, Benjamin Moore produced a lot of leaflets and brochures over the years. It even established a decorating department which allowed customers to pick the brains of its decorating staff – keen DIYers could show up in person or send a letter. In 1930, this led to the creation of marketing character 'Betty Moore'. Played by a series of actors, she offered colour and decorating advice on the radio each week from the 1930s to the 1960s. These talks were based on real queries sent in by customers. Even today, if you visit the company website, there is a 'Betty' chatbot to help.

During the Second World War, the company worked on advancements in tough, 'military-grade' industrial coatings. These products created a great springboard for offering civilian equivalents after the war, from swimming pool paint to bridge paint. The technical coatings division also developed coatings used for both rigid and flexible packaging, vacuum metalising (which creates a layer of metal on a substrate by heating the metal coating material until it vaporises inside a vacuum chamber) and coil stock coating (rolls of, say, coloured aluminium to trim house cladding).

In the 1960s, Benjamin Moore started to offer financial assistance – usually around $200,000 – to certified dealers who were keen to open neighbourhood paint stores. Once profitable, the entrepreneur was expected to start buying back their stock until they fully owned the operation.

In 1982, long before the dawn of the digital age, Benjamin Moore's technical team created a machine to match colours instore. It contained both a spectrophotometer (colour analyser) and a minicomputer. The device received a lot of media attention, both because it was an astonishing innovation and because architects, designers and ordinary families could get just the colours they wanted.

These computerised machines were expensive, at $24,900 a pop; so, in 1985, Benjamin Moore introduced a financing plan: 10% down and the rest over four years. This was not a profit-making venture in itself – the machines were offered as a way to boost retailers' paint sales.

The company's reputation was burnished further by its environmentally friendly innovations, which were way ahead of both regulation and industry trends. These ranged from lead-free paints to the removal of volatile organic compounds.

The 1980s and early 1990s saw rapid growth as Benjamin Moore expanded its store network across America and Canada and increased its market share. New plants were also opened in Alabama, New York and British Columbia.

In 1992, Benjamin Moore opened a 90-acre research and development (R&D) facility in Flanders, New Jersey, including a five-acre outdoor test farm housing more than 2,500 test boards of over 70 different substrate types, coated with both Benjamin Moore and competitor products, to observe how they performed over many years.

In 1999, management realised that the company had too many old and inefficient sites, so the directors implemented a restructuring plan, ceasing production at eight plants to leave a further eight in operation.

On the eve of its entry to the Berkshire Hathaway fold, Benjamin Moore had 73 company-owned stores offering a broad array of products. As well as the Benjamin Moore brand, they stocked competitor coatings, wallcoverings, window treatments and related products. The business served both DIY consumers and contractors. But by far the larger side of the business was its servicing of 3,700 independent dealers who owned over 4,700 storefronts. According to its 1999 Annual Report, this group "forms the core of the Company's marketing strength and provides the high level of customer attention, service and colour expertise critical to the maintenance and expansion of the Benjamin Moore brand". By then, the R&D department had grown to 90 chemists and technicians, out of 2,750 employees overall.

The deal

In July 2000, the directors of Benjamin Moore were considering selling the company. One of them, Robert Mundheim, knew Buffett from his time as general counsel at Salomon Brothers after its bond-trading scandal (see Volume 2, Investment 7) and offered to call him. He thought that Benjamin Moore would fit Buffett's criteria perfectly. Buffett recalled: "I knew Bob from Salomon, where he was general counsel during some difficult times, and held him in very high regard. So my answer was 'Tell me more.'"[381]

In late August, Charlie Munger and Buffett met Richard Roob, chairman of Benjamin Moore, and Yvan Dupuy, president and CEO. "We liked them; we liked the business; and we made a $1 billion cash offer on the spot," said Buffett.[382] In his 2000 letter to Berkshire shareholders, he told them: "Make sure you specify our product for your next paint job."

In October, the board of Benjamin Moore met to discuss the transaction. Some mused whether they should reject the price of £1.01

billion in order to push Buffett into paying more, but Mundheim simply told them it would be "futile" to try[383] – Buffett invariably works out a fair price and sticks to it.

The announcement of the acquisition on 8 November stated that a price of $37.82 per share was agreed for all of the common stock, totalling 26.47 million shares. This was a 51% premium to the undisturbed price of the shares trading on the over-the-counter market. However, it was not that much more than the price that prevailed in 1998 and 1999 (see Figure 11.1).

Figure 11.1 Benjamin Moore stock price, quarterly high and low range, 1998 and 1999 ($)

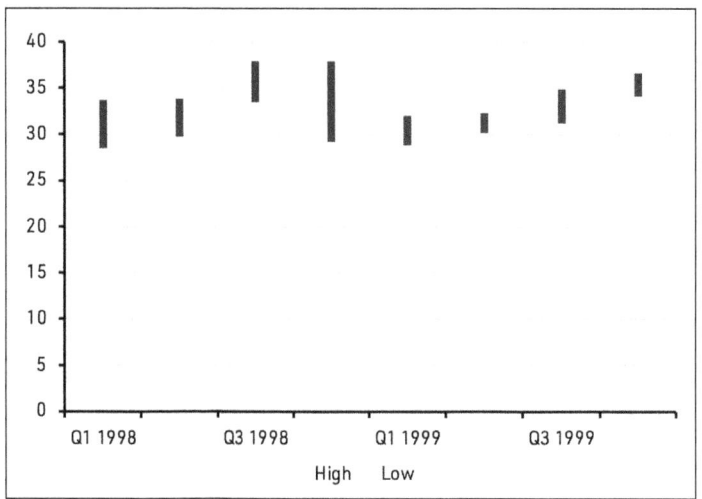

Source: Benjamin Moore Form 10-k 1999.

Richard Roob and Yvan Dupuy wrote in the announcement that:

> this opportunity offers the dual benefit of providing fair value for our shareholders and continuity of the company as a distinct entity. All those, past and present, who have played a part in building this company can feel proud that Warren Buffett and Berkshire Hathaway want to be associated with the name Benjamin Moore.

Buffett responded: "We are extremely excited about the opportunity to add a company with such an outstanding reputation for quality and leadership in its industry to the Berkshire group."

The deal completed on 18 December.

What was bought

In 1999, Benjamin Moore's 73 company-owned stores and the 4,700 independent storefronts produced a combined turnover of £780 million (see Figure 11.2). The United States accounted for 89% of sales and Canada 10%. The company also had a small operation in New Zealand.

Figure 11.2. Benjamin Moore sales, 1994–1999 ($m)

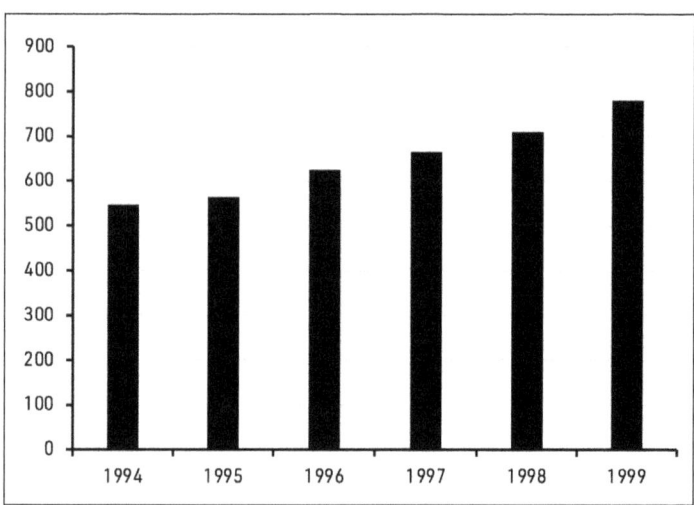

Source: Benjamin Moore Form 10-k 1998 and 1999.

The directors commented on the competitive environment in the 1999 Annual Report:

> The coatings industry is highly competitive and has historically been subject to intense price competition. It is estimated that there are approximately 800 coatings manufacturers in the

United States, many of which are small companies which provide intense competition within regional and local markets, especially with respect to lower priced coatings and custom-made specialty items which are required on a short-time delivery basis.

That didn't sound good. And there was another negative – there were companies in this game much bigger than Benjamin Moore: "Other manufacturers are large diversified corporations, the assets of which are substantially greater than those of the Company, which compete on a nationwide basis" (1999 Annual Report).

So why was Benjamin Moore so profitable (see Figure 11.3)? The following paragraph from the 1999 Annual Report sums it up:

The network … [of] over 4,700 storefronts … forms the core of the Company's marketing strength and provides the high level of customer attention, service and color expertise critical to the maintenance and expansion of the Benjamin Moore brand. It has always been the Company's policy to actively support the continued growth and prosperity of independently owned dealers and retail outlets, through which the Trade Sales Coatings are sold. In 1999, a new color system, the Benjamin Moore Color PreviewTM System was completed … [to] allow the paint buyer to preview their colors before they paint.

Figure 11.3 Benjamin Moore profit after tax, 1994–1999 ($m)

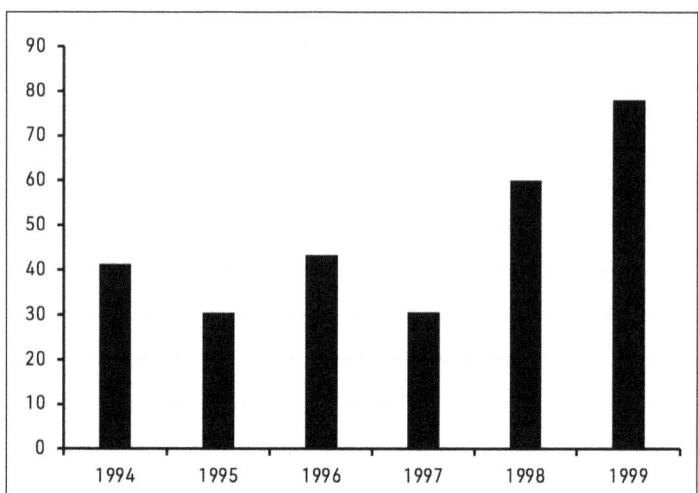

Source: Benjamin Moore Form 10-k 1998 and 1999.

Earnings per share for 1999 were $2.93, so Buffett paid a PER of 12.9. If the average earnings per share over six years is taken as the denominator, the PER is $37.82 ÷ $1.73 = 21.9.

The balance sheet was strong, but shareholders' equity was less than one-third of the buying price (see Table 11.1). At least profit after tax divided by shareholders' equity provided a very satisfactory return on equity capital of over 22%. If incremental capital can be invested in the business at these rates of return, this strengthens the argument for buying the shares at a premium price. Also, there was a spare £100 million of cash and marketable securities sitting in the business. Berkshire Hathaway was able to take high dividends – there are reports of $150 million per year – but the details are sketchy and we don't know how many years of high dividends there were.

Table 11.1 Benjamin Moore balance-sheet items 1998 and 1999

	1999 ($m)	1998 ($m)
Current assets, excluding cash and trading securities	197.6	176.1
Cash and trading securities	100.4	97.2
Current liabilities	−87.4	−67.9
Working capital	210.6	205.4
Total assets	475.6	392.0
Long-term obligations	20.9	20.6
Shareholders' equity	326.9	267.5
Book value per outstanding share of common stock	$12.70	$10.67
Profit after tax/ shareholders' equity	78.0/326.9 = 23.9	60.1/267.5 = 22.5

Source: Benjamin Moore Form 10-k 1999.

Cash flow was impressive relative to the net amount paid for the company (after deducting balance-sheet cash and marketable securities) (see Table 11.2).

Table 11.2 Benjamin Moore cash flows

	1999 ($m)	1998 ($m)
Net income (profit after tax)	78.0	60.1
Add back depreciation and amortisation	13.9	8.6
Add back write-offs of goodwill, intangibles and other non-cash items	0.0	6.9
Deferred income tax	0.6	−1.0
Cash flow after adding back non-cash items	91.3	74.6

Source: Benjamin Moore Form 10-k 1999.

What happened afterwards?

Shortly after the purchase, Buffett starred in a video sent to thousands of Benjamin Moore's independent dealers. He wanted to reassure them that the company would not chase after their bitter rivals, big-box giants Home Depot and Lowe's. He later told *Fortune Magazine*[384] that he made two points in the tape: "First, we buy businesses to keep. We don't resell them. Berkshire was going to be a permanent home for Benjamin Moore … [Second,] I made them a promise that we would forever stick with the dealer system."

Buffett was very pleased with the numbers coming out of Benjamin Moore in the first few years of ownership, writing: "Benjamin Moore … came through the first year with us in great fashion. Charlie and I knew at the time of our purchase that we were in good hands with … Yvan Dupuy."[385] In the second year post sale, the volume of paint and coatings grew by 5% and in 2003 there were record operating earnings. In 2005, sales volumes were up 5% and staff numbers were rising (see Figure 11.4).

Figure 11.4 Benjamin Moore employee numbers, 2003–2023

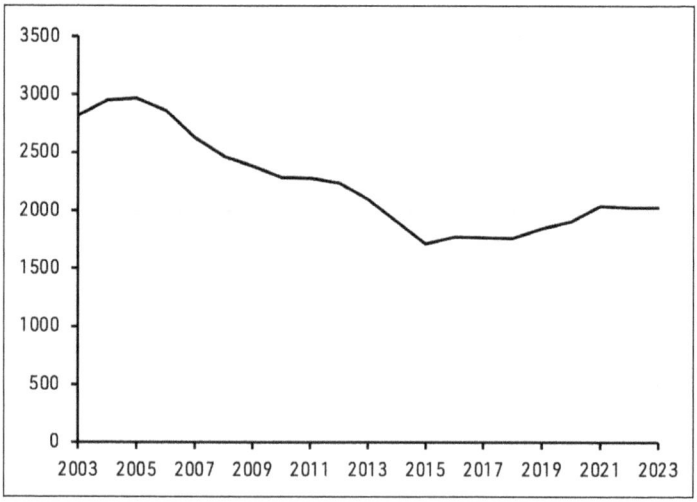

Source: Berkshire Hathaway annual reports.

Then the Great Recession hit. Buffett acknowledged that every Berkshire business connected to residential and commercial construction "suffered severely" in 2009.[386] Remarkably, Benjamin Moore was one of the Berkshire companies in which "profits improved even as sales contracted, always an exceptional managerial achievement".[387]

But that positive situation did not last for long, as Benjamin Moore ran into a crisis entirely of its own making. Abrams, formerly COO, had become CEO in July 2007. He had joined the company in 1995 as a relative neophyte compared with most senior managers when his family business was sold to Benjamin Moore (Yvan Dupuy relinquished the role of CEO but remained as chairman).

Abrams was described as having an "ambitious, impatient temperament"[388] and thought that Benjamin Moore was too constrained by its distribution approach, given that the larger chains of retailers were selling ever more paint. Sales to the big boxes would introduce the brand to new customers, who would surely be impressed by the quality and then buy directly from Moore's dealers – or so the thinking went.

In early 2012, Abrams forged an agreement to supply the company's paint to the 87-store Orchard Supply Hardware and was busy trying to hammer out a deal with home-improvement giant Lowe's – which would have the side effect of undermining the company's independent retail network. This frustrated longstanding employees, who were concerned that sales and market share established through the tried-and-tested routes would fall. But Abrams was adamant: "He told everybody [top executives] to come back to him with reasons why they shouldn't do a Lowe's deal."[389]

Abrams was also accused of strongarming retailers into exclusive distribution deals. "These were family-owned businesses, a lot of them were my friends,"[390] said Rod Mangan, an ex-regional sales manager in Stuart, Florida, who was fired after 31 years at the company. "I used to call them the 'Paint Nazis,'" revealed Frank Harrelson, a Charlotte, North Carolina dealer who ended a 32-year relationship with Benjamin Moore after sales representatives demanded that he throw competing brands out of his store. "You hate to see them coming in the front door."[391]

To rub salt in the wounds of the distributors, the company also began selling paint through its own website, bypassing them further. The ensuing outcry resulted in a modification so that customers who bought online would pick up their purchases from a Benjamin Moore dealer.

One former executive told *The New York Post* that Abrams routinely referred to himself as a "dictator" as he threatened dissenting workers with redundancy. He was accused of meeting his ambitious targets by slashing the sales workforce and the advertising budget, which further eroded revenues and market share.

Unit sales were dropping as price hikes were implemented at a time of recession; and by 2012, sales (excluding acquisitions) were half the peak of $1.1 billion achieved in 2005.[392] But profits still seemed acceptable to Buffett, who was initially unaware of the changes going on at the company – after all, he is famously hands-off. "The numbers looked fine," says Buffett. "That was the problem."[393]

But then dealers started to call Berkshire to complain. When Buffett caught wind of the impending Lowe's deal, he was shocked. Such a move "would have been a complete breach of faith in terms of what I promised them. [So I] made a change".[394] On 14 June 2012, Abrams was escorted from Benjamin Moore's headquarters in Montvale, New Jersey, during a surprise visit from half-a-dozen Berkshire officials.

The rumours among staff, and in a tabloid press story doing the rounds, were that Abrams was sacked because of the amount of company money he had spent on a yacht party in Bermuda in mid-2012 for top executives to celebrate the company's first quarterly sales increase since 2007. The trip had upset the rank-and-file, who had suffered five years of layoffs, reduced commissions and frozen salaries.

On 21 June 2012, Buffett wrote an open letter to Abrams stating: "The recent story coupling a top management convocation on a boat with the decision to make a management change at Benjamin Moore is completely false." He insisted that he would have had "no objection at all" to the party had he been asked about it beforehand, and "there was no reason" to let him know about the event in advance. Then he gave the real reason for Abrams' removal: "a differing view about distribution channels and brand strategy ... It was a decision of key importance and therefore one I needed to make".[395] Buffett elaborated in an interview with Fox Business Network: "We [are] not in the big-box stores nor will we [be] ... We won't hurt our distributors."[396]

It was quite a setback. *Fortune Magazine* reported that Benjamin Moore's revenues rose "a cumulative 40% between 1999 and 2013, while competitors Sherwin Williams and Valspar boosted their revenues, 104% and 196%, respectively".[397] Despite the slow growth in sales, Benjamin Moore made $107 million in profits in 2013.

"We put a lot of trust in people," said Buffett. "And I think when you put trust in people, you get more out of them."[398] Buffett's success with so many other companies suggests that this strategy is generally correct, but clearly the freedom he gives can sometimes backfire.

Buffett's financial assistant, Tracy Britt Cool, aged 29, was asked to recruit a new CEO in the summer of 2012. Cool had recently graduated from Harvard Business School when she joined Berkshire in 2009. Within five years, she was chairman of four Berkshire Hathaway companies (Larson-Juhl, Johns Manville, Oriental Trading Company and Benjamin Moore), and sat on Heinz's board.

Cool recruited Robert Merritt, a former CFO of Outback Steakhouse. He was the husband of Cool's former mentor. Buffett didn't feel the need to interview Merritt: "We looked at his background and everything ... and he seems okay to me."[399]

Merritt went in hard, firing company veterans. He was seen by some as antagonistic and "disrespectful of the company's culture and history";[400] but he also sought to repair relationships with dealers.

In 2013, Buffett stood in for Cool's late father and walked her down the aisle at her wedding. That year, *The New York Post* reported that Merritt was being accused of harassing female employees with dirty jokes, which he denied. Nevertheless, he was let go after just 15 months – a rare second ousting for Buffett.

At the May 2013 Berkshire Hathaway annual meeting, Buffett reflected on the problems he had experienced with this investment:

… at the high end it is the best regarded paint. And we have not lost position in that respect. But when we purchased Benjamin Moore I made a promise. It had a dealer system. People had invested their savings and pensions, and passed on from generation-to-generation dealerships from Benjamin Moore and counted on the company adhering to a dealer system. Even though you could get a huge jump in volume in the first year if you went with big-boxes … they would have loved us to have as a brand, with that kind of identity, in their stores.

But … I don't think it would have worked out as well over time; and I know I would have been essentially, particularly after my pledge, which the management pledged too – there would have been double crossing a network of dealers that had trusted us to continue with the policy.

Dealer policy will work with a first class brand like Benjamin Moore. It will never have the kind of market share as will a Behr, which is distributed through Home Depot. But the company was actually investigating, and went on its way to implementing, some moves that would've, in effect, gutted, or we felt would drastically hurt the dealers and violate the pledge that I'd made to them back when we bought it.

On the day of his son's wedding, Mike Searles – the former CEO of Wilson's Leather – received a call asking if he might be interested in being interviewed for the position of CEO of Benjamin Moore. The prospect excited him so much that he skipped the morning-after breakfast to fly to Omaha to talk with Cool and Buffett. Searles told Buffett that he had admired him for years and had kept in each office he had occupied a framed version of Buffett's aphorism: "I try to buy stock in businesses that are so wonderful that an idiot can run them. Because sooner or later, one will." Once CEO, Searles decided not to put up the 'idiot' quote because "it feels too personal",[401] he said with a laugh.

Searles pointed out that while Benjamin Moore hadn't actually broken Buffett's promise to the independent dealers, it had come close to doing so, and this had caused a loss of trust. It took years to regain the confidence of its dealers. During his five years at the company, he made good progress, increasing the marketing budget, opening stores and recruiting new dealers. "It's like having a breakup with your girlfriend," Buffett said. "It takes you some time to repair the relationship."[402]

In Searles' view, being part of the Berkshire family was a blessing:

> Working for Berkshire and working for Warren is difficult to describe. I've worked in public companies all my life. Working for Warren, working for Berkshire is so unique in that it's hands off. You're constantly focused on the future. The business decisions are not made because of a day or a month or a quarter. They're about the long-term sustainability of the company.[403]

Buffett assisted the restoration of retailer faith by making a new video in which he recommitted to operating through the network: "We came close to violating that pledge, and it'll never happen again."[404]

Buffett understood that Benjamin Moore had carved a niche in the market as a high-end product – what he called "the best paint out there".[405] He added:

> They're not the paint for everybody. We're not in, and we won't be in, the low-priced paint set … We will not be the top ever in market share. The mass market is going to be bigger than the high-end market. But there will always be a high-end market.[406]

Buffett drew an analogy:

> If you go back to the mid-1930s, Packard was an aspirational auto brand. It was above Cadillac. Around 1936 they came out with a considerably lower-priced model. It did wonders for them immediately, but they destroyed the brand over time. If you're a high-end brand, you can always pick up a lot of sales by dropping down. I'm not saying that's what Valspar does; they probably have a bunch of different brands that are doing that. But it would be a big mistake for Benjamin Moore to try and take the Benjamin Moore name downscale and have a cheaper paint.[407]

If there's one thing we need to acknowledge about being an investor, warned Buffett, it's that you will make many errors: "I've made plenty of mistakes. I'm making them right now. I'll make more. It's the nature of things. We don't want to break promises."

And if this commitment limited Benjamin Moore's growth? "We'll stick with the promise," insisted Buffett. "Whether we make or lose money in [a] business is not necessarily in our control, but we can be held accountable for sticking to our promises."[408]

Interviewed by CNBC in 2013, Buffett indicated that the ship was being righted, adding: "Incidentally, Benjamin Moore is making a lot of money."[409] *The New York Post* reported that Buffett had "boasted that Benjamin Moore has raked in $1.5 billion in profits over the past decade despite the housing crash".[410] To make good profits, it is not always necessary to have sales growth – just ask See's Candies managers, who have not noticeably increased the number of stores since it was bought in the early 1970s (see Volume 1, Investment 20). In the case of Benjamin Moore, profits were good, despite falling sales and employee numbers dropping from almost 3,000 in 2005 to 1,715 ten years later – an example of a company focus on profits resulting in few labour costs and lower turnover (a concept that many managers find difficult to conceive).

A recovery in the mid-2010s saw employee numbers rise a little, helped by an expansion in the number of independent retailers, with over 5,000 storefronts in the network. In 2019, Cool resigned as chairman at Benjamin Moore with the intention of launching her own investment group acquiring and building businesses, similar to Berkshire. Also in 2019, Searles retired and 32-year veteran Dan Calkins took over as president and COO, reporting to Berkshire vice chairman Greg Abel. "Benjamin Moore & Co. has long established itself as an industry leader, and under Dan Calkins' guidance, we believe they are primed for an accelerated trajectory into the future," said Abel.[411] Calkin was particularly proud of the brand's growing architect and designer customer base.

Benjamin Moore enjoyed a further boost in 2019 when Ace Hardware Stores expanded its relationship with the company by naming it the preferred paint supplier for approximately 3,300 Ace stores. Participating stores carried either a full-line premium assortment of Benjamin Moore products or a streamlined collection. Benjamin

Moore also assumed responsibility for manufacturing a couple of Ace's private label paint brands.

The relationship with Ace has since deepened and as a result, Benjamin Moore now has 8,000 independently owned and operated paint and decorating and hardware retailers, of which approximately 3,800 are Ace Hardware stores in the United States and Canada, as well as 75 countries globally.

However, the fact that the company has only slightly over 2,000 employees today, compared with 2,968 in 2005, suggests that there has been limited volume growth over the past 20 years (or exceptional productivity improvements). Nonetheless, the brand remains strong and continues to exploit its valuable niche.

Learning points

- **Never lose one ounce of integrity**. Buffett was angry with the actions of the senior team when they made moves to break his word to retail partners. The company had made a binding commitment – whether or not it was in writing – that it would continue to supply the market through its network of distributors and not through big-box stores.
- **Short-term sales and profits may be enhanced by selling to large customers, but care is needed to ensure that this strategic move brings long-term shareholder value**. Big-box retailers, for example, will beat suppliers on price sooner or later, unless they offer a 'must-have' product line (and there are not many of those).
- **Product differentiation is often more important than volume**. If return on capital employed is the objective, then low or zero growth in sales is often the way to go if this strategy permits pricing power in niches (e.g., premium paint at premium prices).

Investment 12

CTB INTERNATIONAL

Summary of the deal

Deal	CTB International
Time	October 2002
Price paid	$140 million
Proportion of equity	100%
Status	Still held

CTB started out in the 1950s, when entrepreneur Howard S Brembeck sought to reduce the burdens on chicken farmers. His products made it easier to do the daily farm chores, so he called his first company Chore-Time – hence the first two letters in CTB. The 'B' came when Brembeck set up a separate company, Brock, to produce storage hoppers for grain. The two companies united in 1976.

Brembeck's founding mission still pertains today: to make life easier for livestock farmers. But worldwide annual sales now top $1 billion and the range of equipment that the company provides to farmers is very broad, from pigpens to computer software and food processing equipment. At its heart, we have here an unassuming business manufacturing everyday bulky items, built on low-cost strategic positioning plus a degree of innovation and branding. While the company cannot charge bargain-hunting farmers a premium price for differentiated products, its "top-flight management", as Warren Buffett called them, nonetheless produce impressive profits.

Buffett agreed to pay $140 million for CTB in 2002 after it had reported annual net income of $14.2 million. It took less than eight years for CTB to return everything Berkshire had paid for it and more: by the end of 2010, it had handed over $160 million in dividends to Berkshire Hathaway and had eliminated the $40 million of debt it was carrying. In 2010 alone, the company earned $106 million pre-tax.

And things just kept getting better: in 2011, CTB distributed another $20 million, after earning $124 million pre-tax that year. Despite handing over so much, it still held $109 million in cash at year-end. So, even if we assumed a failure to produce profits since 2011, we could surmise that this has been one of Buffett's best investments. And in any case, that assumption would be wrong, because Buffett has hinted that the company is making a good income, albeit without providing numbers.

An innovative founder

In 1930, Brembeck was in his first year at the University of Chicago, majoring in economics. The country was reeling from the Wall Street Crash and the first rumblings of the Great Depression had begun to reverberate. Back home in Urbana, Indiana, the Brembecks lost their life savings when the bank in which the money had been deposited collapsed. The family owned a hardware store in Urbana[412] which, of course, was hurt by the Depression. Brembeck quit university and moved back home to help out.

In July 1931, Brembeck attended the first international poultry show in Detroit. There he met up with his mother's cousin, who owned an Urbana-based manufacturer of agricultural spreaders – machines which spread seeds and fertilisers.[413] He offered the 21-year-old Brembeck an apprenticeship at $5 per week. With jobs difficult to come by, Brembeck accepted: "It was probably the best deal I ever made in my life, for Mr. Speicher did more for me than he promised. He did his best to teach me how to become a manufacturer," he told the *Poultry Times* in 1994.[414]

The company, Cyclone, made canvas bags with hand cranks that farmers could turn to scatter feed and fertilisers. While the device was simple, the process through which it was made taught Brembeck a great deal about supply chain management, product design, accounting, sales and management. He absorbed all this and duly ascended to the position of general manager.

Brembeck's talent was spotted by a farm implement distributor in Alliance, Ohio, 440 miles east of Urbana, who promptly poached him. Thus, in 1944, he and his young family[415] moved to Alliance. He regularly met with farmers to discuss their problems, most of which related to their backbreaking daily routines. He thought long and hard about innovations that might help to reduce this burden.

As Brembeck grew in confidence, he itched to strike out on his own; he had already thought of ways to feed and water chickens more efficiently. Eventually, one day in 1952, he woke "in the darkness of early morning", driven "in a very powerful and personal way" to start a business: "I felt compelled to take action … It was almost as if I didn't have any choice in the matter."[416] He heeded the call and duly established his own firm.

The basement of the Brembeck family home in Alliance was the manufacturing hub of this enterprise for the first two years. There was a lot of galvanised steel around the place as tall circular feeders to hold grain were made. Because his aim was to reduce the labour-intensiveness of chicken farming, he called his company Chore-Time Equipment Inc.

In 1954, Brembeck moved his business to Milford in his home state of Indiana, about 37 miles from his childhood home. Today, there is a sprawling Chore-Time factory in Milford that takes up a good proportion of this small town (population 950 in 1952; 1,600 today). His products caught on fast and by 1955, sales had reached over $100,000.

While the feeders he produced significantly improved the lives of poultry farmers, Brembeck was not entirely satisfied with the design. "I still thought there had to be a more efficient way to feed chickens," he explained in an August 2000 interview with the *Indianapolis Star*.[417] He came up with all sorts of feeders and put them into production during the 1950s: for broilers, for turkeys and a monoline feeder. He also developed other product lines, such as egg washers and drink fountains for poultry.

In 1957, Brembeck started manufacturing small hopper bins for the bulk storage of feed. This business was first set up as a separate company in Milford, called Brock Manufacturing Inc.

A real breakthrough was the introduction of the Flex-Auger feed delivery system in 1961. This was a large metal spiral within a flexible tube (an Archimedes' screw) that, when turned by a motor, transported grain from a storage bin dozens of feet away. It could bend around corners and go up or down. It saved farmers from having to lug animal feed around in bulk bags.

Chore-Time continued to pump out innovations in feeders and related items – more than 100 patents were filed over the years. A major extension to the range at Brock was the introduction of grain storage bins in 1964. These were much bigger than the feed bins – often larger than several houses. Today, these enormous rounded-steel drums can be seen dotted around the rural landscape, shining in the sun.

And then came international expansion, with the establishment of the company's first European office, in Belgium, in 1967. Brembeck partnered with a longstanding employee, Forrest Lee Ramser, to create Chore-Time's European manufacturing and marketing base, which offered similar feeding and storage equipment to the Indiana operation. In particular, it brought the first feeder pans for broilers and 'centreless flexible augers' to Europe.

By combining Chore-Time and Brock in 1976, cost savings were realised in a number of departments. However, the separate trade names were retained because they had so much value in the marketplace. It then made sense to create three parts to the business, so that staff could concentrate on particular customer segments:

- products for poultry/egg producers;
- grain-related products, and;
- products for pig producers.

Also in 1976, Brembeck's daughter, Caryl Chocola, joined the board of directors, aged 38. She lived with her family over 150 miles away in

Michigan, where she taught art classes and owned an art shop. While not a full-timer at the company, she makes a significant contribution by developing ideas for the vinyl fence part of the business. Chocola was a keen horsewoman in a cold part of the country. PVC fencing works well in the cold, because it is longer lasting than wood. Chocola would experiment with lengths of PVC pipe to fence off her horses in the fields.

The 1980s saw the emergence of a major exporting business from Milford, called Chore-Time/Brock International. The European business was sold to Ramser, who changed its name to Roxell (an amalgam of 'rock', indicating solidity, and 'excellence', the aim for all activities). Roxell went on to buy a number of European companies focused on manufacturing poultry and swine rearing gear. It too expanded into many countries, including the United States in 1991 and later Brazil. After operating separately for 14 years, in 1999 Roxell was finally brought back into the CTB fold. But Milford HQ had to pay up for its former offspring: the price was $39 million in cash (by then, Roxell had sales of $41 million and net income of $1.9 million).

Buyout

By the early 1990s, annual sales had hit $100 million. As well as expanding Chore-Time and Brock plants in Milford, CTB opened a production facility and warehouse in Uruguay to serve the major countries of South America.

In July 1993, Chris Chocola – son of Caryl – became executive vice-president of CTB. He advanced pretty quickly, rising to the post of CEO the following March. A law major, he had worked at the firm as the company's counsel since graduating in 1988.

Brembeck retired from CTB at the end of 1995, aged 85. At the International Poultry Exposition in Atlanta that year, some 1,500 people gathered to honour him. Chris Chocola gave a keynote address thanking Brembeck for his "achievements and accomplishments", adding that CTB had recorded its strongest sales year ever in 1994 and had launched a 52,000-square-foot expansion to the Milford plant. He said:

We believe the most important action we can take is to continue to pursue the prime goal of Howard Brembeck set when he founded Chore Time-Brock. That goal, 'to make systems for the case of poultry and livestock that users consider the best in the world'. Like other innovators who have had a major influence on their respective fields, Howard Brembeck's innovations have had a profound effect on the shaping of the modern poultry industry ... Businesses need a strong foundation on which to stand in the winds of change. For CTB, a dedication to product leadership with its focus on customer needs will serve as our anchor.[418]

Family control of the company was diluted a few months later when, in January 1996, New York-based private equity firm American Securities Capital Partners bought a controlling stake. However, the Brembeck family, led by Caryl and Chris Chocola, both retained a minority holding and Chris remained as the company's president and CEO.

To enable further growth in 1997, CTB made an IPO of common stock on the Nasdaq stock market. Five million shares were sold to investors at $14 each, raising $70 million in the offering. The shares sold represented just under 40% of the total number of shares, indicating a market capitalisation of slightly less than $175 million. That still left American Securities owning a controlling interest of roughly two-fifths of the ordinary shares. By then, sales were over $200 million and net income $13.9 million.

Acquisitions came thick and fast:

- **Butler Manufacturing**: This Kansas City company – a pioneer in the grain bin business – sold its grain bin division to CTB in 1997. This allowed Butler dealers to sell CTB bins within an expanded region. CTB's primary grain bin business was stronger in the east, but Butler's focus was on the western grain belt. In addition, the deal extended the range of products offered, providing economies of scope – Butler's bins came in different shapes and sizes from CTB's line. Also, a second bin manufacturing plant was brought into the group, doubling the company's grain business.

- **Fancom BV**: This manufacturer and marketer of agricultural computerised climate-controls and software for poultry and livestock was located in the Netherlands, with a subsidiary in France. It was acquired in 1997.
- **Rota Industria de Maquinas Agricolas**: In 1998, this Brazilian manufacturing company entered into a joint venture with CTB, called Rota Brock, to produce commercial grain storage silos, feed bins and grain- and seed-handling equipment.
- **Sibley Industries**: Bought in 1998, Sibley manufactures brooders and heaters and is located in Anderson, Missouri.
- **STACO**: Shaefferstown, Pennsylvania-based STACO – a producer of pig feeders, ventilation products and other swine-rearing equipment – was acquired in 1998.
- **Roxell, NV**: As discussed previously, this company was brought back into the CTB fold in 1999.
- **ABC Industries**: Some assets of ABC Industries, a maker of grain-handling equipment, were bought in 2000. These included patents, trademarks and trade names for a line of products manufactured and marketed by ABC Industries. The company manufactured dry-bulk-handling equipment and dust-control devices; bin sweeps for use in grain-bin unloading; a dust-control product used in grain and industrial receiving facilities; and a line of bucket elevators and conveyors used to move grain.

Trouble comes

But the late 1990s were difficult for CTB. It had to withstand a major downturn in the US hog industry, which hit in 1998; as prices dropped lower than they had been in decades, farmers were reluctant to invest in capital equipment. That same year, the Asian economic crisis affected many of the company's overseas markets, especially Brazil – as a result, Brazilian joint venture Rota Brock was soon dissolved, before it had even started manufacturing. Then, in 1999, there was a softening in the egg market.

This combination of domestic and foreign woes caused net income to deteriorate by 34%, from $13.9 million in 1997 to $9.2 million in 1998. Profits recovered a little in 1999 to $10.2 million on net sales of $273 million.

Having long held political ambitions, Chris Chocola resigned as CEO in April 1999 to become chairman of the board, before running for Congress in 2000. Although he lost to the Democrat candidate at the time, on his second attempt in 2002 he was elected as the US representative for Indiana's second congressional district.

Victor A Mancinelli joined the company in 1999 as president and CEO. The holder of a mathematics degree and an MBA, Mancinelli was already a veteran of the agricultural manufacturing industry, having spent the previous seven years as executive vice-president and COO of Gehl Company, a manufacturer of construction and agricultural equipment used by dairy and livestock farmers. He was also appointed as company chairman in 2014 and still holds both positions today.

Back in 1999, Mancinelli had some tough decisions to make. A streamlining plan was put in place to improve efficiency and reduce costs. For example, the Milford employee count was cut by 12% (support, sales and administrative positions were lost), and Fancom in the Netherlands shed nearly 20% of its staff. Plant layouts were improved and new manufacturing techniques introduced. Perhaps most significantly, most employees were placed into one of three business units, each focused on serving specific customer groups:

- the protein group (equipment for the production of pork, poultry and eggs, primarily in the United States and Canada);
- the grain group (products for the storage, handling and conditioning of grain, primarily in the United States and Canada); and
- the international group (all product lines).

At first, sales fell – not least because the vinyl products business was sold, but also because the company was now focused on holding on to profitable activity while cutting out empty sales. Group sales, which stood at $273 million in 1999, dropped to $233 million in 2001. While sales fell, profits rose from $10.2 million after tax in 1999 to $14.2 million in 2001.

Today, the Mancinelli-led strategy of the firm is expressed as follows:

- Emerge as the best-cost manufacturer.
- Emphasise a product-driven focus.
- Expand global physical presence.
- Fortify through acquisition.
- Enhance financial strength.

The first two points above represent the core of the strategy, with the first ensuring competitive edge for the products that emerge from the second. This is a low-cost strategy with some degree of incremental innovation, rather than a highly differentiated strategy allowing for large gaps between sales price and marginal cost of production. Farmers are tough customers – they will go elsewhere if CTB does not supply good products at low prices – so efficiency is vital.

The deal

Trading on the Nasdaq was not working well for CTB, in the opinion of its directors. Mancinelli echoed the complaints of many small companies: "As a small-capitalization, public company with limited research coverage, we were not widely followed by public market investors."[419] He was frustrated by having such limited access to capital to support the firm's longer-term growth strategy. Michael Fisch, president of American Securities, the 42% shareholder, said that because the stock was very thinly traded, with a small float, "if any investor buys or sells even a small block of stock, as has happened, the stock price can move materially".[420]

During 2000 and 2001, CTB's shares had traded in the depressingly low range of $6.19 to $11.50 – far less than the $14 at the time of the IPO in 1997. Market sentiment was not helped by the company's failure to pay a dividend on its common stock and a statement in its 2002 accounts that it "does not anticipate paying any dividends in the foreseeable future, and intends to retain all earnings, if any, for general corporate purposes … the company's credit agreement contains certain restrictions on CTB's ability to pay dividends".

Investment 12. CTB International

In March 2002, the directors announced that they had hired financial advisers "to develop strategic alternatives … to enhance shareholder value … These alternatives may include a merger or sale of the company".[421] In anticipation that CTB might find a buyer willing to pay a generous price, for a month or so its shares traded in the range of $15 to $18.50. But Nasdaq then suffered a substantial decline, down over 27% in four months. CTB's shares fell below $11 in July as it reported poor second-quarter numbers.[422]

Buffett saw that CTB was "a strong company with great American values. It has an excellent franchise, strong market share in a basic industry and top-flight management".[423] In Mancinelli, it had a manager who had chalked up an "impressive record".[424] Buffett was fully aware that CTB operated in an industry characterised by "tough economics", but it also had "important competitive strength [enabling the firm] to earn decent returns on capital".[425]

The deal agreed with Berkshire Hathaway in August was for CTB shareholders to receive $12.75 per share in cash for all the shares. The total value of the transaction, including roughly $40 million of assumed debt, was approximately $180 million. The equity portion was $12.75 × 10.952 shares = $139.6 million.

Just before the deal was announced, on 19 August 2002, the shares traded up to $14.67, so the question was raised in the press as to why the directors thought that $12.75 was fair. "The deal enables us to find an outstanding permanent home for this business,"[426] said Mancinelli in a statement. "It's good for our customers, our loyal employees and managers, and the local communities in which we operate, as well as providing an assured return on our shareholders' investments."[427] He was looking forward to expanding the business under the Berkshire umbrella, both organically and through a series of acquisitions.

American Securities, the Chocola family and certain members of management had agreed to accept the deal offered by Berkshire before the announcement. Taken together, they controlled more than 55% of the shares. Meanwhile, Fisch was pleased with the outcome for American Securities clients: "At the $12.75 acquisition price, our partners will achieve a very substantial return on their initial investment."[428] These private equity guys had also been hurt by the decline in share prices generally following the dot-com bust of 2000, so to get out of CTB at a profit during the post-bubble malaise was considered impressive.

The takeover was completed on 31 October 2002. Following the announcement, one anonymous wag observed: "First we have Charlie getting into women's underwear [a reference to the purchase of Fruit of the Loom in 2002]. Now Warren goes for cute chicks and a pig that does not need any lipstick."[429]

The shape of the business bought – some numbers

By 2002, CTB – which employed 1,100 people – was supplying complete systems for farmers looking after chickens and hogs, from grain storage to augers moving grain, feeders and in-house climate control. CTB also supplied water drinkers, ventilation gear, mechanical nests, roller belt conveyors, fans and heaters for grain conditioning, software and seed-handling equipment.

It sold its products primarily through a network of independent distributors/dealers who offered targeted geographic coverage in key poultry-, hog-, egg- and grain-producing markets throughout the world. The distributors/dealers provided technical support and services to end users and maintained warehouse facilities for systems and spare parts. CTB ensured through its training system that this network could provide end customers with a good installation package and subsequent quality servicing.

While the company made much of its intellectual property portfolio, affording a degree of competitive shielding in terms of design and customer recognition, it remained the case that "the market for the company's products is competitive",[430] so price was vitally important in attracting and retaining customers. Despite this fact, the company had a competitive advantage in areas such as reputation and customer service. Also, its ability to offer integrated systems to poultry, egg and hog producers, thus reducing overall costs, gave it a further competitive edge.

We can gain some insight into what Warren Buffett saw in CTB's numbers in 2002 by looking at Figures 12.1 and 12.2. The most recent annual net income was $14.2 million, so Berkshire paid a PER of around ten. Taking a longer-term perspective, we could use average earnings per share over the five years, which gives a PER of $12.75 ÷ $1.11 = 11.5 – hardly expensive if there is a reasonable chance of these earnings levels at least being maintained.

Figure 12.1 CTB, sales and profits 1997–2001 ($m)

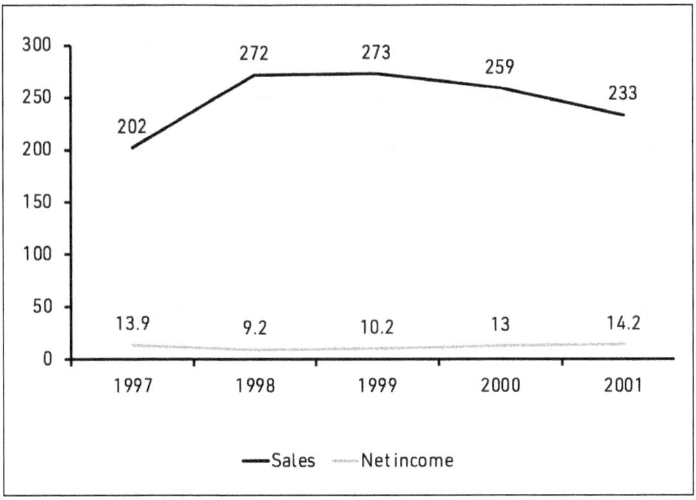

Year	Sales	Net income
1997	202	13.9
1998	272	9.2
1999	273	10.2
2000	259	13
2001	233	14.2

Source: CTB International Corporation Form 10-K 2001.

Figure 12.2 CTB earnings per share ($)

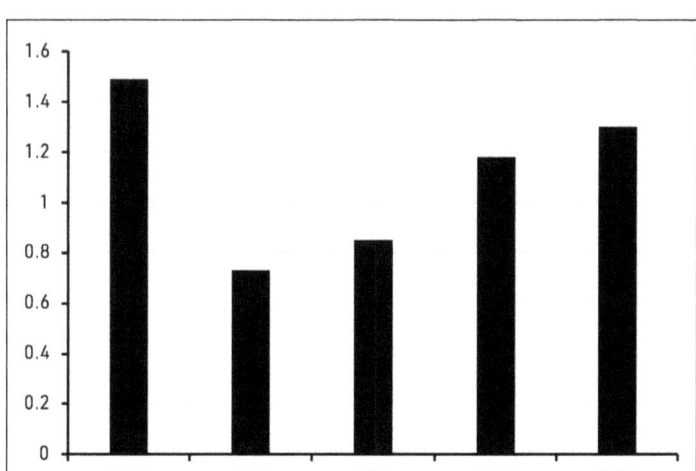

Source: CTB International Corporation Form 10-K 2001.

The managers of CTB kept capital committed to the business at relatively low levels, at around $100 million for shareholders and $40 million from lenders (see Table 12.1).

Table 12.1 Balance-sheet summary ($m)

	June 2002	Dec 2001	Dec 2000	Dec 1999	Dec 1998	Dec 1997
Working capital	30.8	23.9	28.9	29.8	40.9	26.3
Total assets	194	178	195	208	195	167
Debt	40	38	63	78	71	49
Total shareholders' equity	103	99	87	81	77	74
Total shareholders' equity after excluding intangible assets (mostly goodwill)	30	22	5			

Source: CTB International Corporation Form 10-K 2001 and quarterly report Form 10-Q to June 2002.

Profits as a percentage of shareholders' funds were respectable – for example, 15.3% for 2001 ($14.2 million of net income divided by average shareholder funds over 2001 of (99 + 87) ÷ 2 = 93).

But the really interesting statistics were the returns that managers were achieving on the net assets they actually had to use. To explain: most of the shareholders' funds figures consisted of goodwill from acquisitions – that is, when a company is bought for, say, $15 million but it only has $5 million of identifiable (tangible assets), the remaining $10 million goes into the balance sheet as 'goodwill'. The managers only have the tangible assets to work with – the extra $10 million has gone into the pockets of the selling shareholders. If we deduct the goodwill and other intangible assets from the shareholders' funds figures to gain an idea of what the managers were actually working with, we find very small numbers – for example, for June 2002, this was $30 million. The returns on net tangible assets were thus very large percentages – for example, 105% for 2001 ($14.2 million divided by ($22 million + $5 million) ÷ 2). On the other hand, you could say that the managers used shareholder money to buy that goodwill, so this use of capital should not be ignored.

CTB sales were pretty evenly split across the three divisions, as were operating profits (see Figure 12.3).

Figure 12.3 CTB divisional sales and profits, 2001 ($m)

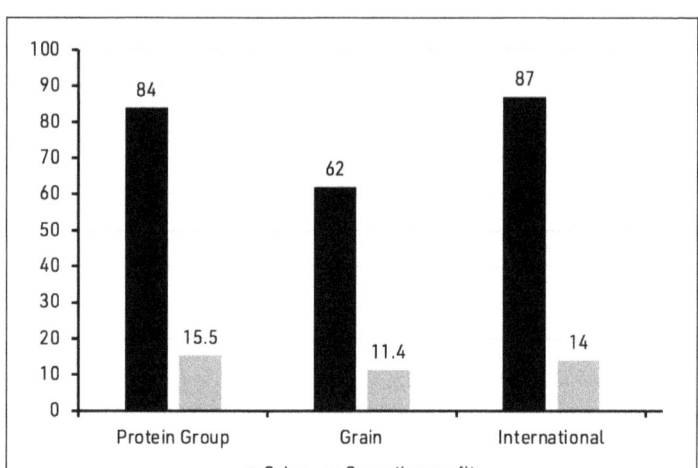

Source: CTB International Corporation Form 10-K 2001.

The company's home market of America remained by far the largest destination for its products (see Figure 12.4).

Figure 12.4 Sales by destination, 2001 ($m)

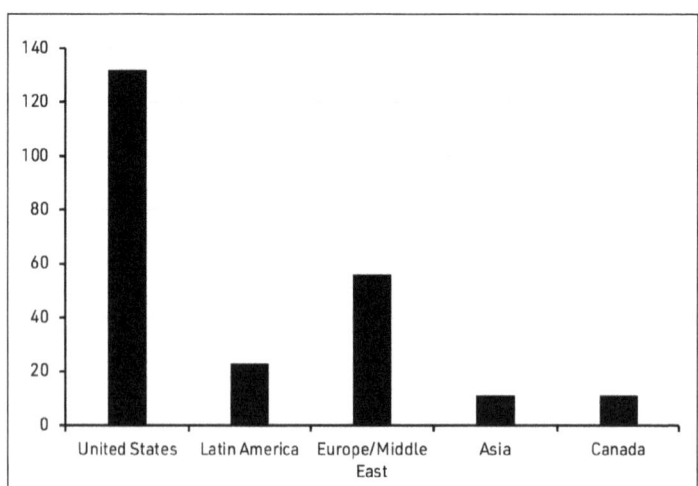

Source: CTB International Corporation Form 10-K 2001.

What happened afterwards?

Mancinelli told Bloomberg News that he typically approaches Buffett when an idea for a deal "picks up steam". He said that Buffett can usually see immediately whether the proposal is rational and can then act fast to help the CTB team if needed. "He's so quick and he understands business so well that what could take hours or days for someone else" takes just minutes, said Mancinelli: "When things come together just correctly, we pounce."[431]

Table 12.2 lists the acquisitions and other major business deals executed by CTB between 2002 and 2010. The sheer volume of activity is striking. Also, while CTB managers sometimes bought entire corporations, they often shrewdly purchased only those specific parts of a business that they were interested in. This not only meant that CTB did not need to deal with units outside its core strategy, but also avoided many explicit or hidden hazards, such as legal liabilities, lease liabilities and less-than-ideal personnel.

In most cases, economies of either scope or scale were very obvious, allowing CTB to offer customers a more complete package or to reduce the cost per unit of output, respectively.

And the company stayed within its circle of competence, buying into product lines and markets with which it was familiar or in adjacent sectors. The managers at CTB would have known many of the people brought on board and therefore could more easily assess their strengths. In many cases, the key people – often entrepreneurial founders – were persuaded to stay on and work under CTB's ownership.

Table 12.2 Major acquisitions and advances, 2002–2010

Year	Company	Bought	Products	Reason
2002	European logistics centre **Chore-Time Europe** established, with locations in the Netherlands and Poland.	Purchased a controlling interest in **Veldmaster BV**, a master distributor in the Netherlands for CTB.	Primarily selling CTB's products for raising poultry throughout Europe, the Middle East and in northern Africa.	Customers can be served quicker and can purchase less than a container load. Reduced tariffs and use of more European components.
2002	**Beard Industries** of Frankfort, Indiana.	Substantially all of the operating assets.	Grain dryer manufacturer and electronic grain-drying controls.	Annual sales of approximately $7 million and about 40 people. Provides grain industry customers with a more complete product package.
2002	**Shenandoah Manufacturing** of Harrisonburg, Virginia.	Substantially all the assets – that is, production machinery, patents, trademarks and trade names.	Manufacturer of poultry heaters, nests, incinerators and commercial heating products.	Acquired the 'leading line' of poultry heaters, nests and incinerators with sales of $15 million. Operational synergies achieved by relocating Shenandoah's poultry heater and nest manufacturing to CTB's Missouri plant, where existing lines of heating systems are made.

Investment 12. CTB International

Year	Company	Bought	Products	Reason
2002	**Jay-Dee Industries** of Dassel, Minnesota.	Minority stake in Jay-Dee, but bought outright poultry nest-related assets: patents, production machinery, trademarks and trade names.	Poultry nest manufacturing.	Synergies achieved by transferring production of Jay-Dee nests to CTB's Missouri plant. Benefit from Jay-Dee's manufacturing. Able to use the Dassal facility to manufacture Shenandoah poultry incinerators and waste-oil heaters.
2004	**Swine Service Specialists** of Lyons, Nebraska.	Substantially all of the assets: machinery and equipment, designs, trademarks and trade names.	Manufacturer of pig-feeding equipment.	Synergies achieved through transferring manufacture and marketing to CTB Milford. Extended the CTB package for the hog industry.
2006	**Yan Agro Logic**, Israel.	A controlling interest bought by CTB. Founders retained an interest and continued as co-managing directors.	Manufacturer of climate controllers, feed and poultry weighing systems and other integrated systems. Almost all sales were to the Far East (none to the US).	To leverage existing global sales channels along with CTB's extensive distribution to further penetrate key markets worldwide. Its cost-efficient designs complement CTB's array of products. Its tech can be employed elsewhere in the business.

Year	Company	Bought	Products	Reason
2007	**Porcon Beheer BV,** the Netherlands.	Acquired the company.	Designer, manufacturer and marketer of equipment for the care and raising of pigs – including stalls, crates and pens – packaged with a variety of other equipment to offer customers system solutions.	Continued to manufacture in Porcon's facilities while leveraging existing global business sales channels to increase CTB's presence in the worldwide pig-production equipment market. Expanded line of products. Tapped into expertise at Porcon.
2007	**Laake GmbH,** Germany.	Acquired the company.	Designer, manufacturer and marketer of sow gestation and farrowing stalls, including free-access gestation stalls. Also stables, paddock doors and feeders for the equine market.	To leverage CTB's existing global business sales channels to increase its presence in the worldwide hog-production equipment market. CTB had previously marketed Laake's sow stalls in the US and Canada. Able to enter the equine market. 45,000-square-foot manufacturing facility useful.
2008	**B Mannebeck Landtechnik GmbH,** Germany (with a facility in Poland).	Acquired the company.	Designer, manufacturer and marketer of equipment for pig production (e.g., electronic sow-feeding and other feeding systems, animal-friendly stalls and crates, and plastic flooring for piglets and sows).	To tap into Mannebeck's original designs and its ongoing commitment to R&D and additional innovations. Mannebeck could exploit CTB's worldwide distribution network and other resources.

Investment 12. CTB International

Year	Company	Bought	Products	Reason
2008	**Uniqfill International BV**, the Netherlands.	Acquired the company.	Designer of chemical and combination chemical/biological air scrubbers for animal livestock and other applications (used to remove ammonia, undesirable odours and particulate matter from the air before it exits a pig house, poultry house, etc.).	Knowledge of this technology brought into the firm to expand its offering. CTB's money and infrastructure used to add distribution channels for air scrubbers.
2010	**Shore Sales** of Rantoul, Illinois.	Bought individual assets rather than the holding company	Designer and marketer of moisture testers for the grain, seed, coffee, milling, processing and farm markets. Also grain-grading equipment.	A complement to CTB's grain-management systems. Shore Sales able to use CTB's distribution network.
2010	**Ironwood Plastics**, of Ironwood, Michigan.	Acquired the company.	Highly engineered, precision-moulded plastic components serving the industrial, automotive, military, agricultural and electronics markets.	Two manufacturing facilities: a 60,000-square-foot design and production facility and a 25,000-square-foot production facility. CTB to learn from Ironwood's plastics processing skills. Opened up opportunities to apply plastics knowledge to the agricultural sector, and to offer existing product-line sales outside the US and Canada.

Year	Company	Bought	Products	Reason
2010	Established **CTB Malaysia Sdn Bhd**, an Asian-based logistics centre.		A 27,000-square-foot logistics centre.	CTB's business units can better serve customers in Southeast Asia – initially broiler producers in Malaysia, Indonesia, Thailand, Vietnam, the Philippines and others. Later encompassed other CTB product lines as well as local manufacturing. Allowed faster delivery times and gave customers the ability to purchase in less-than-container-load quantities, along with the ability to do business using local languages and without the delays that can result from time-zone differences.

Buffett was astounded by what Mancinelli had achieved over the nine years to the end of 2010. In his 2010 letter to shareholders, he enthused that the CTB CEO "just keeps getting better". His team had successfully integrated a slew of companies into CTB. This was a feat in itself, requiring considerable planning and sensitive handling. They had shrewdly developed a cadre of managers capable of helping acquired teams to feel welcome and get the most out of joining the CTB family, thus holding on to the most talented.

Perhaps the highest praise that Buffett bestowed was in his 2008 letter to shareholders:

> Vic Mancinelli, its CEO, followed Berkshire-like operating principles long before our arrival. He focuses on blocking and tackling, day by day doing the little things right and never getting off course. Ten years from now, Vic will be running a much larger operation and, more important, will be earning excellent returns on invested capital.

The numbers reflected the commercial prowess of CTB's managers. Buffett wrote in his 2010 letter:

> Berkshire paid $140 million for CTB in 2002. It has since paid us dividends of $160 million and eliminated $40 million of debt. Last year it earned $106 million pre-tax. Productivity gains have produced much of this increase. When we bought CTB, sales per employee were $189,365; now they are $405,878.

While revenue was jumping by double-digit percentages year on year, employee numbers merely crept up from around 1,100 in 2002 to 1,505 in 2010, despite the great number of acquisitions and organic growth in terms of geographical coverage, size of factories and sales.

In December 2010, founder Howard Brembeck passed away, aged 100. Mancinelli said of him:

> Howard created a legacy of innovation embodied in products of quality and endurance that lives on. We are fortunate to have had Howard as our founder. He combined the rare talent of people development and product excellence with a devotion to innovation that guides us still.[432]

Unfortunately, the profits made by CTB for Berkshire Hathaway in the years after 2010 are not in the public domain. However, the confidence of the managerial team is illustrated by a continuing pattern of acquisitions. We also know that annual sales now exceed $1 billion and that the employee count stands at 2,590.

As Table 12.3 illustrates, CTB's managers have since stuck to their knitting by continuing to deepen their commitment to the poultry- and pig-production sectors, enhancing competitive advantage by offering a more complete package to customers and gaining greater economies of scale and scope. But they also bought into adjacent fields, most notably meat processing.

Table 12.3 Major acquisitions and advances, 2011–2024

Year	Company	Bought	Products	Reason
2012	**Martin Industries, Corp** of Des Moines, Iowa.	Acquired the assets of five subsidiaries: LeMar Industries Riley Equipment Hall Industries Midwest Bearing & Supply The Grain Reclaim Machine Company.	**LeMar Industries**: Designer and manufacturer of grain-handling equipment and related structures, including catwalks, towers, bucket elevators, conveyors and sweeps. **Riley Equipment**: Designer and manufacturer of bucket elevators, grain conveyors and other bulk-material-handling equipment. **Hall Industries**: Custom designer, metal fabricator, metal powder-coater. **Midwest Bearing & Supply**: Bearing and power transmission supply. **The Grain Reclaim Machine Company**: Grain pickup service.	A wider range of products could be offered to customers that handle, store, condition and dry grain, amounting to a complete grain-preservation package. Additional engineering expertise and talented people – two subsidiaries mostly supplied customers outside of agriculture. Useful 300,000 square feet of manufacturing space.

Year	Company	Bought	Products	Reason
2012	**Meyn Holding BV**, with production facilities in the Netherlands, the US and Poland.	Acquired the company.	Designer and manufacturer of poultry-processing equipment (to transport, kill, clean and package birds). Sells in 90 countries.	This vertical integration meant that CTB could offer poultry producers equipment both to raise poultry and to process the end product. Meyn's innovation and customer support skill was instructive for CTB's team. Meyn had about 1,000 employees and annual sales of $269 million.
2016	**Volito Group BV**, the Netherlands.	Acquired the company.	Designer and manufacturer of poultry cage-free layer housing systems, with nests, rearing systems, egg-collection equipment, slats and perches.	CTB extended into additional market areas. Complements CTB's laying system offerings, feeding systems, drinkers, egg collectors and ventilation equipment. Provides customers with a complete line of aviary and nest systems through worldwide CTB distribution network. Volito team's expertise added to CTB's.

Investment 12. CTB International

Year	Company	Bought	Products	Reason
2016	**Cabinplant A/S**, based in Denmark with subsidiaries in Poland, Germany, Spain and the US.	Acquired a majority share.	Processing and weighing equipment used in a wide range of businesses, particularly fish and shellfish, fruit and vegetables, poultry and convenience foods. Part of its expertise includes system customisation achieved through close collaboration with its customers.	Poultry-processing equipment complements Meyn's poultry processing. Broadens range of poultry-processing options that CTB offers customers. Expanding into new market areas for processing, such as seafood and vegetables. Knowledge of the food industry. Employs nearly 300 people and operates in 30 countries.
2016	**Holding Hamon Développement**, parent company of **Serupa SAS and Mafrel SAS**, France.	Acquired the company.	Serupa is a turnkey designer and manufacturer of poultry buildings and buildings used for meat processing and other industries. Mafrel supplies building kits and poultry equipment, such as that supplied by CTB's Roxell, Fancom and CTB business units.	Broadens CTB's offering to the poultry industry. Enhances CTB's overall position in French-speaking markets, where Serupa has a strong customer base. Serupa and Mafrel can expand to additional markets where CTB companies already have a strong presence.

Year	Company	Bought	Products	Reason
2018	**Cat Squared (M-Tech International Inc)**, of Conway, Arkansas; also has a location in Mexico.	Acquired a controlling interest.	Global provider of software solutions for food processing. Real-time data collection and reporting from plant floor, planning tools, traceability and machine learning.	Product line supports CTB's mission of providing a single source of supply to its processing industry customers. Offered customers the ability to collect processing plant data, to produce production and inventory reports, and to access traceability information. Thirty of the top 50 meat- and poultry-processing companies in North America were already customers of Cat Squared. Potential efficiency improvements for a wide variety of processing equipment, including processing customers new to CTB, such as pork and beef. Already operating on six continents.

A few of the businesses purchased contained within them manufacturing or distribution subsidiaries which were less connected to CTB's core product markets. Thus, today we find quite a mix, including architectural doors and windows; oil containment systems; aviation ground-support products, such as towbars for jets; bearings and belts for machinery in many industries; and automotive equipment. Despite these few anomalies – presumably held because they are good businesses in their own right – the vast majority of group sales come from products that help with the production of food from poultry and pigs, the processing of meat, grain storage and so on.

The team at CTB take great pride in what they do for society. This was boosted by what Buffett told them in 2012, when 600 current and former Milford employees gathered to celebrate the company's 60th anniversary: "You've got to have a good feeling about what you do at CTB. You're helping feed the world, and nothing is more important than that." Buffett concluded: "I couldn't feel better about being your partner."

What happened to the people

Chris Chocola resigned from CTB's board in 2002 to focus on serving his country as congressman between 2003 and 2007. In that role, he worked on the Congressional Committees of Agriculture, Small Business, Transport and Infrastructure and Ways and Means. From 2009 to 2014, he was president of the Club for Growth, which promotes fiscal conservativism, such as low taxes, reform of entitlements (state-funded benefits) and limited government. He also serves on American Securities' executive council, helping to identify investment candidates and providing industry insights.

Caryl Chocola resigned from CTB's board in 2002 and continued her many interests. She taught art classes, ran an art store and bred and showed horses before passing away in 2019, aged 81.

Mancinelli is still chairman, CEO and president of CTB, as he approaches his 82nd birthday. Buffett likes to hold on to experienced and talented old hands, saying: "[W]e find it difficult to teach a new dog old tricks. We like people who have been around for a while."[433]

Learning points

- **Intense focus on a single market segment can bring great rewards.** Such singlemindedness can lead to deeper knowledge of customer needs, lower-cost products and greater brand recognition. CTB stuck to its knitting over seven decades: its speciality remains poultry- and pig-raising equipment, despite expanding into ancillary and adjacent areas such as grain storage and meat processing.

- **Successful integration of acquired firms is a challenge but can supercharge earnings growth.** Most mergers do not increase shareholder value, for various reasons, from a failure to motivate newly acquired personnel to poor strategic fit and alien cultures. CTB's top team worked hard to make its acquisitions work.

- **Gaining economies of scale and scope can help to maintain a company's leadership position.** CTB raised capital to enable expansion in the same or related fields, allowing it to provide a more complete offering to customers and achieve unit cost reductions that smaller players could not match.

- **Not all great businesses offer highly differentiated products generating high margins as customers are persuaded to pay premiums.** Some great businesses, such as GEICO and CTB, have a simple offer of good quality at low prices.

- **Investors should not try to teach distinguished managers how to suck eggs.** Buffett knew he had a good leader and a team with depth at CTB, so he did not impose his ideas on strategy or other managerial decisions. He placed great trust in people who deserved it. They responded with gratitude, pride in their performance and loyalty to Berkshire Hathaway.

Notes

1. Michael Santioli, "They've Got Class", *Barron's*, 10 September 2007.
2. Warren Buffett and Carol J Loomis, "Mr. Buffett on the Stock Market", *Fortune Magazine*, 22 November, (1999). The article is based on a Buffett talk given in September 1999 to a group of friends (including Loomis) and a videotape of a speech he gave in July at Allen & Co's Sun Valley, Idaho gathering for business leaders.
3. *Ibid.*
4. *Ibid.*
5. *Ibid.*
6. *Ibid.*
7. *Ibid.*
8. *Ibid.*
9. *Ibid.*
10. *Ibid.*
11. *Ibid.*
12. *Ibid.*
13. Warren Buffett's 2000 letter to Berkshire Hathaway shareholders.
14. *Ibid.*
15. *Ibid.*
16. *Ibid.*
17. *Ibid.*
18. *Ibid.*
19. *Ibid.*
20. *Ibid.*
21. *Ibid.*
22. *Ibid.*
23. *Ibid.*
24. *Ibid.*
25. In the period 2000–2006, Berkshire bought 86.6% of the common stock for $5 billion.

26 Andrew Kilpatrick, *Of Permanent Value: The Story of Warren Buffett* (AKPE Publishing, 2006), p75.
27 The Public Utility Regulatory Policies Act.
28 It went public in 1987.
29 It also supplied all the electricity needs at the US Navy's China Lake Weapons Center, where the geothermal field was located.
30 Maria Shao, "Cal Energy: Out of Hot Water?", *Bloomberg*, 23 June 1991.
31 Ronald W Chan, *Behind the Berkshire Hathaway Curtain* (John Wiley and Sons Inc, 2010), p150.
32 Walter Scott Jr and Perry L Cochell, *From Point A to Point B, Lessons in Leadership* (Boy Scouts of America, 2018).
33 David L Sokol, *Pleased, But Not Satisfied* (self-published, 2007), p8.
34 Ronald W Chan, *Behind the Berkshire Hathaway Curtain* (John Wiley and Sons Inc, 2010), p133.
35 *Ibid.*
36 *Ibid*, pp133–134.
37 David L Sokol, *Pleased, But Not Satisfied* (self-published, 2007), p10.
38 *Ibid*, p11.
39 Walter Scott in Walter Scott Jr and Perry L Cochell, *From Point A to Point B, Lessons in Leadership* (Boy Scouts of America, 2018).
40 Maria Shao, "Cal Energy: Out of Hot Water?", *Bloomberg*, 23 June 1991.
41 Joe Castaldo, "The Oracle of Edmonton: Meet the Canadian Who Might Succeed Warren Buffett", *The Globe and Mail*, 7 May, 2019.
42 *Ibid.*
43 Ronald W Chan, *Behind the Berkshire Hathaway Curtain* (John Wiley and Sons Inc, 2010), p134.
44 *Ibid*, pp135–136.
45 CalEnergy Annual Report 1993.
46 MidAmerican Energy Annual Report 1999.
47 David L Sokol, *Pleased, But Not Satisfied* (self-published, 2007), p12.
48 CalEnergy Annual Report 1996.
49 *Ibid.*
50 *Ibid.*
51 Technically, the buying party was a trust affiliated with Walter Scott, Jr.
52 MidAmerican Energy Annual Report 1996.
53 David Batstone, "The Private Lives of America's Top Managers", *Good Faith Media*, 16 March, 2006. www.googfaithmedia.org.
54 In Ronald W Chan, *Behind the Berkshire Hathaway Curtain* (John Wiley and Sons Inc, 2010), p13
55 *Ibid.*

56 David Batstone, "The Private Lives of America's Top Managers", Good Faith Media, 16 March, 2006, goodfaithmedia.org.
57 David L Sokol, *Pleased, But Not Satisfied* (self-published, 2007), p12.
58 *Ibid*.
59 In Ronald W Chan, *Behind the Berkshire Hathaway Curtain* (John Wiley and Sons Inc, 2010), p137.
60 Buffett's 1999 letter to Berkshire Hathaway shareholders.
61 GuruFocus.com "Why Warren Decided to Enter the Utility Business in 1999", *Yahoo Finance*, 30 October, 1999.
62 Buffett's 2009 letter to Berkshire Hathaway shareholders.
63 MidAmerican Energy Holdings, "Berkshire Hathaway, Walter Scott and David Sokol to acquire MidAmerican Energy Holdings; Transaction Priced at 29% Premium to Market", press release, 25 October 1999.
64 Andy Serwer, "The Oracle of Everything", *Fortune Magazine*, 11 November, 2002.
65 *Ibid*.
66 Buffett's 1999 letter to Berkshire Hathaway shareholders.
67 MidAmerican Energy Holdings, "Berkshire Hathaway, Walter Scott and David Sokol to acquire MidAmerican Energy Holdings; Transaction Priced at 29% Premium to Market", press release, 25 October, 1999.
68 *Ibid*.
69 Buffett's 2007 letter to Berkshire Hathaway shareholders.
70 Berkshire Hathaway Annual Report 2002.
71 Berkshire Hathaway Annual Report 2007.
72 Berkshire Hathaway Annual Report 2000.
73 Annie Leibovitz, "Warren Buffett Speaks Candidly to Vanity Fair About Who Might Succeed Him at Berkshire Hathaway", *Vanity Fair*, 5 January, 2011.
74 Ronald W Chan, *Behind the Berkshire Hathaway Curtain* (John Wiley and Sons Inc, 2010), pp137–138.
75 David L Sokol, *Pleased, But Not Satisfied* (self-published, 2007), p13.
76 Reuters (2004), 27 February.
77 Berkshire Hathaway Annual Report 2005.
78 Berkshire Hathaway Annual Report 2008.
79 In 2011, the company initiated two solar projects in California, with construction costs totalling $3 billion.
80 Berkshire Hathaway Annual Report 2020.
81 David L Sokol, *Pleased, But Not Satisfied* (self-published, 2007) p12.
82 David L Sokol, *Pleased, But Not Satisfied* (self-published, 2007).
83 He resigned from BYD in April 2011.

84 In an interview with CNBC (29 March 2011), Sokol said that while he had invested in companies which he then recommended for acquisition in the past, if he had it all to do again, he would have invested in Lubrizol for himself and not passed the recommendation on to Buffett. He had not expected Buffett to want to buy the company and was surprised at how quickly he had moved. Sokol also pointed out that other Berkshire executives had held shares in companies which they then recommended for investment or acquisition, citing the example of Munger owning a stake in BYD before suggesting it for Berkshire to invest in. Nonetheless, he understood how the sequence of events looked, even if he believed he did nothing wrong.
85 Andrew Bary, "How Berkshire Hathaway's Utility Business Became a $90 Billion Win for Warren Buffett", *Barron's*, 13 July 2023.
86 https://givingpledge.org.
87 Ellen D Wernick, *International Directory of Company Histories*, vol 26, ed. by Jay P Pederson (St James Press, 1999), pp100–103.
88 Jerry Knight, "A stock burst that was a quarter century in the making", *Washington Post*, 19 October 1997.
89 *Ibid.*
90 *Ibid.*
91 CORT Form 10-K 1998.
92 Buffett's 2000 letter to Berkshire Hathaway shareholders.
93 *Ibid.*
94 Quoted in Wesco, "Wesco Financial Corporation to Acquire CORT Business Services Corporation For $28.00 Per Share in Cash", press release, 14 January 2000.
95 *Ibid.*
96 Wesco Annual Report 1999.
97 Because Wesco owned it for only 10 months of 2000, it benefited by $29 million of profits.
98 Wesco Annual Report 2000.
99 *Ibid.*
100 *Ibid.*
101 Wesco Annual Report 2001.
102 Wesco Annual Report 2003.
103 Wesco Annual Report 2007.
104 Wesco Annual Report 2009.
105 Pederson retired in 2024. The new CEO, Mike Davis, is yet another veteran of the firm, having joined in 1997.
106 Buffett's 2023 letter to Berkshire Hathaway shareholders.
107 Munger quoted in *ibid*.
108 Buffett's 1996 letter to Berkshire Hathaway shareholders.

109 Moody's, "Moody's Role in the Global Capital Markets", www.moodys.com.
110 Alice Schroeder, *The Snowball* (Bloomsbury Publishing, 2009), p149.
111 Buffett speaking to Columbia University students in 1993. Andrew Kilpatrick, *Of Permanent Value: The Story of Warren Buffett* (AKPE Publishing, 2006) p84.
112 Brent Schlender, "The Bill and Warren Show", *Fortune*, 20 July 1998.
113 Buffett speaking to Columbia University students in 1993. Andrew Kilpatrick, *Of Permanent Value: The Story of Warren Buffett* (AKPE Publishing, 2006), p84.
114 *Ibid*, p85.
115 Alice Schroeder, *The Snowball* (Bloomsbury Publishing, 2009), p165.
116 *Ibid*, p173.
117 Andrew Kilpatrick, *Of Permanent Value: The Story of Warren Buffett* (AKPE Publishing, 2006), p117.
118 Financial Crisis Inquiry, Transcript of Interview with Warren Buffett, 26 May 2010, www.fraser.stlouisfed.org.
119 *Ibid*.
120 *Ibid*.
121 Following the 2005 2:1 share split, the effective price paid becomes $10.40.
122 Elroy Dimson, Paul Marsh and Mike Staunton, *Triumph of the Optimists: 101 Years of Global Investment Returns* (Princeton University Press, 2002).
123 Financial Crisis Inquiry, Transcript of Interview with Warren Buffett, 26 May 2010, www.fraser.stlouisfed.org.
124 *Ibid*.
125 *Ibid*.
126 Warren Buffett speaking at the 2006 annual general meeting of Berkshire Hathaway shareholders.
127 Financial Crisis Inquiry, Transcript of Interview with Warren Buffett, 26 May 2010, www.fraser.stlouisfed.org.
128 *Ibid*.
129 *Ibid*.
130 *Ibid*.
131 *Ibid*.
132 *Ibid*.
133 *Ibid*.
134 There is a summary of Graham's methods in Glen Arnold, *The Great Investors: Lessons on Investing from Master Traders* (Pearson Education, 2011).
135 Financial Crisis Inquiry, Transcript of Interview with Warren Buffett, 26 May 2010, www.fraser.stlouisfed.org.
136 *Ibid*.

137 *Ibid.*
138 Office of Public Affairs, "Justice Department and State Partners Secure Nearly $864 Million Settlement with Moody's Arising from Conduct in the Lead up to the Financial Crisis", press release, 13 January, 2017.
139 James Hart, "Before H&R Block: Founder Talks About His Days as a Small Business Owner", *Thinking Bigger*, 13 May 2014, www.ithinkbigger.com.
140 *Ibid.*
141 *Ibid.*
142 *Ibid.*
143 H&R Block Company website, "H&R Block Founders", https://www.hrblock.com/tax-center/founders/.
144 During the tax season, most H&R Block offices were open 9am to 9pm weekdays, and 9am to 5pm Saturdays and Sundays. By the late 1990s, tax returns were prepared on computer in the presence of the customer, in most instances in less than one hour, on the basis of information furnished by the customer. There was also a premium service for those with more complex returns.
145 The company helped 13% of US individuals file their tax returns in 1998. In addition, it had 1,348 offices outside of the US – mostly in Canada (with almost 2 million clients), but also Australia (0.4 million) and the UK, as well as four other countries (Annual Report 1998).
146 Option One originated $1.9 billion in mortgage loans in the 10 months after its acquisition up to 30 April 1998. In the same period, it sold $1.8 billion in the financial markets. As of 30 April 1998, it was earning fees by servicing 42,800 loans totalling more than $4.3 billion.
147 H&R Block Form 10-k for 1998.
148 *Ibid.*
149 *Ibid.*
150 "Accounting and auditing services, tax planning and reporting services, profitability improvement and strategic planning, business valuation, litigation support and fraud investigation, public finance verification services to its business clients, and individual tax, estate planning and financial planning services", *Ibid.*
151 H&R Block Annual Report 2000.
152 *Ibid.*
153 Buffett speaking to Columbia University students on 9 May 2002, https://tilsonfunds.com/BuffettColumbiaspeech.pdf.
154 ABC News, "H&R Block's Wall Street Success", 4 April 2001, www.abcnews.go.com.
155 H&R Block Annual Report 2001.
156 *Ibid.*

157 Associated Press, "H&R Block under fire for pushing its lucrative refund loan program", *Cape Cod Times*, 30 March 2002.
158 H&R Block Annual Report 2005.
159 *Ibid.*
160 H&R Block Annual Report 2006.
161 *Ibid.*
162 A quote from Claudius in Shakespeare's *Hamlet*.
163 Generally, an IRA provides a tax-deferred way to save for retirement, providing investors with a variety of investing options, including stocks and mutual funds. But H&R Block's IRAs only allowed clients to save into interest-bearing money market accounts; the interest received frequently didn't cover the fees the company charged.
164 Reuters, "H&R Block Flubs Its Own Taxes", 24 February 2006, www.foxnews.com.
165 H&R Block Annual Report 2007.
166 Richard Breeden quoted in Victoria Kim and Deborah Brewster, "Dissident slate wins H&R Block seats", *Financial Times*, 6 September 2007.
167 Marion and Henry Bloch Family Foundation website, https://blochfamilyfoundation.org/.
168 Berkshire Hathaway Annual Report 2010.
169 Steve Feldman, "One on One with 'Mr.' Shaw", *Floor Covering News*, 4 August 2022.
170 'JC' stands for 'Julius Clarence'. The oldest of Clarence and Essie Evans Shaw's four children, he was born on 18 December 1929.
171 It was later listed on the NYSE and the Pacific Stock Exchange.
172 Chandrani Ghosh, "Floored", *Forbes*, 15 November 1999, p174.
173 *Ibid.*
174 *Ibid.*
175 *Ibid.*
176 Shaw Industries Annual Report 1999.
177 Saul quoted in FCNews Staff, "Looking back: Julian Saul: An allergy to Rayon and cotton rugs was parlayed into Hall of Fame career", *Floor Covering News*, 10 August 2021.
178 *Ibid.*
179 By now, JC Shaw had long since stepped back from day-to-day involvement in the business. He acted as mentor and encourager of the Shaw managerial 'family'. He served as chairman until 1996, when he retired to become chairman emeritus. He died in January 2015 aged 85.
180 Buffett's 2000 letter to Berkshire Hathaway shareholders.
181 *Ibid.*

182 Carrick Mollenkamp and Devon Spurgeon, "Shaw Industries Got Berkshire as Investor Simply by Asking", *The Wall Street Journal*, 20 November, 2000.
183 Quoted in Malcolm Fleschner, "Pile It On", *Selling Power*, 2010, www.sellingpower.com
184 21 January 2002.
185 Berkshire Hathaway Annual Report 2004.
186 The federal corporate income tax rate from 1993 to 2017 for companies with over $10 million of taxable income was 35%.
187 We are also assuming that additional working capital was not required. This is likely to be true in approximate terms because revenue in the final year 2009 ($4.0 billion) was much the same as in 2001 ($4.3 billion), so Shaw would not need to devote money to additional receivables and inventories.
188 Vance Bell transitioned to executive chairman in 2021 and then retired in 2022; Randy Merritt retired in 2017.
189 Floor Daily Staff, "Robert Shaw's Shift of Focus", *Floor Daily*, 28 July 2006.
190 Buffett's 2006 letter to Berkshire Hathaway shareholders.
191 Steve Feldman, "One to One with 'Mr.' Shaw", *Floor Covering News*, 4 August 2022.
192 Buffett's 1997 letter to Berkshire Hathaway shareholders.
193 Robert P Miles, *The Warren Buffett CEO* (John Wiley and Sons Inc, 2002), p200.
194 *Ibid*.
195 *Ibid*.
196 *Ibid*, p201.
197 Lecture given by Melvyn Wolff at the University of Houston, 8 March 2005 (Distinguished Leaders Series, Bauer College of Business).
198 Robert P Miles, *The Warren Buffett CEO* (John Wiley and Sons Inc, 2002), p204.
199 Buffett's 1997 letter to Berkshire Hathaway shareholders.
200 Andrew Kilpatrick, *Of Permanent Value: The Story of Warren Buffett* (AKPE Press, 2006), p653.
201 *Ibid*, p564.
202 Robert P Miles, *The Warren Buffett CEO* (John Wiley and Sons Inc, 2002), p205.
203 Kimberley Wray, "Buffett's Galaxy Grows: Investor Inks Deal for Star Furniture", *Home Furnishing News*, 30 June 1997.
204 Andrew Kilpatrick, *Of Permanent Value: The Story of Warren Buffett* (AKPE Press, 2006), p653.
205 Buffett's 1997 letter to Berkshire Hathaway shareholders.
206 Robert P Miles, *The Warren Buffett CEO* (John Wiley and Sons Inc, 2002), p206.

207 *Ibid*, p206.
208 *Ibid*, p207.
209 *Ibid*.
210 *Ibid*, pp209–213.
211 Staff editors, "Star Furniture Chairman, Melvyn Wolff, Dies at 86", *Furniture Today*, 26 May 2017.
212 Jessica Navarro, "Remembering a Legacy: Bauer College Celebrate Donor and Philanthropist Melvyn Wolff", *Inside Bauer Magazine*, Fall/Winter 2017.
213 Joshua Myerov, "Jordan's Shutdown Marks Era's End", *Boston Globe*, 24 October 2004.
214 Edward's other son was Milton. Edward and Barbara also had two daughters, Shyrlie and Mildred.
215 Patti Doten, "A Matched Set", *Boston Globe*, 25 January 1999.
216 Robert P Miles, *The Warren Buffett CEO* (John Wiley and Sons Inc, 2002), p217.
217 Ronald W Chan, *Behind the Berkshire Hathaway Curtain: Lessons from Warren Buffett's Top Business Leaders* (John Wiley and Sons Inc, 2010), p57.
218 Edward Tatelman, in Robert P Miles, *The Warren Buffett CEO* (John Wiley and Sons Inc, 2002), p217.
219 Ronald W Chan, *Behind the Berkshire Hathaway Curtain: Lessons from Warren Buffett's Top Business Leaders* (John Wiley and Sons Inc, 2010), p59.
220 Barry Tatelman, "Corporate Culture at Jordan's Furniture", *Furniture World Magazine*, 11 June 2004.
221 Ronald W Chan, *Behind the Berkshire Hathaway Curtain: Lessons from Warren Buffett's Top Business Leaders* (John Wiley and Sons Inc, 2010), p58.
222 Floor Daily, "Jordan's ends long time Massachusetts location'", *Floor Daily*, 25 October 2004 www.floordaily.net/flooring-news/jordan39s-ends-long-time-massachusetts-location.
223 *Ibid*.
224 *Ibid*.
225 Arthur Lubow, "Wowing Warren", *Inc Magazine*, 1 March 2000.
226 Barry Tatelman, in Robert P Miles, *The Warren Buffett CEO* (John Wiley and Sons Inc, 2002), p218.
227 Arthur Lubow, "Wowing Warren", *Inc Magazine*, 1 March 2000.
228 Eliot Tatelman, in P Doten, "A Matched Set", *Boston Globe*, 25 January 1999.
229 Ronald W Chan, *Behind the Berkshire Hathaway Curtain: Lessons from Warren Buffett's Top Business Leaders* (John Wiley and Sons Inc, 2010), p60.
230 *Ibid*, p62.

231 Perry Eaton, "For the Past 23 Years, This Has Been the Hottest Mom in Massachusetts", *Boston.com*, 7 May 2015. www.boston.com/culture/entertainment.
232 Clint Engel, "Jordan's path to success: Entertainment that gets customers all the way through the store", *Furniture Today*, 1 May 2017.
233 *Ibid.*
234 Barry Tatelman, "Corporate Culture at Jordan's Furniture", *Furniture World Magazine*, 6 June 2004.
235 The Anti-Defamation League's founding mission was to "stop the defamation of the Jewish people and to secure justice and fair treatment to all". It has since broadened its scope to combat all forms of bias, extremism and bigotry, and to protect democracy and ensure a just and inclusive society. www.adl.org.
236 Ronald W Chan, *Behind the Berkshire Hathaway Curtain: Lessons from Warren Buffett's Top Business Leaders* (John Wiley and Sons Inc, 2010), p63.
237 Writing in the 11 October 1999 Berkshire Hathaway announcement about the purchase.
238 Barry Tatelman, in Arthur Lubow "Wowing Warren", *Inc Magazine*, 1 March 2000.
239 Ronald W Chan, *Behind the Berkshire Hathaway Curtain: Lessons from Warren Buffett's Top Business Leaders* (John Wiley and Sons Inc, 2010), p63.
240 Kimberley Blanton, "Berkshire Hathaway to acquire Jordan's", *Boston Globe*, 12 October 1999, p47.
241 Arthur Lubow, "Wowing Warren", *Inc Magazine*, 1 March 2000.
242 Andrew Kilpatrick, *Of Permanent Value: The Story of Warren Buffett* (AKPE Press, 2006), p683.
243 Ronald W Chan, *Behind the Berkshire Hathaway Curtain: Lessons from Warren Buffett's Top Business Leaders* (John Wiley and Sons Inc, 2010), p55.
244 "Berkshire Hathaway unit to acquire Jordan's Furniture", *Boston Business Journal*, 11 October 1999. www.bizjournals.com/boston/stories/1999/10/11/daily1.html
245 Joshua Myerov, "Jordan's Shutdown Marks Era's End", *Boston Globe*, 24 October 2004.
246 Eliot Tatelman, in Robert P Miles, *The Warren Buffett CEO* (John Wiley and Sons Inc, 2002), p221.
247 Eamon Convey and Loretta McLaughlin, "Buffett is sold on Jordan's: Billionaire to Buy Furniture Chain", *Boston Herald*, 12 October 1999.
248 After the sale, June Tatelman continued to work as a schoolteacher.
249 Buffett's 1999 letter to Berkshire Hathaway shareholders.
250 Robert P Miles, *The Warren Buffett CEO* (John Wiley and Sons Inc, 2002), p223.

251　*Ibid*, p224.
252　*Ibid*, p224.
253　Clint Engel, "Jordan's Takes It to the IMAX", *Furniture Today*, 26 August 2002.
254　Joshua Myerov, "Jordan's Shutdown Marks Era's End", *Boston Globe*, 24 October 2004.
255　Staff writer, "Whatever happened to… Barry Tatelman of Jordan's Furniture?" *WickedLocal.com*, 23 April 2014.
256　Robert P Miles, *The Warren Buffett CEO* (John Wiley and Sons Inc, 2002), pp231–232.
257　Ronald W Chan, *Behind the Berkshire Hathaway Curtain: Lessons from Warren Buffett's Top Business Leaders* (John Wiley and Sons Inc, 2010), p66.
258　It also moved location within downtown Seattle.
259　Herb Bridge, *Building Bridges, as told to Maureen Lander* (Lifetime Legacies, 2012), p21.
260　*Ibid*, p24.
261　*Ibid*, p26.
262　*Ibid*, p28.
263　*Ibid*, p30.
264　*Ibid*, p38.
265　*Ibid*, p51.
266　*Ibid*, p54.
267　*Ibid*, p62.
268　*Ibid*, p91.
269　*Ibid*, p102.
270　*Ibid*.
271　*Ibid*, p103.
272　Interviewed by the *Puget Sound Business Journal*, 17 July 1992.
273　Herb Bridge *Building Bridges, as told to Maureen Lander* (Lifetime Legacies, 2012), p104.
274　*Ibid*, p105.
275　*Ibid*, p113.
276　*Ibid*, p114.
277　*Ibid*, p116.
278　*Ibid*, pp117–118.
279　*Ibid*, p118.
280　*Ibid*, p168–170.
281　*Ibid*, p166.
282　*Ibid*, p178.
283　*Ibid*.

284 *Ibid.*
285 Buffett's 2000 letter to Berkshire Hathaway shareholders.
286 *Ibid.*
287 Carol Loomis, "The Value Machine", *Fortune Magazine*, 19 February 2001.
288 Robert P Miles, *The Warren Buffett CEO* (John Wiley and Sons Inc, 2002), p308.
289 Carol Loomis, "The Value Machine", *Fortune Magazine*, 19 February 2001.
290 Herb Bridge, *Building Bridges, as told to Maureen Lander* (Lifetime Legacies, 2012), p178.
291 Carol Loomis, "The Value Machine", *Fortune Magazine*, 19 February 2001.
292 Berkshire Hathaway, "Berkshire Hathaway Inc. Acquires Ben Bridge Jeweler", 18 May 2000.
293 *Ibid.*
294 *Ibid.*
295 Herb Bridge, *Building Bridges, as told to Maureen Lander* (Lifetime Legacies, 2012), p178.
296 Rob Bates, "Interview with Lisa and Ed Bridge, the future and current heads of Ben Bridge", *JCK Online*, 26 November 2018 www.jckonline.com/editorial-article/interview-ed-lisa-ben-bridge.
297 *Ibid.*
298 *Ibid.*
299 Carol Loomis, "The Value Machine", *Fortune Magazine*, 19 February 2001.
300 Herb Bridge, *Building Bridges, as told to Maureen Lander* (Lifetime Legacies, 2012), p179.
301 *Ibid*, p180.
302 Buffett's 2000 letter to Berkshire Hathaway shareholders.
303 Herb Bridge, *Building Bridges, as told to Maureen Lander* (Lifetime Legacies, 2012), p178.
304 Rob Bates, "Interview with Lisa and Ed Bridge, the future and current heads of Ben Bridge", *JCK Online*, 26 November 2018, www.jckonline.com/editorial-article/interview-ed-lisa-ben-bridge.
305 *Ibid.*
306 Michelle Graff, "Warren Buffett Picks a Woman to Head Ben Bridge", *National Jeweler*, 7 November 2017.
307 *The Centurion*, "Lisa Bridge named CEO of Ben Bridge", 14 November 2018.
308 Marc Bridge, "Ben Bridge Stories—Marc Bridge", Ben Bridge Jeweler, 4 November 2009, www.benbridgejeweler.wordpress.com.
309 *Ibid.*

Notes

310 *At Present*, "Betting on yourself: Marc Bridge, Founder and CEO", 26 September 2023. https://atpresent.com/
311 Lenore Fedow, "Ben Bridge is selling its Pandora franchise stores back to the brand", *National Jeweler*, 12 January 2022.
312 *Businesswire*, "Ben Bridge Jeweler Signs Letter of Intent to Transfer Pandora Stores to Pandora" Group", 10 January 2022.
313 Interviewed by Nancy Blasé, Jewish Archives Committee, 10 March 2020, www.digitalcollections.lib.washington.edu/digital/collection/ohc/id/3333.
314 Herb Bridge, *Building Bridges, as told to Maureen Lander* (Lifetime Legacies, 2012), p152.
315 Women were admitted in 1989.
316 *Ibid*, p197.
317 Shirley had passed away in 2008.
318 Herb Bridge, *Building Bridges, as told to Maureen Lander* (Lifetime Legacies, 2012), pp184–185.
319 *Ibid*, pp195 and 201.
320 Frank See, interviewed in the *McAllen Monitor*, in Hidalgo, Texas on 22 January 1932.
321 Irvin Farman, *Standard of the West: The Justin Story* (Texas Christian University Press, 1996), p30.
322 Enid Justin's 1985 memoir, quoted in *ibid*, p51.
323 *Ibid*.
324 *Ibid*, p68.
325 *Ibid*, p92.
326 *Ibid*, p94.
327 *Ibid*.
328 *Ibid*, p95.
329 *Ibid*, p96.
330 *Ibid*.
331 *Ibid*, p97.
332 *Ibid*, p98.
333 *Ibid*, p98.
334 *Ibid*, p99.
335 *Ibid*, p101.
336 *Ibid*, pp103–104.
337 *Ibid*, p105.
338 Irvin Farman, "You'll get a boot out of this, girls", *New York Daily News*, 2 November 1952.
339 Irvin Farman, *Standard of the West: The Justin Story* (Texas Christian University Press, 1996), p133.

340 *Ibid*, p172.
341 *Ibid*.
342 Bill Beck, *Acme Brick Company: 125 Years across Three Centuries* (The Donning Company Publishers, 2016).
343 Irvin Farman, *Standard of the West: The Justin Story* (Texas Christian University Press, 1996), p177.
344 *Ibid*, p178.
345 *Ibid*.
346 *Ibid*.
347 *Ibid*, p179.
348 *Ibid*, p181.
349 *Ibid*, pp182–183.
350 *Ibid*, p184.
351 *Ibid*, p192.
352 Nina Hyde, "Wear 'Em, Cowboy", *Washington Post*, 13 February 1979.
353 Irvin Farman, *Standard of the West: The Justin Story* (Texas Christian University Press, 1996), p241.
354 *Ibid*.
355 Ronald W Chan, *Behind the Berkshire Hathaway Curtain: Lessons from Warren Buffett's Top Business Leaders* (John Wiley and Sons Inc, 2010), p27.
356 *Ibid*.
357 According to Harrold Melton's recollections as reported in Bill Beck, *Acme Brick Company: 125 Years across Three Centuries* (The Donning Company Publishers, 2016).
358 Buffett's 2000 letter to Berkshire Hathaway shareholders.
359 Robert P Miles, *The Warren Buffett CEO* (John Wiley and Sons Inc, 2002), p319.
360 *Ibid*.
361 Russ Banham, "The Warren Buffett School", *Chief Executive Magazine*, December 2002 (Vol 184).
362 Acme Brick Company press release, "America's Most Successful Investor Discovers Value of Acme Brick", 20 March 2001.
363 Bill Beck, *Acme Brick Company: 125 Years across Three Centuries* (The Donning Company Publishers, 2016), p117.
364 *Ibid*.
365 Robert P Miles, *The Warren Buffett CEO* (John Wiley and Sons Inc, 2002), p320.
366 *Ibid*.
367 Acme Brick Company press release, "America's Most Successful Investor Discovers Value of Acme Brick", 20 March 2001.

Notes

368 Andrew Kilpatrick, *Of Permanent Value: The Story of Warren Buffett* (AKPE Publishing, 2006), pp722–723, quoting from *Fort Worth Star-Telegram*, 21 June 2000.
369 Berkshire Hathaway announcement, 20 June 2000.
370 *Ibid.*
371 Bill Beck, *Acme Brick Company: 125 Years across Three Centuries* (The Donning Company Publishers, 2016), p117.
372 Robert P Miles, *The Warren Buffett CEO* (John Wiley and Sons Inc, 2002), p321.
373 Ronald W Chan, *Behind the Berkshire Hathaway Curtain: Lessons from Warren Buffett's Top Business Leaders* (John Wiley and Sons Inc, 2010), p32.
374 Bill Beck, *Acme Brick Company: 125 Years across Three Centuries* (The Donning Company Publishers, 2016), p118.
375 *Ibid*, p113.
376 *Ibid.*
377 Ronald W Chan, *Behind the Berkshire Hathaway Curtain: Lessons from Warren Buffett's Top Business Leaders* (John Wiley and Sons Inc, 2010), pp79–80.
378 Bill Beck, *Acme Brick Company: 125 Years across Three Centuries* (The Donning Company Publishers, 2016), p144.
379 Benjamin Moore, "Once Upon a Time in America: The Legendary Benjamin Moore Brand", www.benjaminmoore.pl/en/once-upon-a-time.
380 Jay P Pederson, *International Directory of Company Histories, Volume 38* (St James Press, 2001).
381 Buffett's 2000 letter to Berkshire Hathaway shareholders.
382 *Ibid.*
383 Lawrence A Cunningham, *Berkshire Beyond Buffett: The Enduring Value of Values* (Columbia Business School Press, 2014).
384 Colleen Leahey, "The Wrath of Warren Buffett: How Benjamin Moore Almost Broke His Promise", *Fortune Magazine*, 6 October 2014.
385 Buffett's 2001 letter to Berkshire Hathaway shareholders.
386 Buffett's 2009 letter to Berkshire Hathaway shareholders.
387 *Ibid.*
388 Colleen Leahey, "The Wrath of Warren Buffett: How Benjamin Moore Almost Broke His Promise", *Fortune Magazine*, 6 October 2014.
389 James Covert, "Boxed in by Lowe's", *New York Post*, 29 June 2012.
390 James Covert, "Warren Buffett fired Benjamin Moore CEO after Bermuda Cruise", *New York Post*, 15 June 2012.
391 James Covert, "Brooklyn Paint Dealers Say Buffett Rolled All Over Them", *New York Post*, 14 October 2013.

392 James Covert, "Warren Buffett fired Benjamin Moore CEO after Bermuda Cruise", *New York Post*, 15 June 2012.
393 Colleen Leahey, "The Wrath of Warren Buffett: How Benjamin Moore Almost Broke His Promise", *Fortune Magazine*, 6 October 2014.
394 *Ibid*.
395 Alex Crippen, "Warren Buffett to Fired CEO: Board Party Didn't Sink You", *CNBC*, 27 June 2012.
396 James Covert, "Boxed in by Lowe's", *New York Post*, 29 June 2012.
397 Colleen Leahey, "The Wrath of Warren Buffett: How Benjamin Moore Almost Broke His Promise", *Fortune Magazine*, 6 October 2014.
398 *Ibid*.
399 *Ibid*.
400 *Ibid*.
401 *Ibid*.
402 *Ibid*.
403 Nicole Sinclair, "Benjamin Moore CEO: Warren Buffett is Very Particular About the Promises He Makes", Yahoo Finance, 3 May 2016.
404 Colleen Leahey, "The Wrath of Warren Buffett: How Benjamin Moore Almost Broke His Promise", *Fortune Magazine*, 6 October 2014.
405 *Ibid*.
406 *Ibid*.
407 *Ibid*.
408 *Ibid*.
409 James Covert, "Benjamin Moore Problems Getting Painted Over by Buffett", *New York Post*, 16 October 2013.
410 *Ibid*.
411 Benjamin Moore, "Benjamin Moore & Co. Appoints Company Veteran Dan Calkins Chairman & Chief Executive Officer", 8 January 2019.
412 Brembeck's father had also served as a state representative in the Indiana legislature.
413 The company, called Cyclone Manufacturing, is still going strong today.
414 Bob Braley, "Milford business celebrating 50 years of operation", KPC News, 23 June 2002 www.kpcnews.com.
415 Howard married Myra in 1933 and they had a daughter, Caryl, in 1938.
416 Quoted in Howard S Brembeck's memoir in "Company Profile: Brock Grain Systems", *Grain Journal*, May/June 2012, www.grainjournal.com/profiles/brock-grain-systems-1.
417 Encyclopedia.com, "CTB International Corporation", www.encyclopedia.com/books/politics-and-business-magazines/ctb-international-corporation.

Notes

418 Indiana State Poultry Association, "Reception During Expo Honors Chore Time-Brock Founder", *Wings, Webs, & Wattles*, March 1995.
419 CTB International Corporation, "CTB International Corp. Announces Agreement to be Acquired by Berkshire Hathaway", 19 August 2002.
420 *Ibid.*
421 CTB International Corporation, "CTB to explore strategic alternatives", 18 March 2002.
422 Its accounts for the second quarter of 2002 showed sales down by 5.1% compared with the same period in the previous year. This was mostly attributed to "poor conditions in the US egg market", resulting in protein group sales declining by 13.1%. Gross profit was also down 4%, but through cost control, the managers achieved an increase of 1.8% in operating income.
423 CTB International Corporation, "CTB International Corp. Announces Agreement to be Acquired by Berkshire Hathaway", 19 August 2002.
424 Buffett's 2002 letter to Berkshire Hathaway shareholders.
425 *Ibid.*
426 CTB International Corporation, "CTB International Corp. Announces Agreement to be Acquired by Berkshire Hathaway", 19 August 2002.
427 *Ibid.*
428 *Ibid.*
429 Andrew Kilpatrick, *Of Permanent Value: The Story of Warren Buffett* (AKPE, 2006), p798.
430 CTB International Corporation Form 10-K, 2001.
431 *Bloomberg News*, "Warren Buffett's CEOs are big spenders too", 10 May 2013.
432 CTB International Corporation, "CTB Inc. Announces Passing of Its Founder", 7 December 2010.
433 Adam Smith, "It's difficult to teach a new dog old tricks", *Kingswell*, 16 October 1998, www.kingswell.io/p/its-difficult-to-teach-a-new-dog.

www.ingramcontent.com/pod-product-compliance
Ingram Content Group UK Ltd.
Pitfield, Milton Keynes, MK11 3LW, UK
UKHW021825050825
461579UK00003B/6